Civilian or Combatant?

CIVILIAN OR COMBATANT?
A CHALLENGE FOR THE TWENTY-FIRST CENTURY

Anicée Van Engeland

OXFORD
UNIVERSITY PRESS

OXFORD
UNIVERSITY PRESS

Oxford University Press, Inc., publishes works that further Oxford University's objective of excellence in research, scholarship, and education.

Oxford   New York
Auckland   Cape Town   Dar es Salaam   Hong Kong   Karachi   Kuala Lumpur   Madrid
Melbourne   Mexico City   Nairobi   New Delhi   Shanghai   Taipei   Toronto

With offices in
Argentina   Austria   Brazil   Chile   Czech Republic   France   Greece   Guatemala   Hungary   Italy
Japan   Poland   Portugal   Singapore   South Korea   Switzerland   Thailand   Turkey   Ukraine
Vietnam

Library of Congress Cataloging-in-Publication Data
Engeland, Anisseh van.
  Civilian or combatant? : a challenge for the 21st century / Anicée M. Van Engeland.
    p. cm. — (Terrorism and global justice series)
  Includes bibliographical references and index.
  ISBN 978-0-19-974324-7 (hardback : alk. paper)
1. Combatants and noncombatants (International law) I. Title.
  KZ6515.E54 2011
  341.6'7—dc22   2010045119

1 2 3 4 5 6 7 8 9

Printed in the United States of America on acid-free paper

Note to Readers
This publication is designed to provide accurate and authoritative information in regard to the subject matter covered. It is based upon sources believed to be accurate and reliable and is intended to be current as of the time it was written. It is sold with the understanding that the publisher is not engaged in rendering legal, accounting, or other professional services. If legal advice or other expert assistance is required, the services of a competent professional person should be sought. Also, to confirm that the information has not been affected or changed by recent developments, traditional legal research techniques should be used, including checking primary sources where appropriate.

(Based on the Declaration of Principles jointly adopted by a Committee of the American Bar Association and a Committee of Publishers and Associations.)

Contents

ix   Introduction

1   Chapter 1: The Distinction between Combatants and Civilians, a Cornerstone of International Humanitarian Law

1   I. The Distinction in History: Ethics, Law, and Political Philosophy

2   A. Civilians as Incidental Victims of War: From Association with Territories, Leadership, and Population to the Emergence of the Nation State

6   B. First Attempts and Regulations to Limit War and Protect Civilians

11   C. The Emergence of an Ethic of Protection

13   II. The Distinction as a Cornerstone of Modern International Humanitarian Law

13   A. The Legalization of War: The Laws of War

16   B. The Role of International Humanitarian Law Regarding the Distinction in the Twenty-First Century: New Challenges

20   C. Ethics

24   III. Conclusion

27   Chapter 2: The Distinction between Civilians and Combatants

28   I. The Principle of Distinction

29   A. Who Is a Civilian? A Civilian Is a Noncombatant

29   1. The Distinction Relies on a Negative Definition

31   a. Protection of Civilians, Civilian Populations, and Civilian Property

33   b. Violations of the Principle of Distinction

35   2. The Rationale

37   B. Who Is a Combatant? A Specific Definition

37   1. Who Is a Combatant?

40   2. Other Categories of Combatants

40   a. Rebels, Terrorists, and Insurgents

42   b. Civilians Who Take Part in Hostilities

43   c. Mercenaries and Spies

45   d. Prisoners of War

48   e. The Sick, the Wounded, and the *Hors de Combat*

49   C. Legitimate Military Targets
54   II. The Distinction in Customary International Law
54   A. What Are Customary Rules of Humanitarian Law?
57   B. The ICRC Study
59   III. Conclusion

61   Chapter 3: Protection Afforded to Civilians and Rights of Combatants
61   I. Analysis of the Protection Afforded to Civilians
61   A. The Aim of Geneva Convention IV and the Additional Protocols
62   1. Protection of Civilians as a Principle
63   2. Illustrations of Protection from Effects of War and from
                    Attacks: Articles 31–34 GCIV
64   3. Illustrations of Civilian Protection Granted by Additional Protocol I
66   4. Illustrations of Civilian Protection in Non International Armed
                    Conflicts
68   5. Rights and Fundamental Guarantees
70   B. Protection of Civilian Property
71   II. Concrete Examples of Protection to Civilians
72   A. Safe Zones
75   B. Extra Protection Afforded to Civilians
75   1. Protection
77   2. Extra Protection for Women
78   3. Extra Protection for Children
81   C. Refugees and Internally Displaced People
81   1. Internally Displaced Persons: IDPs
82   2. Refugees
84   D. Journalists
84   1. Journalists Are Civilians
87   2. Embedded Journalists
88   3. Freelance Journalists
89   4. Military Journalists
89   5. Debates Regarding Journalism at War
94   E. Occupied Territories
99   III. Conclusion

101   Chapter 4: The Shift between Categories
102   I. From Civilian to Combatant
102   A. The Concept of Direct Participation in Hostilities
105   B. The ICRC Study
108   C. The Protection Afforded to Civilians Who Participate in Hostilities
110   D. A Sensitive Case: Human Shields
112   II. The Blurring of the Concept of Combatant
113   A. Additional Protocol I and the Extension of the Status of Combatants
                and Prisoners of War
113   1. Extension of the Status of Combatants

115   2. Extension of the Status of POW
116   B. Lawful and Unlawful/Unprivileged Combatants
116   1. Who Are Unlawful Combatants?
117   2. The Argument Against the Notion
119   3. In Practice: the U.S. and Israel
122   III. Civilians or Combatants? The Privatization of War
122   A. Mercenaries
122   1. Who Is a Mercenary?
125   2. Evolution
127   B. Private Military and Security Companies
127   1. What are Private Military/Security Companies?
128   2. Obligations under International Humanitarian Law
130   3. Combatants or Civilians?
131   C. Civilians Working for an Army
132   IV. Conclusion

133   Chapter 5: Concrete Challenges: the Evolution of War—Asymmetric
        Conflicts, Terrorism, and Weapon Technology
134   I. The Definition of Asymmetric Conflict
134   A. What Is an Asymmetric Conflict?
136   B. Asymmetric Conflict in the Twenty-First Century: A Challenge
138   II. Wars of Self-Determination and Armed Struggles: The Distinction
        During Wars of National Liberation
138   A. War of Self-Determination
139   B. International Humanitarian Law and Wars of Self-Determination
139   1. Applicable Law
141   2. Limits of These International Documents
142   3. Protection of Civilians
145   III. Terrorism and the Principle of Distinction
145   A. What Is Terrorism under International Humanitarian Law?
148   B. The War on Terror
149   1. Is the War on Terror an Armed Conflict?
150   2. International Humanitarian Law Does Not Apply to Terrorists?
151   3. Humanitarian Law Does Apply to Terrorists
152   IV. Weapons and the Principle of Distinction
152   A. A New Behavior
153   B. The Regulation of Weapons under International Humanitarian Law:
        Protection of Civilians
155   C. Prohibition to Use Weapons Causing Unnecessary Suffering
155   D. Violations of the Principle of Distinction in Practice—The Principle
        of Distinction versus Military Necessity
157   V. Conclusion

159   Conclusion: Is the Principle of Distinction Still Useful?
163   Index

Introduction

Sometimes I think it should be a rule of war that you have to see somebody up close and get to know him before you can shoot him. ~ Colonel Potter, M*A*S*H[1]

AN OLD PHENOMENON

Not a week passes by without its share of massacres of civilians making the headlines: In Somalia, civilians are caught between the fires of local war lords, Islamists, and foreign armies. Civilians are literally trapped in cities or live in camps on the main roads leading to these cities.[2] In the Democratic Republic of Congo, the area of Kivu has been the theater of violence against civilians including looting, raping, and killings, with a sharp increase since May 2009.[3] The same spring was deadly in Sri Lanka: the government decided to put an end to the Tigers' domination in the

---

[1] Colonel Sherman Tecumseh Potter (portrayed by Harry Morgan) was a fictional character from the *M*A*S*H* television show.
[2] Jeffrey Gettleman, *The Most Dangerous Place in the World*, FOREIGN POLICY (March/April 2009), http://www.foreignpolicy.com/story/cms.php?story_id=4682.
[3] Press Release, International Committee of the Red Cross, Democratic Republic of Congo: Mounting Concern as Civilians' Plight Worsens (July 8, 2009), http://www.icrc.org/Web/eng/siteeng0.nsf/html/congo-kinshasa-update-080609.This is because the ICRC has renewed its website. Here is the update link http://www.icrc.org/eng/resources/documents/update/congo-kinshasa-up-date-080709.htm

Tamil area. Some speak of 20,000 deaths resulting from the eradication of the movement.[4] In Iraq, there were as of November 2010 between 98,872 and 107,934 civilian deaths accounted as a result of the ongoing war.[5] Armed conflicts, whether international or non international, cause many deaths among civilians either because they are directly targeted by Parties to the hostilities or because of the ongoing battles violating humanitarian principles.

Targeting civilians demonstrates a lack of ethics but also disrespect for the law: massacres as acts of revenge, as a means to control a population, or merely in order to spread terror and increase power. The deaths of civilians, the deliberate targeting, and the violations of international humanitarian law are not new phenomena, and history is full of war events during which civilians got caught in hostilities and paid a high price. It is, for example, very complex to control troops when armies are on the move and enter populated areas. It is then difficult to prevent killings, looting, rapes, and abuses when an army ransacks a city, as demonstrated during the fall of Kabul on November 13, 2001: while Kabuli cheered upon the arrival of the Northern Alliance, doom befell villages once the Taliban ran away from the capital. An historical example is the massacre of Melos: Athens besieged the island of Melos during the Peloponnesian War; when the army eventually arrived on the island in 416 BC, the belligerents killed all the men, while women and children were enslaved. The atrocities were later regretted by Athenians. Thucydides wrote an eloquent piece on the Melos massacre, reflecting the responsibility of power, morality, and violence.[6] Attila and his Huns became legendary by "ground[ing] almost the whole of Europe into the dust"[7] in the fifth century. The sack of Jerusalem, which occurred after the Crusaders captured the city from the Fatimid Egypt in 1099, claimed the lives of 40,000 civilians during the siege, the final assault, and the fall of the city.[8]

There was an improvement in the Middle Ages: the war field was delimited and two armies faced one another with limited involvement of the civilian population. That said, this improvement was limited to Christian Europe as the Church attempted to regulate wars and to avoid bloodshed. In other places, it was generally accepted that the civilian population was a target for attack as part of a strategy or was part of war's booty.[9] For example, the armies of Tamerlane starved besieged cities, entered them on the promise that no harm would be done to the population,

---

[4] Catherine Philp, *The Hidden Massacre: Sri Lanka's Final Offensive against Tamil Tigers*, TIMES ONLINE, May 29, 2009, http://www.timesonline.co.uk/tol/news/world/asia/article6383449.ece.

[5] See for regular updates, the website http://www.iraqbodycount.org.

[6] THUCYDIDES, HISTORY OF THE PELOPONNESIAN WAR, Chapter XVII (Benjamin Jowett trans., Oxford: Clarendon Press 1990); *see also* Paul Cartledge, *Might and Right: Thucydides and the Melos Massacre*, 36:5 HISTORY TODAY 11, 11–15 (May 1986).

[7] AMMIANUS MARCELLINUS, ROMAN HISTORY, book 31, 575–623 (London: Bohn 1862).

[8] John & Laurita Hill, *The Jerusalem Massacre of July 1099 in the Western Historiography of the Crusades*, *in* 3 THE CRUSADES 65 (Benjamin Z. Kedar & Jonathan S.C. Riley-Smith eds., Ashgate Publishing Limited 2004).

[9] PHILIPPE CONTAMINE, WAR IN THE MIDDLE AGES 262 (Oxford; New York: B. Blackwell 1984).

then looted the cities, raped women, and exterminated civilians. Tamerlane's calling card was to build pyramids of skulls; his army would then release survivors to run to the next city in order to spread the news of terror and warn them that Tamerlane's troops were coming.[10] In 1387, Isfahan's officials took Tamerlane's ambassadors hostage. When Tamerlane arrived, the officials panicked and opened the gates for rendition. Tamerlane was irritated by the behavior of the Isfahani, and it was a bloodbath: 70,000 people were killed, constituting 35 minarets of 2000 human skulls each.[11] It is worth noting that with all this cruelty, Tamerlane kept craftsmen alive (in Shiraz, Esfahan, and Herat, but also Delhi and Damascus) and sent them to Samarkand and Bukhara, which explains why these two cities of Uzbekistan are so beautiful and why they remind one so vividly of Isfahan, Iran. Tamerlane never shied away from the use of violence and once declared:

I am the scourge of God chosen
To chastise you, since no one
Knows the remedy of your
Iniquity except me. You are
Wicked but I am more wicked
Than you, so be silent.[12]

Despite the attempts of the Christian Church to limit the war field and casualties, there were major atrocities: during the Thirty Years War, which began as a religious conflict between Protestants and Catholics, eight million civilians were either killed or displaced. These historical examples demonstrate that the distinction between civilians and combatants has always been difficult to respect and that civilians had a role to play in military strategies. This crucial role civilians endorse unwillingly has not evolved much: civilians are often deliberately targeted during wars, with no military purpose, for the sake of violence by terrorist groups, or as a demonstration of strength, as illustrated by the horrors committed during the wars in the Former Yugoslavia, on all sides. Consequently, civilians still bear the brunt of war. The situation is quite alarming nowadays as civilians constitute the largest bulk of war victims. This is partly the result of the fast-paced evolution of technology that has allowed for more protection of the military versus the forever-increasing exposure of civilians; aerial bombardment and drone attacks illustrate the phenomenon.

There are concomitant efforts to curb the violence against civilians and to distinguish civilians from soldiers during armed conflicts. In the medieval period, it was seen as an act of chivalry to protect civilians.[13] There were "articles of war" released

[10] MAJOR DAVY, POLITICAL AND MILITARY INSTRUMENTS OF TAMERLANE (Cambridge: Cambridge University Press 1972).

[11] RUY GONZALEZ DE CLAVIJO, LA ROUTE DE SAMARKAND AU TEMPS DE TAMERLAN (Paris: Imprimer Nationale, Collection voyages et Découverts 2006).

[12] WILFRID BLUNT, THE GOLDEN ROAD TO SAMARKAND 144 (London: Hamish Hamilton 1973).

[13] Hugo Slim, *Why Protect Civilians? Innocence, Immunity and Enmity in War*, 79:3 INT'L AFF. 481, 481–501.

by European rulers to avoid massive casualties: the *jus armorum*, the professional code for knights, included prohibitions against civilian attacks.[14] Another instance is the "just war doctrine"[15] elaborated by Christians, according to which there are philosophical, religious, ethical, or political conditions for going to war and rules to respect during war. These rules include the protection of civilians. In Islam, there is a distinction between combatants and non combatants that dates back to the Prophet Mohammed's time: it is prohibited to target civilians, and there is an ethic of saving lives,[16] an ethic that has been tampered with by Classicist and Neo-Classicist authors, later reinterpreted by extremist groups such al Qaeda to justify the killings of civilians.[17] This effort to distinguish civilians and protect them from the effects of war has evolved through history as explained in Chapter One. The principle of distinction became a cornerstone of international humanitarian law in the twentieth century: the 1949 Geneva Conventions (GC) and the 1977 Additional Protocols (AP) legalized the distinction. However, the distinction between civilians and combatants has proven difficult to uphold in practice, as illustrated in this book.

CHALLENGES FOR INTERNATIONAL HUMANITARIAN LAW REGARDING THE DISTINCTION

The most recent efforts to establish the distinction have been legal and are embodied in international humanitarian law: the discrimination between civilians and combatants is indeed a cornerstone of the modern law of armed conflict. The 1949 Geneva Conventions, later completed by the 1977 Additional Protocols, clearly distinguish combatants from civilians.

In the twentieth century, 43 million to 54 million civilians died from war-related causes, which amounts to 50 to 62 percent of all deaths.[18] Numbers are on the rise due to various factors, including the spread of new far-reaching and deadly technologies, with the extreme illustration of the atomic bomb launched on Hiroshima on August 6, 1945. The challenges international humanitarian law faces today regarding the distinction between civilians and combatants and the protection of civilians are numerous and deal with asymmetric wars, terrorism, a lack of ethics, and the development of new technologies. Indeed there are massive casualties in the

---

[14] MAURICE KEEN, THE LAWS OF WAR IN THE LATE MIDDLE AGES 17–22 (London, Routledge & K. Paul 1965).

[15] FREDERICK RUSSELL, THE JUST WAR IN THE MIDDLE AGES (Cambridge; New York: Cambridge University Press 1975).

[16] Sohail H. Hashmi, *Saving and Taking Life in War: Three Modern Muslim Views*, 89: 2 THE MUSLIM WORLD 158, 158–80 (April 1999).

[17] Anicée Van Engeland, *Islam and the Protection of Civilians in the Conduct of Hostilities: The Asymmetrical War from the Transnational Terrorist Groups' Viewpoints and from the Muslim Modernists' Viewpoints, in* JIHAD AND THE CHALLENGES OF INTERNATIONAL AND DOMESTIC LAW (The Hague: Asser Press & Cambridge University Press forthcoming 2009). It was published in 2010

[18] William Eckhardt, *Civilian Deaths in Wartime*, 20:1 BULLETIN OF PEACE PROPOSALS 90 (1989).

field; terrorism takes hostage scores of civilians; the lack of ethics leads to the justification of civilians' deaths in the name of a greater good; and the development of new technologies allows for bombs that suppress all human life without affecting buildings for chemical agents that incapacitate, injure, or kill by attacking the nervous system.[19] The latter were used in Iraq by Saddam Hussein against the Shias and the Kurds, and against Iranian civilians during the 1980–88 war.[20] There is an increasing pressure from the military to lead comprehensive wars including so-called new parameters, which is clearly at the cost of civilians' lives. In a way, it has become acceptable to have collateral damage among civilians in the name of an extended interpretation and understanding of the principle of military necessity.[21] The outcome is that rather than striving for respect of the distinction at all costs, some people try to find cracks in the system and argue on the basis of military logic, justifying therefore, for example, the potential targeting of human shields. It is a rhetoric Saddam Hussein used during the war with Iran in the 1980s: he invoked international humanitarian law while violating it.[22] Iraq bombed civilians' sites on a huge scale in blunt violation of Article 51-5 (b) API, which deals with protection of civilians and states that "an attack which may be expected to cause incidental loss of civilian life, injury to civilians, damage to civilian objects, or a combination thereof, which would be excessive in relation to the concrete and direct military advantage anticipated" is considered indiscriminate. In 1985, the Secretary General of the United Nations tried to encourage a ceasefire and respect for the Geneva Conventions. The government of Iraq replied that "the application of specific conventions and Additional Protocols cannot be conditional upon a cease-fire: they have been adopted precisely to mitigate the effects of the war";[23] As General William T. Sherman

---

[19] Radiological and chemical weapons can contaminate a territory or poison human beings without affecting structures. See, e.g., U.S. CONGRESS/OFFICE OF TECHNOLOGY ASSESSMENT, PROLIFERATION OF WEAPONS OF MASS DESTRUCTION: ASSESSING THE RISKS 3 (Washington DC: US Government Printing Office 1993).

[20] JOOST HILTERMANN, A POISONOUS AFFAIR: AMERICA, IRAQ AND THE GASSING OF HALABJA 150 (New York: Cambridge University Press 2007).

[21] Military necessity is a principle of humanitarian law, along with the principle of distinction and the principle of proportionality. It is a fundamental notion according to which an attack or action must be intended to help in the military defeat of the enemy. It must be an attack on a military objective, and the harm caused to civilians or civilian property must be proportional and not excessive in relation to the concrete and direct military advantage anticipated. There is a debate regarding the manipulations of the concept: there is a trend that tries to extend the concept to cover other situations, in particular collateral damage. The Military Necessity Project at PRIO in Norway works on these attempts of manipulation: http://www.prio.no/Research-and-Publications/Project/?oid=19239363. Questions arise in all fields of humanitarian protection, as demonstrated by the following article dealing with the protection afforded in the medical field: Hans-Ulrich Baer & Jean-Michel Baillat, Military Necessity versus the Protection of the Wounded and Sick: A Critical Balance, 167:8 MILITARY MEDICINE 17–19 (2002).

[22] THE GULF WAR OF 1980–88: THE IRAN-IRAQ WAR IN INTERNATIONAL LEGAL PERSPECTIVE (Ike Dekker & Harry H. G. Post eds., Dordrecht: Martinus Nijhoff 1992).

[23] Report of Secretary General, Field Trip in Iran and in Iraq, UN Doc. S/17097, at 8–9 (Apr. 12, 1985).

put it: "The crueler it [war] is, the sooner it will be over."[24] Michael Walzer explains the rational for such approaches by writing: "the greater the justice of my cause, the more rules I can violate for the sake of the cause—though some rules are always inviolable. The same argument can be put in terms of outcomes: the greater the injustice likely to result from my defeat, the more rules I can violate in order to avoid defeat."[25] It was clear in the case of Saddam Hussein during the war with Iran that he approached war that way which is why he turned to total war targeting civilians (and so did Iran, but for other reasons[26]). This reasoning is based upon raw military necessity and sets aside the humanitarian part of the Geneva Conventions and the Additional Protocols. The outcome was the gassing of the Iraqi Kurds and Shias in Iraq as well as the draining of the Marshland, and the massive bombing of Iranian villages, towns and cities.

This type of behavior highlights the need for a rehumanization of current international humanitarian law, too often construed as the law of armed conflict. The regulation of war through the lens of the law of armed conflict rather than through the eye of international humanitarian law amounts to more than a semantic issue: it results in an increasingly militarized reading of the Geneva Conventions and other documents at the expense of humanitarian principles. An instance of this change is the Blair doctrine, named after Britain's Prime Minister Tony Blair, which justified wars in Iraq and Afghanistan in the name of human rights interests, rather than military interests,[27] blurring therefore the lines between the laws of war and international humanitarian law. Yet, in the end, peace, development, democracy, and human rights were all to be imported through wars and caused the mass killing of civilians. Another illustration of the tendency to speak of the laws of the war as to give all the importance to the military, at the expense of the humanitarian aspect of the law, can be found in the Israeli Defense Forces (IDF)'s strategy of entering Palestinian Occupied Territories with tanks and of bombing the territories. Civilians have paid a high price for the so-called military necessity, with the Israeli army committing abuses when bombarding orphanages, hospitals, and humanitarian organizations' headquarters. The war rhetoric of these belligerents justifies the death of civilians for a greater cause, whether it is the creation of an Islamic world for al Qaeda or the strengthening of peace and security in the world for former Prime Minister Tony Blair and former President George W. Bush.

---

[24] Letter from General William T. Sherman to James Calhoun, September 12, 1864, *in* 2 WILLIAM TECUMSEH SHERMAN, MEMOIRS OF GENERAL WILLIAM T. SHERMAN 600–02 (New York, D. Appleton and Company 1875).

[25] MICHAEL WALZER, JUST AND UNJUST WARS 229 (New York: Basic Books 1992).

[26] Iran avoided targeting civilians at the beginning of the war. Yet when it saw that Iraqi citizens were not rebelling against Saddam Hussein as they were expected under Islamic standards (Muslims are expected to revolt against unjust rulers, and their oppression is one basis for a legitimate jihad), the country opted for total war on Iraq.

[27] C. Abbott & J. Sloboda, *The "Blair Doctrine" and After: Five Years of Humanitarian Intervention*, Open Democracy (Apr. 21, 2004), http://www.opendemocracy.net/globalization-institutions_government/article_1857.jsp.

Establishing a comparison between al Qaeda and the United States is certainly not right considering there is a difference of mind frame, approach and goals: al Qaeda seeks anarchy and never tries to adhere to humanitarian standards, Hussein sought dictatorial control, while Israel and the United States tried to find an appropriate response to violence, although both often act on the fringes on international law. However, in the end, civilians are hurt, maimed, or killed. Additionally, it is not because a war crime is committed by a wealthy nation in the name of ideals that it is more acceptable than the horrible deeds committed by others. The very philosophy of the Blair Doctrine is wrong: to justify a military intervention on humanitarian grounds is contradictory, as illustrated in Afghanistan, where the first victims of the conflict are the very women the coalition promised to free from human rights violations. Other instances of Western double standards include the creation of the International Criminal Tribunal for Former Yugoslavia: it did not emerge to prosecute war crimes committed by NATO; and yet some of NATO's actions in the region were undeniably war crimes. However, since the legal machinery was set up by the Security Council, there was little chance that NATO would ever be prosecuted.

The tragic events of 9/11 have not only cast a light on matters that have been lingering since World War II; they have brought them into broad daylight: civilians die more than combatants. This is the outcome of a shift: before, it was mainly countries from the southern hemisphere whose gross violations of international humanitarian law were publicized. After 9/11, the United States and its Allies could not hide their own violations. In a war like the War on Terror, all codes of ethics have faded in the name of a goal. This is how we have witnessed a slow but sure transition from international humanitarian law to the laws of war as the rubric for military decisions. The Geneva body of law is not so much used to protect civilians and to distinguish combatants from civilians; it is now perceived as laws setting up guidelines for the conduct of hostilities. The focus of these laws has transitioned from civilians to the army's tactics and strategies.

An alternative and dynamic reading of all international documents pertaining to the regulation of war exists; it is encompassed in international humanitarian law and the humanitarian legal philosophy. To switch back to this humanitarian philosophy that focuses on the "human" and the "humanitarian" rather than the army's needs, a strict and rigorous approach to protecting of civilians should be set forward. Additionally, the military approach should be turned on its head by mitigating the concept of military necessity, which pushed to its extreme creates dangerous precedents such as the bloodbath caused by the Sri Lankan army and the Tamil Tigers in 2009. Another approach to the distinction between civilians and combatants, far from the extended understanding of the concept of military necessity and collateral damages, should be advocated. As stressed by Antonio Cassese, the evolution of modern war has led to the increased killing of civilians despite the concomitant emergence of laws to distinguish and protect, and an end should be put to this phenomenon.[28]

Besides the targeting of civilians, there is another issue: there is a constant evolution of the status of civilians and combatants that cannot and should not be ignored as some people seem to fall on the line between the two categories because of their actions. There were for instance debates to know whether or not the status of combatants could apply to the Taliban and al Qaeda fighters in Afghanistan. Questions arise: if a peasant grows vegetables and sells them to the army, does that make him a combatant? What is the status of armed sentinels in Peru's villages ready to defend their people against various guerrilla movements and drug lords? Are the Palestinians living in the Occupied Territories and building new types of bombs without firing them civilians or combatants? What about those who travel underground through a labyrinth of tunnels to bring back medications, food, and weapons? Those who are armed to defend their families against factional struggles and Israeli patrols? What about the Palestinian woman who hides men belonging to the insurgency? Where and how to draw the line between a civilian and a combatant? The conditions under which someone is a civilian have been blurred because some non-combatants take part in the conflict. Indeed, the Conventions and the Additional Protocols give detailed rules regarding the distinction between civilians and combatants, and when the line is blurred, the Protocols provide extra protection via the Conventions and customary law.

FROM MY LAI AND SABRA AND SHATILA TO GUANTANAMO

The blurring between the two categories, combatants and non combatants, is prone to manipulation and the broadening of concepts like military necessity and collateral damage leads to major catastrophes and massacres. The principle of distinction should instead be seen as sacred. There are catastrophes when the principle is not respected either directly or indirectly—if twisted, for example, to answer a military agenda. Two major events illustrating the nonrespect of the distinction can be found in the history of the twentieth century: the massacres of My Lai, and Sabra and Shatila. On March 16, 1968, 347 unarmed civilians were brutally murdered by the U.S. army in South Vietnam. The massacres took place in two small hamlets, My Lai and My Khe, parts of the Son My Village. The U.S. army attacked the village thinking Vietcong were hiding there. Civilians often hid Vietcong among themselves because they supported the rebellion; there were also civilians who sometimes carried out acts of violence. These two elements were enough to blur all ethical lines. When the soldiers reached the two hamlets, orders given by U.S. army superiors to soldiers regarding civilians were vague. The combination of all these factors (and of course other factors such as physical exhaustion, fear, and other psychological factors) resulted in a ruthless, indiscriminate massacre that lasted

---

[28] Antonio Cassese, Fabio Mino e Giorgio Rochat, *Vittime civili il prezzo assurdo delle guerre*, LA REPUBBLICA, and General Fabio Mini, LA REPUBBLICA, Gennaio 20, 2009, at 1.

two days. Some of the victims were raped, tortured, or maimed.[29] The My Son Massacre demonstrates why it is crucial to respect the distinction, to have soldiers educated to understand, respect, and enforce it even under heavy stress, and to have a chain of command deeply committed to the respect and enforcement of international humanitarian law.

The second example is the Sabra and Shatila massacre: 3,500 people were butchered during two days of September 1982 by the Lebanese Forces militia group, with the support of the Israeli Defense Force. The two Palestinian refugee camps located in Lebanon were at the time full of women, children, and elderly people. During three days, the Israeli Defense Force blocked all entrances and exits, trapping refugees who were killed by the Phalangists[30] on the basis that Israel was looking for PLO fighters hiding among civilians.[31] These two events are the very outcome of the rhetoric of the military abusing the very concept of military necessity and of the violation of the principle of distinction. These examples are disturbing because both massacres were committed or backed up by two democratic countries: the United States and Israel. This shows that no army is immune to violations of humanitarian law, and this is why the transition from humanitarian law to the laws of war must be fought with energy. The focus of the law must be on civilians and not on war.

Another consequence of the current main trend of thought and interpretation of the "laws of armed conflict" is the existence of the Guantanamo Bay detention center. The very fact that the detention camp at Guantanamo Bay exists shows that some countries do not mind twisting international humanitarian law to fit a political agenda. This leaves hollow the very purpose of international humanitarian law, which is to protect. The laws have been elaborated to protect civilians and combatants as well as people who would fall in between the two categories: it cannot and should not be used and abused, or referred to as being "quaint and obsolete[32]", to explain the existence of Guantanamo Bay and the practice of torture by the United States.

The very philosophy of international humanitarian law seems to be forgotten under the pressure of military necessity. This shift actually illustrates an ongoing semantic debate between, on the one hand, the Hague law that deals mainly with the conduct of hostilities and combatants, and the Geneva law, dealing with civilians'

[29] *Murder in the Name of War—My Lai*, BBC NEWS, July 20, 1998; MICHAEL BILTON & KEVIN SIM, FOUR HOURS IN MY LAI (London: Penguin 1993); for an analysis, see LAWRENCE A. TRITLE, FROM MELOS TO MY LAI: WAR AND SURVIVAL (London; New York: Routledge 2000).

[30] A Lebanese Christian Militia.

[31] BAYAN NUWAYHED AL-HOUT, SABRA AND CHATILA: SEPTEMBER 1982 (London; Ann Arbor, MI: Pluto Press 2004).

[32] The White House's chief legal adviser, Alberto Gonzales, declared the Geneva Conventions to be so in a memorandum: Alberto R. Gonzales, MEMORENDUM TO THE PRESIDENT, RE: DECISION RE APPLICATION OF THE GENEVA CONVENTIONS ON PRISONERS OF WAR IN THE CONFLICT WITH AL QAEDA AND THE TALIBAN, 25 January 2002.

protection. Yoram Dinstein rejects this division as being an effect of fashion.[33] There is certainly no difference between the two laws, both belonging to international humanitarian law and symbolizing an evolution, the Hague laws dating back as far as 1907, while the Geneva Conventions and the Additional Protocols are closer to us in time (1949 and 1977, respectively). There is however no doubt that the two sets of law spring from different philosophies: the Hague law is rather focused on the military aspect while the Geneva law is focused on the human aspect. There is also no denial that today armies and armed groups tend to approach the regulation of war through the regulation of the conduct of hostilities while humanitarian law focuses on human victims of war. Organizations that should fight this trend keep welcoming more advocates of the extended approach to military necessity in their ranks by awarding them humanitarian prizes for academic articles or hiring them as security consultants. If it is a normal trend to have the military interacting with organizations devoted to protect civilians, especially since members of the army bring in knowledge about the reality of war, it remains a symptom of a shift to accommodate the army's needs. The participation of the military in humanitarian studies is not a problem in itself: on the contrary, it brings a variety of thought to the field. The problem lies with the import of a new philosophy that violates the creed of international humanitarian law. An example of this influence can be seen in the International Committee of the Red Cross (ICRC) interpretative guidance as to how the concept of "direct participation to hostilities" should be understood. The series of expert meetings that produced the guidelines seems to have given in to a military viewpoint. Indeed, if the guidance brings a much-needed clarification to the concept of "direct participation in hostilities," it also creates some doubts. It is said that members of organized groups belonging to a non state party to the armed conflict cease to be civilians and lose their protection for as long as they assume a combat function. This rule raises several questions pertaining to the time factor: when does one become a fighter and cease to be a fighter? The ICRC seems to be going down the path that a farmer who cultivates during the day and turns into a fighter at night is a combatant even when he attends to crops. Does that mean that a Hamas leader not in arms and attending a wedding can be a legitimate target, despite the presence of all the civilian guests? Would the farmer-by-day/fighter-by-night working on his crops with his children be a legitimate target? Considering the behavior of Israel and the United States with regard to targeted killings, some clarifications are needed; otherwise, it seems like the ICRC guidance might pave the way to the membership-based argument that targets all members of an armed non state actor that belong to that movement. There are however clarifications in the document that indicate quite clearly the importance of the time factor: the civilian is a combatant for the time he is in arms, as clarified in chapter 4. The ICRC needs to provide more explanations as to what the time of being in arms means to avoid having the membership argument take over the field.

---

[33] Yoram Dinstein, The Conduct of Hostilities under International Armed Conflict 12 (Cambridge: Cambridge University Press 2004).

The need to protect civilians will be argued throughout the book, which will also analyze other challenges, issues, and threats, such as wars of self determination; the changing face of modern warfare with new technology and new weaponry; the expansion of guerrilla methods; the permanency of terrorism; asymmetric conflicts; and other issues affecting the distinction between civilians and combatants in the twenty-first century.

1 The Distinction between Combatants and Civilians, a Cornerstone of International Humanitarian Law

The necessity of distinguishing between civilians and combatants in war has been clear since early in history. The development of the distinction has been influenced by the evolution of warfare, legal traditions, and historical events. Some of these elements are presented in this chapter. The inclusion of the principle of distinction within positive law in the 1949 Geneva Conventions, completed later by the 1977 Additional Protocols, was, in that regard, an important step. However, the rapid evolution of warfare has raised numerous questions; civilians are still deliberately targeted and are victims of war and attacks. Before arguing and explaining why the distinction is still relevant, and before addressing all issues arising under the principle of distinction between the two categories, it is necessary to describe the history of the distinction while briefly explaining the role that philosophy, ethics, law, culture, and religion have played in its development.

I. THE DISTINCTION IN HISTORY: ETHICS, LAW, AND POLITICAL PHILOSOPHY

The duty to protect civilians and to distinguish civilians from combatants is quite ancient. It is therefore not surprising that the principle of distinction between civilians and combatants, so deeply entrenched in law, philosophy, and ethics, is one of the cornerstones of modern international humanitarian law. A brief look at history shows there has been an effort to spare civilians in wartime and war zones, despite the records of massacres.

1

A. Civilians as Incidental Victims of War: From Association with Territories, Leadership, and Population to the Emergence of the Nation State

Despite early attempts to codify behaviors during war, civilians were left to the mercy of belligerents and to their beliefs as to whether or not they should spare civilians. Approaches to the issues varied according to places and civilizations: one of the cornerstones of the Islamic humanitarian philosophy was the distinction between civilians and combatants, as well as several other humanitarian principles, from the protection of cattle to the rights of prisoners of war.[1] There were however discordant voices, in particular among Classicist and later among Neo-Classicist jurists: for example, Al Shaybani allowed the killing of captives,[2] and Al Mawardi agreed with the killing of old men.[3] Humanitarian standards were therefore lowered by these intellectuals because of the higher purpose of the war, which was to universalize Islam through jihad.[4] Bin Laden and al Qaeda's ideologues refer to these authors to justify the deliberate targeting of civilians today. This is a clear demonstration of how humanitarian standards that are clear in Islam can be distorted to fit a political agenda and how different philosophies affect civilians. This illustration shows that restraints depend upon the ethics of the belligerent, with the understanding that ethics is a subjective element. It was so until the codification of the distinction between civilians and combatants and of the principle of protection in the Geneva Conventions and the Protocols.

An example of how civilians depended about philosophies and ethics can be found in the Bible in Numbers 31:7–8, which reflects the philosophy of the time:[5]

They fought against Midian, as the LORD commanded Moses, and killed every man. Among their victims were Evi, Rekem, Zur, Hur and Reba—the five kings of Midian. They also killed Balaam son of Beor with the sword. The Israelites captured the Midianite women and children and took all the Midianite herds, flocks and goods as plunder.

---

[1] *See, e.g.*, Mian Rashid Ahmad Khan, Islamic Jurisprudence 211 (Lahore: SH Muhammad Ashraf ed., 1978); Marcel A. Boisard, *The Conduct of Hostilities and the Protection of the Victims of Armed Conflicts in Islam*, 1: 2 *in* Hamdard Islamicus 10 (1978); Ayatollah Mohaghegh Damad, *International Humanitarian Law in Islam and Contemporary International Law*, *in* Islamic Views on Human Rights: Viewpoints of Iranian Scholars 253, 253–93 (Husayn Salimi & Homeyra Moshirzadeh eds., Kanishka Publishers 2003); Hilmi M. Zawati, Is Jihad a Just War? War, Peace, and Human Rights under Islamic and Public International Law 89 (Edwin Mellen Press, Studies in Religion and Society Series No. 53, 2001); Harifah Abdel Haleem, Oliver Ramsbotham, Saba Risaluddin, & Brian Wicker, The Crescent and the Cross: Muslim and Christian Approaches to War and Peace 67 (Palgrave-UK-USA 1998).

[2] Troy S. Thomas, *Jihad's Captives: Prisoners of War in Islam*, 12 J. Legal Stud. 87–101 (2002/2003).

[3] Hassan al Mawardi, Al Akram as-Sultaniyyah [The Laws of Islamic Governance] 192 (Ta Ha Publishers 1996).

[4] Sayyid Qutb, Fi Zilal al Quran [In the Shade of the Quran] (Al Zarahba Al Shariah ed., 1980).

[5] The author is using the online Bible available on www.biblica.com

They burned all the towns where the Midianites had settled, as well as all their camps. They took all the plunder and spoils, including the people and animals, and brought the captives, spoils and plunder to Moses and Eleazar the priest and the Israelite assembly at their camp on the plains of Moab, by the Jordan across from Jericho.

This is not an exception in the Bible and, under certain circumstances, it was allowed to kill an enemy and seize his property.[6] This is a realistic approach of war as being part of the human realm, an approach that is also found in the Quran: when the Holy Book was revealed and the Prophet was alive, there were many wars and feuds going on,[7] and this is reflected in Islamic law. There are rules (*siyar*) to instruct Muslims how they should deal with conflicts and war. However, just as the Bible does, *siyar* contain humanitarian principles. For example, the Quran says: "Fight in the cause of Allah those who fight you, but do not transgress limits; for Allah loveth not transgressors." (Quran 2:190).[8] A good example of a *hadith* (Abu Dawud) regulating a humanitarian principle is: "Do not kill an old person, a child, a woman; do not cheat on the booty, do well: God likes the ones who act right."[9] Another *hadith* reports that the Prophet Muhammed said: "Prisoners are your brothers and companions. It is because of God's compassion that they are in your hands. They are at your mercy, so treat them well as if you were treating yourself, with food, clothes and housing."[10] Or, "[d]o not be eager to meet the enemy but ask God for safety; yet, if you meet them, persevere and have patience; and know that Paradise is under the Shadow of Swords."[11] This said, the Quran has a very controversial verse called the Verse of the Sword, verse 9:5, that is rather violent:

But when the forbidden months are past, then fight and slay the Pagans wherever ye find them, and seize them, beleaguer them, and lie in wait for them in every stratagem [of war]; but if they repent, and establish regular prayers and practice regular charity, then open the way for them: for Allah is Oft-forgiving, Most Merciful.[12]

---

[6] For more regarding Christian philosophy of war, see also CROSS, CRESCENT, AND SWORD: THE JUSTIFICATION AND LIMITATION OF WAR IN WESTERN AND ISLAMIC TRADITION (James Turner Johnson & John Kelsay eds., Greenwood Press 1991).

[7] Ayatollah Morteza Mottahari, *Introduction* to JIHAD VA MAVAREDE MASHRUYIAT-E DAR QURAN [JIHAD AND ITS LEGITIMACY IN THE QURAN] (Islamic Culture and Relations Organization 1998).

[8] Yusuf Ali, translation, http://www.usc.edu/schools/college/crcc/engagement/resources/texts/muslim/quran/009.qmt.html.

[9] Hadith quoted in Hamed Sultan, *La Conception Islamique [The Islamic Approach]*, *in* LES DIMENSIONS INTERNATIONALES DU DROIT HUMANITAIRE 57 (Institut Henry Dunant & UNESCO eds., Paris: Pedone 1986).

[10] Quoted in M. K. Erekoussi, *Le Coran et les Conventions Humanitaires [The Quran and Humanitarian Conventions]*, 503 REVUE INTERNATIONALE DE LA CROIX ROUGE 650 (1960).

[11] Hadith reported by Bukhari and quoted by Mian Rashid Ahmad Khan, ISLAMIC JURISPRUDENCE 211 (Lahore: S. H. Muhammad Ashraf ed., 1978).

[12] *See supra* note 8.

This verse is invoked by fundamentalists and Islamic terrorist groups. Real divergences regarding the distinction between civilians and combatants date from Classicists and in particular Neo-Classicists. The two examples above borrowed from religious sacred texts show that although there was an attempt to limit civilian casualties, war is part of the human reality and should be addressed, which is the same approach adopted by international humanitarian law: it mitigates the effects of war on people but it does not seek to prohibit war. Interpretations made of these religious texts also try to reflect the harsh reality of a war zone. These sacred texts have influenced generations of warriors in their approach to civilians, whether during the Crusades or during different jihads.

The language of the Quran, like that of the Bible, seems to associate a people with the leadership: territories were not organized like today, in States, but rather in small territories where all inhabitants owed an allegiance to a lord, or in small territories belonging to a tribe or clan elsewhere.[13] Therefore, because of the oath of allegiance, the population was assimilated to the lord or the tribe and had to bear all consequences. Hugo Grotius made a long list of massacres of civilians in ancient history.[14] The existence of such a long record of killings can be explained by the nature of war before the emergence of Nation States: war was a contest of territories, a pursuit to extend empires, with inhabitants considered part of the war booty and seen as enemies. In ancient times Servius,[15] commenting on a passage of Virgil, stated that the poet said that war "will authorize mutual acts of destruction and rapine."[16] As stated above, this reflects the social and traditional beliefs of the time: the population gave allegiance to a leader and had to pay the price if or when he lost to others. In one of Euripides' tragedies, *The Children of Herakles*, it is explained that killing an enemy in a war is not a murder, and non combatants were perceived as enemies.[17] This play is challenging, in particular for the time, since it questions the treatment of prisoners of war and refugees as well as the ethical behavior on the war field, while in the Greek or Roman ethics, killing was part of a war. Grotius cites several authors, politicians, and jurists who confirm this approach: Caesar said to the Eduans that "it was an act of kindness in him, to spare those whom the laws of war would have authorized him to put to death."[18] What probably best reflects the environment of the time and the approach regarding civilians is the following dialogue in Thucydides' history of the

---

[13] HANS MORGENTHAU ET AL., POLITICS AMONG NATIONS (7th ed. McGraw-Hill Humanities/Social Sciences/Languages 2005).

[14] *See* HUGO GROTIUS, ON THE LAW OF WAR AND PEACE (Louise R. Loomis trans., published for the Classics Club by W. J. Black 1949) (1625).

[15] Maurus Servius Honoratus was a grammarian who lived in the fourth century AD. He authored a book of commentary on Virgil, *In tria Virgilii Opera Expositio*, which was the first manuscript to be printed in Florence by Bernardo Cennini in 1471.

[16] Servius is quoted by Hugo Grotius, *supra* note 14, chapter 4, "On the Right of Killing an Enemy in Lawful War, and Committing Other Acts of Hostility."

[17] EURIPIDES, CHILDREN OF HERAKLES (Henry Taylor & Robert A. Brooks trans., Oxford University Press 1981).

[18] GROTIUS, *supra* note 14, at 259.

Peloponnesian war: The people of Melos, a small island in the Aegean, wanted to remain neutral and had no desire to join the Athenian Empire, so the Athenians forced them to chose a side. When they refused to do so, Athenians invaded Melos, in 416 BCE. Thucydides presents an account of a dialogue between the Athenians and the Melians.[19] The Athenians offer the Melians a choice: become a subject of Athens, or resist and be annihilated. The Melians reply by saying that justice is on their side and they have the right to remain neutral. The answer from the Athenians is swift: the population of Melos was massacred or enslaved. There were laws of war regulating combat in ancient times[20]—although most laws were customary—but civilians were not considered *per se* in these laws: they were approached as being part of the war booty.[21] The laws of war were based upon religious beliefs and a code of honor but had little consideration for non combatants. Civilians were either killed, enslaved, or captured for ransom. However, natural law called for restraints and, indeed, the Athenians later regretted the Melos massacre. In Roman history, civilians did not fare better, as reflected by Juvenal in his *Satires*. In one episode, it is explained that prisoners of war do not dare complain against violence made against them because soldiers were perceived as all-empowered.[22]

The idea that an entire population represents an entity to conquer slowly disappeared with the emergence of the Nation State and the apparition of the concept of citizens: civilians are not seen as swearing allegiances to a leader anymore but as a separate entity. As stressed by Von Clausewitz, armies become professionals and a code of ethics begin to emerge, in which the fighting is restricted to soldiers. However, such justification for the attacks on the Twin Towers in New York City on September 11, 2001, can be found in al Qaeda's rhetoric: Saudi Sheikh Ali al Khudeir justifies the 2001 killings by saying that civilians working in the Twin Towers were involved in capitalism, and were working for the State or for offices linked to the American system. They had also elected George W. Bush as president and therefore supported his policies. Consequently, they were combatants indirectly representing their government.[23] Rashid al Ghanouchi,[24] a Tunisian Islamist and the exiled leader of Tunisia's Hizb al-Nahda (Renaissance-Party)—a banned Islamist opposition political party in Tunisia—issued a *fatwa*, which is a legal decision, in which he allows the killing of Israeli civilians because "there are no civilians in Israel.

---

[19] THUCYDIDES, HISTORY OF THE PELOPONNESIAN WAR, 5.89 (Benjamin Jowett trans., Oxford Clarendon Press 1990).

[20] *See, e.g.,* Everett L. Wheeler, *Ephorus and the Prohibition of Missiles,* 117 TRANSACTIONS OF THE AMERICAN PHILOLOGICAL ASSOCIATION 178–82 (1987); Josiah Ober, *Classical Greek Times, in* THE LAWS OF WAR: CONSTRAINTS ON WARFARE IN THE WESTERN WORLD (Michael Howard et al. eds., Yale University Press 1994).

[21] Adrian Lanni, *The Laws of War in Ancient Greece,* 26:3 LAW AND HISTORY (2008).

[22] JUVENAL, SATIRES (Cambridge University Press 1996).

[23] Ali bin Khudeir al-Khudeiri, *fatwa* published in AL-HAYAT, Feb. 13, 2002.

[24] It is important to stress that al Ghannouchi is a very controversial figure in Islam: some consider him a dangerous extremist, while others see him as a democrat.

The population—males, females, and children—are the army reserve soldiers, and thus can be killed."25

Despite such exceptions, there has been a clear evolution with the emergence of a Nation State: war is led by a State against another State, and professional armies oppose each other; it is then that civilians cease to be considered incidental victims of war and part of the war booty. The emergence of transnational wars have come to question this way of waging wars, and civilians are again at the core of conflicts, especially with regard to terrorism.

B. First Attempts and Regulations to Limit War and Protect Civilians

What seems to be one of the first attempts to regulate war can be found in the Old Testament. Deuteronomy 20:19 puts a limit on collateral damages as well as damages to the environment:

When thou shalt besiege a city a long time, in making war against it to take it, thou shalt not destroy the trees thereof by wielding an axe against them; for thou mayest eat of them, but thou shalt not cut them down; for is the tree of the field man, that it should be besieged of thee? Only the trees of which thou knowest that they are not trees for food, them thou mayest destroy and cut down, that thou mayest build bulwarks against the city that maketh war with thee, until it fall.

Additionally, Deuteronomy 21:10–15 says that female captives should be treated according to proper human standards. Similar rules can be found in Islamic law.[26] The Prophet Muhammad had a lot of interactions with other tribes and nations. He soon needed a set of rules that would regulate Islamic behavior in international relations.[27] He prepared for war but also included humanitarian standards from the viewpoint of the Quran. An example of such a standard is the distinction between civilians and combatants: civilians cannot be targeted.

[25] Rashid al Ghannouchi, *fatwa* from his 1993 book, FREEDOM IN THE ISLAMIC STATE, cited in John C. Zimmerman, *Roots of Conflict: The Islamist Critique of Western Value*, 30:4 JOURNAL OF SOCIAL, POLITICAL, AND ECONOMIC STUDIES 455: 425–58 (2005).

[26] Anicée Van Engeland, *The Differences and Similarities between International Humanitarian Law and Islamic Humanitarian Law: Is There Ground for Reconciliation?* 10:1 THE JOURNAL OF ISLAMIC LAW & CULTURE 81–97 (2008); Anicée Van Engeland, *Islam and the Protection of Civilians in the Conduct of Hostilities: The Asymmetrical War from the Transnational Terrorist Groups' Viewpoints and from the Muslim Modernists' Viewpoints, in* JIHAD AND THE CHALLENGES OF INTERNATIONAL AND DOMESTIC LAW (The Hague: Asser Press & Cambridge University Press, 2010).

[27] Murielle Paradelle, *Une Approche Sociologique de la Théorie Classique du Droit International Islamique, in* DROITS ET SOCIETES DAN LE MONDE ARABE: PERSPECTIVES SOCIO-ANTHROPOLOGIQUES 25–35 (Gilles Boëtsch et al. eds., Presses Universitaires de Marseille 1997).

This is a divine order that cannot be transgressed.[28] Caliph Abu Bakr is reported to have said:

Stop, O people, that I may give you ten rules for your guidance in the battlefield. Do not commit treachery or deviate from the right path. You must not mutilate dead bodies. Neither kill a child, nor a woman, nor an aged man. Bring no harm to the trees, nor burn them with fire, especially those which are fruitful. Slay not any of the enemy's flock, save for your food. You are likely to pass by people who have devoted their lives to monastic services; leave them alone.[29]

Greek philosophers spoke of moderation: Plato in *Republic* and *Laws* speaks about war and urges for limits to war. In *Republic*, he harshly criticized the way the Greeks led war with no constraints. Aristotle also calls for limits and says that the very nature of men is to be reasonable, rather than be carried away by passion and violence. Later, Cicero, a Roman lawyer, believed war must be led justly, which included refraining from attacking unarmed civilians. His thoughts about human treatment during war were quite important[30] and were developed by Bishop Ambrose of Milan (fourth century) and integrated into Christian thinking.[31] Another attempt to humanize war in antiquity is the code of Emperor Maurice, who compiled *Strategica* (Articles of War) toward the end of the sixth century AD. The document states that a soldier who hurts a civilian and makes no effort to repair the damage will be requested to repay the damage twofold.[32] The *Ex Ruffo Leges Militares* (*Military Laws from Rufus*) applied harsher judgments, with physical maiming of soldiers when they attacked civilians. These are a few examples of attempts to "humanize" war.

In practice, in antiquity, there were formal and informal rules of war, and restraints on excesses were clearly an issue since it is mentioned by many authors, although most of them approach civilian causalities as incidental to war. An event related by Herodotus demonstrates the emergence of an awareness regarding the need to avoid massacres. Persian envoys sent by Darius I were slaughtered by Alexander I of Macedon. The Spartans did the same. Both the Athenians and the Spartans acknowledged they had transgressed the laws of man, as well as the laws applicable to Barbarians.[33] Xerxes, King of Persia, pondered doing the same later but then

---

[28] HARIFAH ABDEL HALEEM ET AL., THE CRESCENT AND THE CROSS: MUSLIM AND CHRISTIAN APPROACHES TO WAR AND PEACE 69 (New York: MacMillan 1998).

[29] YUSSEF ABOUL-ENEINE & SHERIFA ZUHUR, ISLAMIC RULINGS ON WARFARE 22 (Strategic Studies Institute, U.S. Army War College 2004).

[30] Marcus Tullius Cicero, senator and philosopher, is a father of the theory of "just war." *See* CICERO, DE OFFICIIS (M. Ponsot trans., Paris: F. Tandou 1864).

[31] *See, e.g.*, JOSEPH FRANCIS KELLY, THE WORLD OF EARLY CHRISTIANS 164–65 (The Liturgical Press 1997).

[32] C. E. BRAND, ROMAN MILITARY LAW 195–96 (University of Texas Press 1968) (quoting from a Greek translation of *Strategica*, Chapter VI, 10).

[33] *See* Timothy L. H. McCormack, *From Sun Tzu to the Sixth Committee: The Evolution of International Criminal Law Regime, in* THE LAW OF WAR CRIMES: NATIONAL AND INTERNATIONAL

opted out: he considered these acts of violence a violation of the laws of nation.[34] The Greeks also considered war excesses to be violations of law that could bring a soldier to court, although trials were set up on a rather ad hoc basis.[35]

Attempts to draw a distinction can be found in different legal, religious, or philosophical sources other than the West. The renowned *Art of War* by Sun Tzu (dated to 500 BC) and the *Manu Smriti*, an anonymous Sanskrit treatise (dated between 200 BC and 200 AD), forbade the killings of prisoners of war. The Code of Manu is the oldest code of Hindu law and speaks of the legal regulation of armed conflicts:[36] it prohibits some weapons because of the wounds they make. It dictates that unarmed or wounded soldiers, as well as civilians, cannot be killed. Morality supports the document, along with religious values. That said, it is really law the document talks about, in particular in relation to war: violations of this code would have been judged in a court.[37] In his book, Sun Tzu prescribed humanitarian limitations in the conduct of hostilities.[38] He does not refer to any particular ethics or religion to justify these limitations but evaluates the effects of the war and tries to be rational: there is no point destroying the environment and cities or killing people, since all of them are useful once the conquest is over. There is no sense in ruling a ruined and deserted city. Modern utilitarian philosophers would add that it is counterproductive since the battle for hearts and minds is as important as the war itself. Rather, Sun Tzu's theory is about making the most out of a conflict, and that includes keeping civilians alive. In both documents, the distinction between civilians and combatants appears but is not directly addressed. The humanization of warfare and the respect of the civilian status are analyzed: for example, both Sun Tzu and the *Smriti* suggest, instead of killing civilians to integrate them into the army, enslaving them or asking for a ransom. Mao Tse Tung based his actions on Sun Tzu's theory when he opted for the integration solution, after the Chinese Nationalists, led by Chang Kai Chek, were defeated.[39]

In the fourth century, in the West, the philosophy of St. Augustine of Hippo to restrain war and its effects was crucial. He advocated a civilian-based approach to

APPROACHES 33 (Timothy L. H. McCormack & Gerry J. Simpson eds., Kluwer Law International 1997).

[34] M. C. Bassiouni, *Crimes Against Humanity, in* INTERNATIONAL LAW 154 (Dordrecht; Boston: Norwell, MA: M. Nijhoff Publishers 1992), citing COLEMAN PHILIPSON, THE INTERNATIONAL LAW AND CUSTOM OF ANCIENT GREECE AND ROME 60 (London: Macmillan and Co. 1911) (citing HERODOTUS, HISTORY, VII, 136).

[35] For more about war in antiquity, see, e.g., DAVID J. BEDERMAN, INTERNATIONAL LAW IN ANTIQUITY (Cambridge University Press 2001).

[36] The Laws of Manu (G. Buhler trans., Motilal Banarsidass 1964).

[37] K. P. JAYASWAL, MANU & YAJNAVALKYA: A COMPARISON AND A CONTRAST—A TREATISE ON THE BASIC HINDU LAW 106 (INDIA: BUTTERWORTH 1930).

[38] SUN TZU, THE ART OF WARFARE (Ballantine Books 1993).

[39] Howard S. Levie, *History of the Law of War on Land*, 838 I.R.C.C. 339–50 (2000).

war, sparing innocent civilians to avoid guilt.[40] Violence was advised as a response to violence, but innocents could not be dragged into the conflict. The killing of a person in war had to be justified as being the only appropriate treatment and response.[41] His theology of just war says that war can only be acceptable when led for a good and just purpose, rather than for self-gain or as an exercise of power. Secondly, just war must be waged by a properly instituted authority, such as the State. Thirdly, love must be a central motive, even in the midst of violence. Therefore, the reason for not killing was not based upon ethics or law, but rather on religion.[42] Consequently, the Catholic Church invoked religion to stress that the killings might not be in agreement with religious precepts and beliefs, and might not be ethical. After St. Augustine came the Peace of God, or the *Pax Dei*, a movement that originated in what is currently France and was linked to the Catholic Church.[43] The movement aimed at limiting violence in the private wars of feudal societies. The real aim was to Christianize people and pacify the societal structures of the time. The Peace of God was a proclamation issued by the clergy that granted to civilians immunity from violence. The peasants and the clergy were the first to benefit from the concept. The *Pax Dei* prohibited nobles engaged in war from entering churches, harming non combatants, or burning houses. Civilians were consequently under the protection of the Church. While Christians were drawing on religion to explain the concept of just war and sketch the attempts to formally distinguish the two categories and protect civilians, Islam focused on the prohibition to kill civilians and the distinction which is deeply entrenched and rests on a godly command: killing a civilian demonstrates a lack of *kufr* (faith). This is a legal as well as a moral prohibition: the *Shari'a* encompasses every aspect of life, and each Muslim must conform with it. Since the *Shari'a* prohibits killing, any good Muslim must comply with that rule. Therefore, the distinction between civilians and combatants, which is clearer in Islamic legal sources than in any other document until the 1949 Geneva Conventions, rests on religious, legal, and ethical values.

The Middle Ages was a time marked by several concrete attempts to protect civilians from combatants. At the time, most battles took place far away from the cities, in designated areas and at specific times of the day and week. Campaigns were led with the orders of sparing civilians (meaning women, children, and the elderly) as much as possible. Religious principles, coupled with chivalric traditions, were merged with Roman law and the ideas of *ius naturale* and *ius gentium*. The *jus armorum*, the code of knightly behavior established in the thirteenth century and providing for an ethic

---

[40] Colm McKeogh, *Civilian Immunity in War: From Augustine to Vattel, in* CIVILIAN IMMUNITY IN WAR 62 (Igor Primoratz ed., Oxford University Press 2007).

[41] *Id.* at 65.

[42] For more about this philosophy, see Richard Shelly Hartigan, *Saint Augustine on War and Killing: The Problem of the Innocent, in* 27:2 JOURNAL OF THE HISTORY OF IDEAS 194–204 (1966).

[43] THOMAS HEAD & R. LANDES, PEACE OF GOD: SOCIAL VIOLENCE AND RELIGIOUS RESPONSE IN FRANCE AROUND THE YEAR 1000 (Cornell University Press 1992).

of fighting,[44] was adamant about the distinction between combatants and civilians as well as about the protection of civilians.[45] Ransoms were more popular in the Middle Ages as a source of income[46] and there were exchanges of prisoners when the latter were not enslaved. It was actually a custom of chivalric warfare that gave a price to life and popularized ransoms: a civilian alive had a price while a dead civilian had none. For example, after Jerusalem fell, Saladin did not kill Frank civilians, and instead put a price on each of them according to gender. Those who were not exchanged for a ransom were enslaved.[47] In the Christian Middle Ages, civilians, in particular children and women, were often considered part of the war booty and were enslaved, sold, or killed. This is explained by the linkage established between civilians and the leader they swore allegiance to. When they were not killed, civilians lived a hard life as slaves, and women were sexually exploited.[48]

There were also judicial attempts in the Middle Ages to draw the line between civilians and combatants. In 1268, in Naples, Conradin von Hohenstafen was judged and sentenced to death.[49] He was accused of initiating an unjust war which led to the killing of civilians. Another attempt, which was judicial but also very political, was the 1305 trial of William Wallace, the Scottish national hero, for murder of civilians during wartime. He allegedly spared "neither age nor sex, monk nor nun"[50] and was punished for his excesses. The first prosecution for war crimes was held against Peter Von Hagenbach in 1474, when he was judged for his cruelty against the people of Breisach when he occupied the city to put an end to a rebellion.[51] He was tried by an hoc tribunal of the Holy Roman Empire and beheaded for the violation of his duty to prevent crimes. He argued that he was following orders from the Duke of Burgundy[52], which of course reminds us of the Nuremberg Trials and the landmark decision that obeying the chain of command is not an acceptable justification: one is responsible for his own crimes.

---

[44] BEN LOWE, IMAGINING PEACE: A HISTORY OF EARLY ENGLISH PACIFIST IDEAS 34 (Pennsylvania State University Press 1997).

[45] THEODORE MERON, HENRY'S WAR AND SHAKESPEARE'S LAW: PERSPECTIVES ON THE LAW OF WAR IN THE LATER MIDDLE AGES 9 (Clarendon Press/Oxford University Press 1993).

[46] Major Gary D. Brown, *Prisoner of War Parole: Ancient Concept, Modern Utility*, 156 MIL. LAW REV. 200–23 (1998).

[47] FRANCESCO GABRIELI, ARAB HISTORIANS OF THE CRUSADES 142–43 (University of California Press 1969).

[48] YVONNE FRIEDMAN, ENCOUNTER BETWEEN ENEMIES: CAPTIVITY AND RANSOM IN THE LATIN KINGDOM OF JERUSALEM: CULTURES, BELIEFS, AND TRADITIONS 162–86 (Leiden: Brill 2002).

[49] McCormack, *supra* note 33, at 37.

[50] Georg Schwarzenberger, *The Judgment of Nuremberg*, 21 TUL. L. REV. 329–44 (1947).

[51] Edoardo Greppi, *The Evolution of Individual Criminal Responsibility under International Law*, 835 I.R.C.C. 531–53 (1999).

[52] WILLIAM SCHABAS, AN INTRODUCTION TO THE INTERNATIONAL CRIMINAL COURT 1 (Cambridge University Press, 2007).

C. The Emergence of an Ethic of Protection

The principle of distinction that appeared in different documents—religious edicts, laws, philosophical beliefs, and other sources—is based upon the belief that it is wrong to kill people who do not take part in hostilities or play a role in war. With the Middle Ages and the emergence of the idea of protection of civilians as a matter of ethics or religion, the concept of distinction began to take shape. For example, Honoré Bonet, a heraldist from Provence, France, wrote a book (between 1382 and 1387), *Arbre des Batailles (The Tree of Battles)*, that deals with heraldry and the behavior and responsibilities of officers in war.[53] The book became a manual for the commanders of King Charles V of France. Bonet approaches civilians' deaths as unfortunate and unintended and stated that they should be avoided. It is another book, anonymous this time, *Les Voeux du Héron (Vows of the Heron)*, that clearly breaks with previous tradition.[54] It takes an original stance in the sense that it blames the nobility for the death of civilians and condemns their clear intent to destroy and kill.[55] Therefore, a concept of civilian immunity that had already emerged within major religions and civilizations is strengthened in the Middle Ages mainly because of the chivalric tradition.

The concept of just war was also developed during the Middle Ages. Theologians like Thomas Aquinas and Augustine of Hippo developed that concept,[56] which also relied on morality.[57] St. Thomas Aquinas set up conditions for a just war. His definition of a just war is a war that must be started and controlled by the leader of a State; it should be waged for a just cause; it must be waged for good or against evil; law must be respected or established quickly; war should be the last resort; and the principle of proportionality must be respected. This last principle is crucial when it comes to civilians: the philosopher makes a difference between targeting civilians, which is illegitimate, and the legitimate targeting of military objectives.[58] Francisco de Vitoria later contributed to the concept of just war. He stated that "it is lawful to

---

[53] Honore Bonet, The Tree of Battles (G. W. Coopland trans., Liverpool University Press 1949).

[54] Anonymous, The Vows of the Heron (John Grigsby & Norris J. Lacy eds., Norris J. Lacy trans., Garland Pub. 1992).

[55] Patricia DeMarco, *Inscribing the Body with Meaning: Chivalric Cultures and the Norms of Violence in the Vows of the Heron, in* Inscribing the Hundred Years' War in French and English Cultures 39 (Denise N. Baker ed., State University of New York Press 2000).

[56] The doctrine of just war was developed first by Romans and then by the Catholic Church. It holds that a conflict must meet the criteria of philosophical, religious, or political justice, and follow conditions to be just. The concept goes back to Cicero, was developed by Augustine of Hippo, and Thomas Aquinas, then Vitoria, Grotius, and Hobbes, who secularized the concept. The concept of just war is still influential today.

[57] Frederick H. Russell, The Just War in the Middle Ages 261 (Cambridge University Press 1975).

[58] Richard Shelly Hartigan, The Forgotten Victim: A History of the Civilian 40 (Precedent Pub. 1982).

kill indiscriminately all those who fight against us,"[59] which in a way is the premise of a formal distinction. His reasoning was not yet clear since he allowed the killing of males who could not clearly be identified as civilians. Ethics was constantly in the background, reinforced by religious beliefs.

The next generation of authors influenced by the Just War doctrine were political philosophers and, in particular, the philosophers of the Enlightenment, who clarified the concept of "civilian." Emerich de Vattel published *The Laws of Nations* in 1758. He considered all inhabitants of an enemy territory to be enemies and advised that measures be taken against them, as long as they are not "odious," "unjustifiable," or "prohibited against the law of nature."[60] He also believed women, children, the elderly, and sick people should benefit from protection.[61] He went on by explaining that all non combatants should benefit from this immunity:

The people, the peasants, the citizens take no part in it, and generally have nothing to fear from the sword of the enemy. Provided the inhabitants submit to him who is master of the country, pay the contributions imposed, and refrain from all hostilities, they live in as perfect safety as if they were friends: they even continue in possession of what belongs to them.[62]

The respect for civilians is therefore conditioned on their behavior toward the enemy army. This is explained by the fact that it was expected of civilians not to participate in hostilities. This explains why guerrilla war is prohibited by Vattel.[63] Later, Jean-Jacques Rousseau developed a theory regarding the treatment of the population during wartime. His main argument is that war is a battle between nations and not between individuals; consequently, civilians had to be protected.[64]

War is in no way a relationship of man with man but a relationship between States, in which individuals are enemies only by accident; not as men, nor even as citizens, but as soldiers [...]. Since the object of war is to destroy the enemy State, it is legitimate to kill the latter defenders as long as they are carrying arms; but as soon as they lay them down and surrender, they cease to be enemies or agents of the enemy, and again become mere men, and it is no longer legitimate to take their lives.

---

[59] Francisco de Vitoria, *On the Law of War, in* VITORIA: POLITICAL WRITINGS 319 (Anthony Pagden & Jeremy Lawrence eds., Cambridge University Press 1991).

[60] EMERICH DE VATTEL, LAWS OF NATIONS 321, Book III, chap. 5, para. "69–70 (London G. G & J. Robinson 1797).

[61] *Id.*

[62] *Id.* at 147.

[63] *Id.* at 226.

[64] JEAN-JACQUES ROUSSEAU, SOCIAL CONTRACT AND DISCOURSES (J. M. Dent & Sons, Ltd.; E. P. Dutton & Co. 1973).

Military strategists later made the transition from ethics, religion, and philosophy to law by developing the laws of war. The reason for this change was that war became a professional matter during the seventeenth and eighteenth centuries, with State armies opposing each other. Civilians were not considered as actors bearing rights, but were seen as unfortunate victims of the conflict. This was a radical change. Although philosophical and ethical considerations kept developing, the distinction also became a legal issue. However, attempts to regulate the conflict focused hostilities rather than on civilians' protection.[65]

II. THE DISTINCTION AS A CORNERSTONE OF MODERN INTERNATIONAL HUMANITARIAN LAW
A. The Legalization of War: The Laws of War

With the beginning of the seventeenth century, several States began drafting military codes. This was an outcome of the emergence of the Nation State and the professionalization of armies. The most influential of all codes was the General Order number 100, known as the Lieber Code, presented by the lawyer and philosopher Francis Lieber and issued in 1863 by Abraham Lincoln.[66] The document focused on the regulation of war and was used for future developments in international humanitarian law. It was also used as the basis of the 1874 conference on the harmonization and codification of the laws of war that took place in Brussels. The code focused on the regulation of war and the notion of military necessity, with a final aim of defeating the enemy. Some rules pertaining to civilians already appeared based upon the principle of humanity. Article 15 said: "Military necessity admits of all direct destruction of life or limb of armed enemies, and of other persons whose destruction is incidentally unavoidable in the armed contests of the war."[67] Article 22 states

... as civilization has advanced during the last centuries, so has likewise steadily advanced, especially in war on land, the distinction between the private individual belonging to the hostile country and the hostile country itself, with its men and arms. The principle has been more and more acknowledged that the unarmed citizen is to be spared in person, property and honor as much as the exigencies of war will admit.[68]

And Article 23 added: "Private citizens are no longer murdered, enslaved, or carried off to distant parts, and the inoffensive individual is as little disturbed in his

---

[65] ANTONIO CASSESE, INTERNATIONAL LAW IN A DIVIDED WORLD 255 (Oxford: Oxford University Press 1989).
[66] FRANCIS LIEBER, LIEBER'S CODE AND THE LAW OF WAR (Richard Shelly Hartigan ed., Precedent 1983).
[67] *Id.*
[68] *Id.*

private relations as the commander of the hostile troops can afford to grant in the overruling demands of a vigorous war."[69] However, practicality and pragmatism were the heart of the manual; it was a manual to conduct hostilities at war and thus focused on the military.

Later, the Declaration of St. Petersburg in 1868 prohibited the use of a specific type of bullet for humanitarian reasons. The discrimination between combatant and non combatant could be inferred from the following article: "the only legitimate object which States should endeavor to accomplish during war is to weaken the military forces of the enemy."[70] The Brussels Conference in 1874 drafted an international agreement on the laws and customs of war, the Brussels Declaration, which was never ratified. It said that belligerent forces are not granted "unlimited power as the choice of injuring the enemy." This rule appeared also in Article 22 of the Hague Regulations of 1907. There were also basic rules regarding bombardment: a warning had to be issued to the population before the beginning of the bombardment. The distinction can again be inferred from all these rules, but the protection of civilians is never addressed directly.

In the nineteenth century, war became an instrument of national policy. It meant that armies knew they would be fighting each other and that war would determine States' foreign policy, as summarized by Carl Von Clausewitz. Consequently, they expected professional behavior from each other. This had an impact on the distinction: it seemed clearer that war was taking place between States via their armies, and civilians were to be left aside. The first Geneva Convention dates back from 1864. It sought to codify the conduct of war or, rather, principles that should govern "civilized nations" at war. It was said that attacking defenseless citizens or towns was a war crime. To take from the civilian population more than what was necessary to feed and sustain an occupying army was a war crime. Then there was the Martens clause, which came as preamble to the 1899 Hague Conventions. It referred to the principle of humanity as prohibiting means and methods of war which are not necessary for the attainment of a definite military advantage.[71]

After the American Civil War and the wars in Europe in the nineteenth century, the distinction took a more legal aspect with the Hague Peace Conferences of 1899 and 1907, which were the first internationally codified documents stating that civilians should not suffer from the effects of hostilities. These two Conventions did not establish the principle of distinction but said that the means and methods of war should not lead to indiscriminate attacks against civilians and combatants. The protection of civilians appears in the texts, with articles prohibiting the bombardment

[69] *Id.*

[70] The Declaration of St. Petersburg, Nov. 29, 1868, DIETRICH SCHINDLER & JIRI TOMAN, THE LAWS OF ARMED CONFLICTS (Martinus Nihjoff Publisher 1988).

[71] Edward Kwakwa, The International Law of Armed Conflict: Personal and Material Fields of Application 36 (Dordrecht: Kluwer Academic 1992).

of defenseless towns, villages, and other places. They also created safe zones (safe havens) where the population could be protected. The distinction at the time served military purposes rather than civilians' interests: the goal was to limit civilians' casualties but not to protect non combatants. The extensive treaty in the Land Warfare Regulations, annexed to the 1907 Hague Convention IV, Articles 25-8 and 42-56, laid down rules about the protection of civilians in the conduct of hostilities and in occupied territories. The treaty includes the principle of proportionality, according to which the parties to a conflict cannot use unlimited means and methods of war. Using means or methods that might have caused indiscriminate pain and suffering among the civilian population as well as the combatants was prohibited. This led in part to the acceptance of the non-targeting of civilians, but the focus of the documents remained the conduct of hostilities and the laws of war rather than humanitarian principles. Protection of civilians was not yet at the core of the law.

The attempts to enforce the distinction between civilians and combatants was challenged during World War I and, mostly, during World War II. New technology appeared and increased the mobility of soldiers, resulting in the spread of conflict zones and an increase of civilian victims. During World War I, the number of civilian casualties was larger than the number of soldiers' deaths. One of the outcomes was the exposure of civilians during wars due to the two factors stated above. In addition to soldiers becoming more mobile, there has been an increasing blur between the status of civilians and combatants: it is not rare today to see civilians armed to defend themselves, as in the streets of Sarajevo, or civilians who joined active resistance to the occupation of their lands.[72]

What comes out of this brief historical study is that the principle of discrimination between civilians and combatants is not a new idea but has taken time to take shape. Despite all of the efforts to codify the laws of war, little was done regarding the codification of the principle of discrimination: distinction remained a principle of customary law until the 1949 Geneva Conventions were drafted. Until then, the rule of distinction was rather abstract, and the reason for war and the regulation of hostilities overcame principles of humanity.[73]

The outcome of all this evolution was a codification of the laws of war with a focus on the protection of human beings, whether they were combatants or non combatants, with the 1949 Geneva Conventions, later completed by the 1977 Additional Protocols. The four Conventions and the two Protocols were a landmark in the attempts to shift from a law of war, focused on combatants, conduct of hostilities, and the battlefield, to humanitarian law aimed at protecting civilians. The Conventions represent the interests of civilian populations better as well as broadened humanitarian concerns, since they address for the first time the protection of

---

[72] UN Security Council, Commission of Experts, The Battle of Sarajevo and the Law of Armed Conflict, S/1994/674/Add.2 (Vol. I) (Dec. 28, 1994) (prepared by William J. Fenrick & Major A. J. van Veen), http://www.ess.uwe.ac.uk/comexpert/ANX/VI-B.htm.

[73] JUDITH GAIL GARDAM, NON-COMBATANT IMMUNITY AS A NORM OF INTERNATIONAL HUMANITARIAN LAW 27 (Dordrecht: Martinus Nijhoff 1993).

civilians as such, with a balanced relation to military strategy and necessity. They humanize the laws of war previously codified by shifting the focus from war realities to human beings at war. The Conventions are also very detailed regarding populations living under occupation.

The Geneva Conventions draw from previous experiences: for example, Article 53 of the Fourth Geneva Convention that deals with civilians expressly prohibits collective punishments. This article is a clear response to the German army's massacres of villages as a form of collective punishment for acts of rebellion committed by a few individuals. On June 10, 1944, 642 French citizens of the village of Oradour-sur-Glane, mainly women and children, were killed as a form of collective punishment. The 1977 Additional Protocols complete the Conventions since they are more detailed and address new issues, such as the development of technology and struggles for self-determination and guerrilla warfare. This bulk of documents has become the governing law. The most relevant documents for the distinction between civilians and combatants is the Fourth Convention relative to the Protection of Civilian Persons in Time of War and the two Additional Protocols to the Geneva Conventions of August 12, 1949. In addition to the principle of distinction, the two documents address several other principles regarding the protection of civilians in hostilities and the protection of combatants. This is how the distinction became a cornerstone of international humanitarian law. The Third Geneva Convention addresses the status of combatants.

The existence of these legal documents has not put an end to targeting or deliberate attacks against civilians. Even though the rule is clear, civilians are still the first victims of war, as demonstrated by the wars in Iraq and Afghanistan: 296 Iraqi civilians died a violent death in November 2008 alone.[74] The same month, a U.S. air strike killed forty Afghan civilians gathered for a wedding.[75] Furthermore, there are issues regarding the interpretation of the Conventions and a debate regarding their relevance to the so-called new types of conflicts as well as to different types of conflicts from the ones expressly worded in the Geneva Conventions.

B. The Role of International Humanitarian Law Regarding the Distinction in the Twenty-First Century: New Challenges

The principle of distinction between combatants and civilians is now a cornerstone of international humanitarian law, which requires that the parties to an armed conflict distinguish between civilians and combatants as well as between civilian objects and military targets. Civilians who do not participate in the hostilities cannot be targeted and must be spared by parties at war. They should be respected, protected, and treated humanely. The principle of distinction is also linked to

---

[74] Mohamed Abbas, *Iraq Civilian Death Toll Up in November*, REUTERS UK, Dec. 1, 2008.
[75] Abdul Waheed Wafa & John F. Burns, *US Airstrike Reported to Hit Afghan Wedding*, N.Y. TIMES, Nov. 5, 2008.

the principle of proportionality:[76] indiscriminate and disproportionate attacks against civilians are prohibited. Means and methods of warfare are restricted in order to spare civilians or avoid damages to civilian objects. This fundamental rule protects civilians from suffering from the effects of war and military operations. To enforce this protection, there are international treaties and customary international law.

The Geneva Conventions establish the protection of civilians, individually and at the population level. The two Additional Protocols complete this distinction and stress the need to protect civilians during wartime. Customary international law completes the picture. This is now the law when it comes to armed conflicts, and all countries that have ratified the Geneva Conventions (most countries in the world) and their Protocols are bound by international humanitarian law. The same applies to non signatories since most rules of international humanitarian laws are also customary law, which explains why the International Committee of the Red Cross published an extensive study on humanitarian customary rules.[77] There is a positive obligation to make the distinction between civilians and combatants. Those who violate these rules and commit war crimes can be prosecuted, as illustrated by the Nuremberg Trials, which took place before the Geneva Conventions were drafted, and subsequent international courts.

The principle of distinction is challenged today for various reasons. One factor is the fast-paced evolution of warfare technology. Other reasons include the blurring between the two categories, and the resurgence of asymmetrical warfare and terrorism. All will be analyzed in subsequent chapters.

The intentional violation of the principle of distinction remains a major violation of international humanitarian law. The deliberate targeting of civilians is sometimes part of a military strategy to spread terror. The message is then to denounce a government's inability to protect its citizens in order to weaken that State. When in the fourteenth century Tamerlane butchered all civilians in the cities he conquered, erected towers of skulls, and left only a few civilians to tell the tale, he wanted to demonstrate to civilians that their rulers could not help them. When in the twenty-first century al Qaeda targeted the Twin Towers, it sent the same message to Americans, demonstrating the so-called weakness and decadency of a government unable to protect its own people. The targeting of civilians might sometimes be incidental or accidental but violate the bombardment on the Former Yugoslavia violated the distinction between civilians and combatants in the name of a greater good. NATO can certainly not be comparable to al Qaeda, but a strategy that aims at democratizing a country or bringing human rights to a people via a war that will

---

[76] FRANCOISE BOUCHET-SAULNIER, THE PRACTICAL GUIDE TO HUMANITARIAN LAW 331 (Laura Brav & Clémentine Olivier trans., Rowman & Littlefield 2007) (explaining that "the principle of proportionality states that the effect produced by the means and methods of warfare used in a given situation must not be disproportionate to the military advantage sought.").

[77] JEAN-MARIE HENCKAERTS & LOUISE DOSWALD-BECK, CUSTOMARY INTERNATIONAL HUMANITARIAN LAW (Cambridge University Press 2005).

affect civilians and might have many of them killed should be questioned. The grounds for war are then discussable and yet civilians are indirectly targeted, and labeled collateral damage. As in the U.S. invasion of Iraq to end a dictatorship many die on a daily basis in the name of democratization. Additionally, it happens some-times that armies in the Iraqi field prefer to shoot down anyone standing on a street and staring at a convoy, even if it is a child, in the name of precaution.[78] Some ana-lysts believe that the Israeli attack on Lebanon in 2006 was a demonstration of force aimed at the Islamic republic of Iran.[79] As General William T. Sherman put it when he expelled the population of Atlanta, "[w]ar is a cruelty and you cannot refine it."[80] Tenants of realpolitik believe there are incompressible variables grounded in reality that have to be taken into account while at war, such as the fact that civilians will be killed. The approach of international humanitarian law to the issue of distinction is, in that sense, very utilitarian: It does not take a stance on whether a war is just or not. It simply limits war's effects in the field while attempting to protect civilians. It strikes a balance between military necessity and the distinction between civilians and combatants. International humanitarian law is very pragmatic: it deals with war as an unavoidable evil.

The reflection should take us further: if we adopt a realpolitik stance, does that mean that using smart bombs that aim at hurting, maiming, and killing can be used in a war, since there will be civil victims no matter how hard we try? Is a war only an army's defense gets destroyed possible? Experts said that the 1991 Gulf War was a step forward regarding the possibilities of leading such a sophisticated war. The reality of such a war was that 314 civilians, most of them children, died in a "smart" bomb attack on al Firdos bunker in Baghdad on February 13, 1991.[81] The U.S. army *believed* it was headquarters for *Mukhabarat*, the Ba'ath Party's secret police. One of the criticisms addressed after this disaster was that the U.S. army did not try hard enough to avoid harming civilians and should have gathered more information *to be sure* that it was a headquarters.[82] There were calls to stop strategic attacks since information might not always be reliable. This is why the real battle nowadays is the acquisition of information and intelligence to make sure bombs meet their aims. Although, tactics, operations, and strategy are very precise, they do not prevent surgical bombings from falling far from their targets or from accidents happening. Besides, the military should always make sure that the target is

---

[78] Richard A. Oppel & Riyadh Muhammad, *8 Civilians Killed in 2 Disputed Attacks, Iraq Says*, N.Y. TIMES, June 26, 2008; Jomana Karadsheh, *Bloody Weekend Includes 2 Iraqi Deaths Involving U.S. Forces*, CNN, July 12, 2009.

[79] Vali Nasr, *After Lebanon, There Is Iran*, CHRISTIAN SCIENCE MONITOR, Aug. 9, 2006.

[80] Letter from General William T. Sherman to James Calhoun (Sept. 12, 1864), *in* 2 WILLIAM TECUMSEH SHERMAN, MEMOIRS OF GENERAL WILLIAM T. SHERMAN 600–02 (D. Appleton and Company 1875).

[81] Michael W. Lewis, *The Law of Aerial Bombardment in the 1991 Gulf War*, 97:3 AM. J. INT'L L. 481–509 (July 2003).

[82] HUMAN RIGHTS WATCH, NEEDLESS DEATHS IN THE GULF WAR 128–29 (Washington DC: Human Rights Watch 1991).

acceptable regarding the principles of distinction, proportionality, and military necessity. Seeking the destruction of a bridge does not justify the killing of fourteen people (including children and a pregnant woman) and the wounding of sixteen others, as happened on April 12, 1999, with the Grdelica train bombing in the Balkans.[83] General Wesley Clark, who was the leader of the Allies in that campaign, declared that the train was traveling too fast for the pilot to divert his target, which was the bridge the train was traveling on. The first missile had been fired and all the pilot could see was a flash of light. He then realized he had hit the train and decided to complete the mission by striking the end of the bridge. Instead, the second missile also hit the train.[84] A manipulated video surfaced in which the images were accelerated to give the impression that the train was moving so fast that the behavior of the pilot would look acceptable.[85] As Amnesty International stressed at the time, the pilot should have stopped the attack instead of launching a second missile.[86] The second missile violated the principle of proportionality, while the first violated the principle of distinction. Additionally, the attack violated Article 57 of Protocol I, according to which an attack must "be cancelled or suspended if it becomes clear that the objective is a not a military one… or that the attack may be expected to cause incidental loss of civilian life… which would be excessive in relation to the concrete and direct military advantage anticipated."[87] Furthermore, even when

[83] Elmer Schmähling, *More or Less Exposed: Non-Combatants and Civilian Objects Under the Conditions of "Modern Warfare, in* MATHEMATICS AND WAR 287 (Jens Høyrup et al. eds., Birkhäuser 2003).The Grdelica train bombing, the destruction of a Yugoslav train by a NATO missile, killing fourteen people, was called "an uncanny accident" by NATO supreme commander General Wesley Clark. *See, e.g., Attack on Train Called "An Uncanny Accident,"* S.F. CHRONICLE, Apr. 14, 1999. Michael Parenti explains this extension of the concept of military necessity with the concept of a rational destruction of Yugoslavia: these accidents were part of a campaign to bend Milosevic's rule and to demonstrate to people that they could not be well protected by their government. *See* MICHAEL PARENTI, TO KILL A NATION: THE ATTACK ON YUGOSLAVIA (Verso 2000).

[84] Press Conference, by Jamie Shea and General Wesley Clark, Apr. 13, 1999 http://www.nato.int/kosovo/press/p990413a.htm.

[85] NATO Missile Video "No Distortion, BBC, Jan. 7, 2000.

[86] AMNESTY INTERNATIONAL, NATO/FEDERAL REPUBLIC OF YUGOSLAVIA/"COLLATERAL DAMAGES" OR UNLAWFUL KILLINGS (Amnesty International, May 7, 2000).

[87] A committee was established by the International Criminal Tribunal for the Former Yugoslavia (ICTY) in May 1999 to determine whether the attack had been proportionate or not. With little surprise, the committee decided it was. The ICTY was itself the creation of the Security Council, and multiple members of the Security Council are part of NATO. The reasoning set up in the report is worrisome: "It is the opinion of the committee that the bridge was a legitimate military objective. The passenger train was not deliberately targeted. The person controlling the bombs, pilot or WSO, targeted the bridge and, over a very short period of time, failed to recognize the arrival of the train while the first bomb was in flight. The train was on the bridge when the bridge was targeted a second time and the bridge length has been estimated at 50 meters." *See* ICTY, *Final Report to the Prosecutor by the Committee Established to Review the NATO Bombing Campaign Against the Federal Republic of Yugoslavia,* International Criminal Tribunal for the Former Yugoslavia, June 13, 2000, http://www.icty.org/x/file/About/OTP/otp_report_nato_bombing_en.pdf, A. P. V. Rogers, *What Is a Legitimate Military Target?, in* INTERNATIONAL CONFLICT AND SECURITY LAW: ESSAYS IN MEMORY OF HILAIRE MCCOUBREY 167 (Cambridge University Press 2005). A. P. V. Rogers commented that the committee "must have considered the first missile strike to be a legitimate action against a

attacking a lawful target, precautionary measures to spare civilians have to be taken.

The lesson to be learned from incidents like the destruction of the Grdelica train is the reality of the field: the pilot saw the flash of light that was the train too late. Combatants often operate under heavy stress and have to take swift decisions. The issue then is to know whether to shoot or not. The new rules of engagement established by General Stanley McChrystal imposed in Afghanistan by both the UK and the U.S. army frustrated soldiers who had to retain fire to consider each situation in an effort to curb the civilians' death tolls.[88] They felt endangered, especially as the Taliban knew about these new rules and used them against the foreign soldiers. While the outcome of such rules meant that many Taliban have escaped after attacking troops, it seems that civilian populated areas might in the end be better protected.[89] The principle of "holding fire" in case of a doubt might be frustrating for soldiers, but it remains a must to ensure the respect of the distinction between civilians and combatants as well as the principle of protection: a war might take longer but at least civilians will not pay a heavy cost.

C. Ethics

Ethics still plays a role, despite the existence of normative rules. From an ethical point of view, force is only justified as a response to an act of violence.[90] Therefore, only a combatant can attack another combatant. Innocents should not be dragged into the conflict since they have done no harm. Slowly, and with the evolution of warfare and the notion of the State, ethics has played an increasingly important role putting forward the concept of innocent civilians.[91] Ethics has certainly influenced the law and its evolution regarding the distinction between civilians

---

military objective, the inference being that any civilian casualties of that strike were not disproportionate, and that the firing of the second missile was an error of judgment in the heat of the moment." This decision can be discussed since the ICTY seems to hand in a license to commit "uncanny accidents." The report, while taking military reality into account, seems to set aside the fact that the combatant, a pilot, had been trained in theory to respect international humanitarian law and trained to command his fear and stress level. It also seemed to ignore the fact that the second bombing should have been prevented once the pilot had realized his mistake. Indeed, if the ICTY reasoning is acceptable for the first bombing because the pilot failed to identify the civilian element, the second bombing sounds quite cruel and inhuman. William Fenrick, *Targeting and Proportionality During the NATO Bombing Campaign Against Yugoslavia*, 12:3 E.J.I.L. 500, 489–502 (2001).

[88] Michael Hastings, *The Runaway General*, ROLLING STONE, June 22, 2010.

[89] Miles Amoore, *Strict Battle Guidelines Hampering British Troops in Afghanistan*, SUNDAY TIMES, Feb. 21, 2010, http://www.timesonline.co.uk/tol/news/world/afghanistan/article7034878.ece.

[90] J. T. Johnson, *Maintaining the Protection of Noncombatants*, 37:4 JOURNAL OF PEACE RESEARCH 421–48; 422 (July 2000).

[91] COLM MCKEOGH, INNOCENT CIVILIANS: THE MORALITY OF KILLING IN WAR 116 (Palgrave 2002).

and combatants. For example, Just War doctrine relies heavily on the concept of ethics: when is it just to go to war and what means can be used at war? Most people agree that killing civilians is wrong. An International Committee of the Red Cross (ICRC) study shows that 64 percent of populations of war-torn societies believe that combatants should be the only ones involved in the war and should leave civilians alone. Only 3 percent thought that belligerents could attack combatants and non-combatants alike.[92] So, from an ethical viewpoint, there is an agreement that killing civilians is wrong. In addition, killing is considered counterproductive: it antagonizes populations, whether inside the country or in the international community. It creates resentment and brews hatred like the growing anti-Americanism in Iraq today. Even though the law says killing civilians is wrong, economics says it is a bad strategy, and ethics says it is wrong to kill or target civilians, civilians are still victims. There are still direct challenges to the distinction between civilians and combatants: the concept of total war is one of them. It aims at the complete annihilation of a country's resources or an army (as in the adage "Carthage must be destroyed"[93]). Total war rests on the idea that destroying civilians' infrastructures and killing civilians would prevent the country from running. In addition, this type of total war also relies on demoralizing and terrorizing the population. An example of total war is the war between Iran and Iraq. After some initial restraint, both countries showed a real will to annihilate each other.

In the West, the Just War doctrine finds its sources in Christianity. Further developments in the field of war studies and the field of humanitarian studies have followed the Just War tradition, while secularizing it. It is a doctrine that relies on ethics, saying that a conflict should meet a set of conditions: this helps knowing when resorting to war is morally permissible, when it is right to resort to armed force and what means are acceptable for use. The aim of the doctrine is therefore to acknowledge the reality of war while maintaining humanitarian standards. The principle of distinction between civilians and combatants is part of the conduct of hostilities: in a just war, civilians and combatants should be distinguished. The principle of proportionality is also part of the behavior of belligerents at war: an attack cannot be launched for a military objective with the knowledge that the incidental civilian injuries will be clearly excessive in relation to the anticipated military advantage. Eventually, the principle of military necessity is part of the Just War theory: an attack must be focused on a military objective, and the harm caused to civilians or civilian property must be proportional and not excessive in relation to the concrete and direct military advantage anticipated. This principle is meant to limit excessive and unnecessary death and destruction. However, keeping ethics as the mainstream

[92] Greenberg Research, The People on War Report: ICRC Worldwide Consultation on the Rules of War, Geneva, ICRC 1999, www.icrc.org/eng/resources/documents/publication/p0758.htm
[93] Rome destroyed the city of Carthage during the Third Punic War in 146 BC. The city was set ablaze and ruined.

guideline is not sufficient: law has an important role to play, and this is why legal documents were developed in the twentieth century. The theory of just war remains still at the core of military doctrine and international humanitarian law, but under a legalized shape. This is a victory over other theories, such as militarism, whose adherents believe that war could be beneficial to society; realism, which questions the applicability of morality and justice to the conduct of war; or pacifism, which believes that war is unacceptable. As stressed by the Oxford Institute for Ethics, Law, and Armed Conflict, just war principles have been adapted to modern circumstances, striking a balance between military necessity and distinction.[94]

It is crucial to go beyond a moral edict. Indeed, the first issue with ethics is that each and every one of us has our own code of ethics. Each organization and institution, including armies, has a code of ethics. These codes might differ radically from one another or from an ethical norm or guideline. Al Qaeda has a code of honor: in this code of ethics, the one who does not perform jihad and kill unbelievers in the name of jihad is a "bad Muslim." His refusal to kill in the name of Allah is a weakness that reveals a lack of faith (*kufr*). The Afghan Taliban also has a code of ethics: In July 2009, they issued a code of conduct that reflects the ethics of the new leaders of the movement.[95] The movement has undergone drastic changes since 2008 and the statement issued in November 2009 shows the depth of the changes: it states that the Taliban would keep fighting a jihad, but they also declared that a future Taliban regime will bring peace and non interference from foreign power, which seems to include al Qaeda. They did not speak of imposing *Shari'a* or creating an Islamic State but this does not mean it is not their aim. This might explain why the movement issued a new handbook for its fighters which aims at winning the hearts and minds of the population: the Taliban wish to establish a State under their control. This 2009 code of conduct published in Pashto and entitled, "Afghanistan Islamic Emirate Rules and Regulations," regulates the conduct of hostilities and in particular the one of the mujahedeen. The book is made up of thirteen chapters with sixty-seven articles.[96] It reminds the reader that jihad can only be carried out according to rules. The new code takes into account the distinction between civilians and combatants and includes some rules of international humanitarian law. It talks of limiting suicide attacks, avoiding civilian casualties, and winning the battle for the hearts and minds of the local civilian population. It says: "Suicide attacks should be at high value and important targets because a brave son of Islam should not be used for low value and useless targets [...] In suicide attacks the killing of innocent people and damage to their property should be minimized." The code adds that "all mujahedeen must do their best to avoid civilian deaths and injuries and damage to civilian property." And it says that mujahedeen "should refrain" from disfiguring people, such as the severing of ears, noses, and lips. It is chilling that orders not to mutilate

[94] Http://www.elac.ox.ac.uk/.

[95] Al Jazeera, *Taliban Issue a Code of Conduct*, AL JAZEERA, July 27, 2009.

[96] Taliban handbook, The Islamic Emirate of Afghanistan: A Book of Rules, NEFA trans., Sept. 10, 2009, http://www.nefafoundation.org/miscellaneous/nefa_talibancodeconduct.pdf.

needs to be issued. It reveals that deep down, the Taliban has no understanding that civilians at war must be spared. There is not clear prohibition of suicide attacks or a prohibition on targeting civilians, but instead there seems to be the suggestion that attacking higher targets would be best. There are clear guidelines on how the Taliban will treat its prisoners as well: "Whenever any official, soldier, contractor or worker of the slave government is captured, these prisoners cannot be attacked or harmed [...] The decision on whether to seek a prisoner exchange or to release the prisoner with strong guarantees will be made by the provincial leader." Releasing prisoners in exchange for money is strictly prohibited. The book further states that if a "military infidel" is captured, the decision on whether to kill, release, or exchange the hostage is only to be made by the Imam, a reference to Mullah Omar, or the deputy Imam.[97] This change to new ethics, as limited as it looks compared to international humanitarian law, can also be understood as an attempt to comply with international standards and Islamic standards to wage war. It also indicates that the Taliban have a new politics to the conquest of Afghanistan: the mujahedeen have to behave well and show proper treatment to the nation, in order to win over the hearts of Muslim civilians. This is why "the mujahedeen must avoid discrimination based on tribal roots, language or geographic background." This new approach and the content of the statement are the outcomes of the arrival to leadership of a new generation of Taliban, which is educated and focused on jihad in Afghanistan, with a deadly impact for foreign soldiers on the conduct of hostilities. They are determined and cold-blooded soldiers, with a particular code of ethics. Their mission is to conquer Afghanistan through jihad in addition to winning the hearts and minds of the local population.

Additionally, just war ethics have given rise to much debate. The success of Western institutions and countries in Kosovo led some to believe that war for humanitarian and human rights purposes as well as democracy was acceptable. War is then led for humanitarian motives instead of political motives. There is, thus, a moral duty to interfere in countries that are not respecting universal human rights or humanitarian law, even if that means using force. This is how the concept of humanitarian intervention as an exception to the prohibition of the use of force seems to slowly find its place in international law.[98] Article 2 (4) of the UN Charter prohibits the use of force. There are two exceptions to this rule: one is self-defense (Article 51 of the UN Charter) and the authorization of the use of force by the UN Security Council. It seems now that in practice a third exception is emerging: the use of force for humanitarian purposes. There are still debates as to whether or not this new exception is acceptable and whether it should be included in the

---

[97] Roy Gutman, *Afghanistan War: How Taliban Tactics Are Evolving*, CHRISTIAN SCIENCE MONITOR, Mar. 15, 2010.

[98] Jason Ralph, Tony Blair's "New Doctrine of International Community" and the UK Decision to Invade Iraq, POLIS Working Paper No. 20, August 2005, http://www.polis.leeds.ac.uk/assets/files/research/working-papers/wp20ralph.pdf.

second exception.[99] This means that an authorization from the United Nations would then be necessary. Others promote a third exception as an independant one, believing that force could be used without the support of the UN Security Council when there are massive human rights or humanitarian violations. This readiness to kill in the name of a supreme form of good is another example of an ethical logic that certainly defies the ethics of many. If the answer brought to human rights and humanitarian violations seems wrong in humanitarian terms, it still raises a question: what is the best form of response to such violations? The Responsibility to Protect project brings in some answers. This concept relies on the idea that the principle of sovereignty is a responsibility, and when a State misbehaves and violates human rights, the international community must interfere. Military force seems to be an option. Michael Walzer explains, since we all agree that there are "legitimate occasions for humanitarian intervention," how do we conduct this intervention, keeping ethics in mind?[100]

The hanging of former President Saddam Hussein was yet another illustration of that variety in ethics. Another example would be the cold-blooded targeted assassination of Sheikh Yassin in the Palestinian Occupied Territories. These are illustrations of why we should be wary of ethics. It demonstrates why ethics cannot be the sole basis for the principle of distinction between civilians and combatants. Morality certainly has a role to play:[101] it is crucial to educate troops to respect the distinction based upon the right and wrong argument. However, it is not enough: the distinction must be written in law and violations must be punished. This brings in many questions, such as the type of punishment applicable, as well as the debate as to whether all parties to a conflict should be punished for violating the distinction between civilians and combatants. The Allies were never punished for the mass crimes they committed in order to terminate World War II. No leader was ever legally questioned about the Hiroshima bomb or the dreadful Dresden bombardment during which civilians were massacred for forty-eight hours on February 14, 1945.

III. CONCLUSION

The distinction which is inherited from a long tradition of ethics, law, and philosophy entails that civilians are entitled to the respect of their lives and integrity. Civilians also benefit from legal guarantees described in the Geneva Conventions and the Protocols; they must be protected and treated humanely. There are detailed rules regarding the treatment of a civilian who is under the authority of an enemy

---

[99] Lyal S. Sunga, *The Role of Humanitarian Intervention in International Peace and Security: Guarantee or Threat?*, *in* THE USE OF FORCE IN INTERNATIONAL RELATIONS: CHALLENGES TO COLLECTIVE SECURITY (Hans Kochler ed., Int'l Progress Organization 2006).

[100] Michael Walzer, *The Argument about Humanitarian Intervention*, 53 DISSENT 29–37 (Winter 2002).

[101] *See, e.g.*, Johnson, *supra* note 92.

power (for example, under occupation). A civilian who is in the hands of the enemy must be provided with food, shelter, and medical care. Life, dignity, personal rights, religious rights, and other rights must also be respected. These are the outcomes of centuries of attempts to codify an international approach to the distinction and protection of civilians. This distinction, however crucial, is less and less respected; even though the failure to protect civilians amounts to a war crime, civilians are more and more dragged into wars and constitute the largest group of war victims.

2 The Distinction between Civilians and Combatants

Before technology entered the battlefield, the first victims were the soldiers themselves. This trend is now inverted; civilians are the first casualties during hostilities. During World War I, 5 percent of the victims were civilians, but during World War II, nearly 50 percent of the victims were.[1] This dramatic increase in civilian deaths led to the drafting of the Geneva Conventions, in particular, the Fourth Convention, which deals with civilians' protection. Meanwhile, the distinction between civilians and combatants that is at the root of humanitarian law is often disregarded when states fulfill war's purposes. An example of the violation of the principle of distinction is antipersonnel mines; they cannot distinguish between combatants, legitimate military objectives, and civilians who inadvertently activate them.[2] The use of antipersonnel mines is therefore a violation of humanitarian law. Yet despite the 1997 Mine Ban Treaty, mines are still laid in many locales around the world.

---

[1] JUDITH GAIL GARDAM, NON-COMBATANT IMMUNITY AS A NORM OF INTERNATIONAL HUMANITARIAN LAW 1 (Dordrecht/Boston: Norwell, MA: M. Nijhoff 1993).
[2] Human Rights Watch, *Conduct on the War Ground, in* OFF TARGET: THE CONDUCT OF WAR AND CIVILIAN CASUALTIES IN IRAQ (Washington DC: December 2003).

Civilian or Combatant?

I. THE PRINCIPLE OF DISTINCTION

The distinction between civilians and combatants has become a cornerstone of international humanitarian law. It is also a principle in the 1949 Geneva Conventions, reaffirmed in the 1977 Additional Protocol. For example, Protocol I in Article 48 and Protocol II in Article 13 state that "the Parties to the conflict shall at all times distinguish between the civilian population and combatants and between civilian objects and military objectives and accordingly shall direct their operations only against military objectives." The distinction implies that the civilian population must be protected from attacks; it also means that methods or means of warfare are not unlimited. This distinction is considered to be universal. It applies to individual civilians, as well as to the civilian population generally and civilian property. It includes all those who do not take part in the fighting, such as medical personnel and religious personnel. It also protects those who stopped taking part in hostilities, such as the wounded and shipwrecked, sick combatants, and prisoners of war. Therefore, only attacks against military objectives are legal. This means that targeting a hospital is prohibited. When NATO bombarded buildings next to the Dragisa Misovic hospital in downtown Belgrade, it hit the maternity ward. Several women in labor were injured. The maternity ward was evacuated, and photos of babies coming to birth under a heavy shelling as well as photos of wounded mothers had an important impact on the international community.[3] It was reported by NATO as collateral damage.[4] Many other hospitals were hit during that war, in full violation of humanitarian law.[5]

International humanitarian law establishes the principle of distinction and protects civilians, civilian populations, and civilian objects. The Geneva Conventions and the two 1977 Protocols set forth the principle of protection of civilians and civilian property, which means that civilians must be distinguished from combatants, and civilian property from legitimate targets. Where international humanitarian law grants "a permit to kill" according to the rules laid down for combat, non combatants must be protected. The distinction between civilians and civilian objects from legitimate, lawful combatants and military targets is therefore clear; it is acceptable to bomb a military headquarters, but it is not acceptable to bomb a building with civilian residents. The problem is that in reality, it is sometimes difficult to make this distinction. Is a military headquarters in a densely populated area a legitimate target? Is a computer expert working for an army a legitimate target? What happens if there are military personnel or armed rebels hiding inside a civilian building? The situation indeed is rarely black or white when it comes to qualifying a person or a property as civilian or combatant. This is why it is crucial to explain and

---

[3] *NATO Strikes Heart of Belgrade for the First Time*, CNN, Apr. 2, 1999.

[4] Philipp Hammond, *Reporting "Humanitarian" Warfare: Propaganda, Moralism and NATO's Kosovo War*, 1:3 JOURNALISM STUDIES 365–86 (August 2000).

[5] To see a list of civilians casualties and destruction in Former Yugoslavia in the year of 1999, see http://opinionleaders.htmlplanet.com/casualties.html#hospitals.

describe first, who is a civilian under international humanitarian law, and second, who is a combatant, before looking at cases in between in the next chapters.

A. Who Is a Civilian? A Civilian Is a Noncombatant

Each of the four Geneva Conventions and the two Additional Protocols addresses different types of situations and different types of people. While the Third Geneva Convention applies to combatants (*relative to the Treatment of Prisoners of War*), the Fourth Geneva Convention applies to civilians (*relative to the Protection of Civilian Persons in Time of War*). Both are applicable in times of international armed conflicts. The only article of the Geneva Conventions that applies to non international armed conflicts is Common Article 3. Additional Protocol I relates to the Protection of Victims of International Armed Conflicts, while Protocol II relates to Protection of Victims of Non International Armed Conflicts. We therefore will look at Geneva Convention IV and the two Protocols in this chapter, keeping in mind that there are different types of conflicts: international armed conflicts and non international armed conflicts.[6]

1. The Distinction Relies on a Negative Definition

Civilians are protected by several international documents. The main documents are the Geneva Convention IV and the two Protocols. The Geneva Convention IV (GCIV) and Additional Protocol I (API) apply to international armed conflicts while Common Article 3 and Additional Protocol I (APII) apply to non international armed conflicts. The first crucial step is to understand who a civilian is, in order to be able to distinguish him from a combatant. There is no straightforward definition in any of the aforementioned documents, but rather the following negative definition: a civilian is a non combatant. A civilian is an individual who neither takes direct part in any military action or hostilities nor belongs to armed forces. The civilian is not a member of a militia, a paramilitary police, or a resistance movement. Clearly, it would be easier if international humanitarian law provided a positive definition. A reason for abstaining from giving one was to avoid limiting the concept of civilians; the drafters of the Geneva Conventions and the Protocols also wished to avoid the risk of leaving behind exceptions or specific cases. Any strict definition might indeed exclude certain civilians or the people who fall in between categories.

---

[6] According to the ICRC, International humanitarian law distinguishes two types of armed conflicts, namely:
• international armed conflicts, opposing two or more States, and
• non-international armed conflicts, between governmental forces and non governmental armed groups, or between such groups only.

International Humanitarian Law treaty law also establishes a distinction between non international armed conflicts in the meaning of Common Article 3 of the Geneva Conventions of 1949 and non international armed conflicts falling within the definition provided in Article 1 of Additional Protocol II. *See* http://www.icrc.org/web/eng/siteeng0.nsf/html/armed-conflict-article-170308.

Even though Article 50 API says that in the case of doubt, a person will be considered a civilian, it would be hazardous to provide a clear-cut definition of the term civilian. History has proven that international humanitarian law can be manipulated in times of war, when leaders and armies are under pressure to make decisions. This is why it is not necessary to provide anyone with more tools to abuse the limits that might exist in this branch of law. This is also why Article 50 API provides a negative definition rather than positively defining the concept of civilian.

This negative definition works by opposition and elimination; a person who is not a combatant is a civilian. This means that the concept of combatant must be defined clearly. Articles 4a of the Third Geneva Convention (GCIII) and 43 API provide us with answers by defining who can be a prisoner of war, knowing that only combatants benefit from that status. Article 4a tells us that prisoners of war are people who belong to one of the following categories:

1. Members of the armed forces of a Party to the conflict, as well as members of militias or volunteer corps forming part of such armed forces.
2. Members of other militias and members of other volunteer corps, including those of organized resistance movements, belonging to a Party to the conflict and operating in or outside their own territory, even if this territory is occupied, provided that such militias or volunteer corps, including such organized resistance movements, fulfill the following conditions:
    (a) that of being commanded by a person responsible for his subordinates;
    (b) that of having a fixed distinctive sign recognizable at a distance;
    (c) that of carrying arms openly;
    (d) that of conducting their operations in accordance with the laws and customs of war.

This list helps us understand how a combatant can be identified. Additionally, Article 43 API gives a definition of armed forces, which also helps determine who is a noncombatant:

1. The armed forces of a Party to a conflict consist of all organized armed forces, groups and units which are under a command responsible to that Party for the conduct or its subordinates, even if that Party is represented by a government or an authority not recognized by an adverse Party. Such armed forces shall be subject to an internal disciplinary system which, inter alia, shall enforce compliance with the rules of international law applicable in armed conflict.
2. Members of the armed forces of a Party to a conflict (other than medical personnel and chaplains covered by Article 33 of the Third Convention) are combatants, that is to say, they have the right to participate directly in hostilities.
3. Whenever a Party to a conflict incorporates a paramilitary or armed law enforcement agency into its armed forces it shall so notify the other Parties to the conflict.

Article 44 (3) API is also particularly relevant since it gives the following guidance regarding the distinction: "In order to promote the protection of the civilian population from the effects of hostilities, combatants are obliged to distinguish themselves from the civilian population while they are engaged in an attack or in a military operation preparatory to an attack." Article 44 API is very important since it relaxes the standards to be a combatant and extends the category to people in armed groups. It means that all fighters belonging to armed groups struggling for national determination are combatants. Therefore, if a person satisfies none of the above criteria, he is a civilian.

Article 50 API states that in a case of doubt, the person will be considered a civilian. There was a debate during the *travaux préparatoires* for Additional Protocol I since some delegates believed that paragraph 1 of Article 50 API was in some way contradictory to paragraph 2 of Article 5 GCIII. The latter states that in case of doubt regarding the status of a person who has committed acts of belligerency, the person will be protected by GCIII until his status is determined by a competent tribunal. After debates, it was decided that there was no contradiction between the two articles because they deal with different situations; in the case of Article 5 GCIII, the individual who has committed a belligerent act and who claims to be a combatant can expect when caught by the enemy to be treated as a prisoner of war. Article 50 API deals with a person who has not committed acts of belligerency but whose status is doubtful because of the context. In that case, the person will be considered a civilian.[7] For example, a civilian who is accused of spying will remain a civilian absent formal proofs that he is a combatant. This article is of particular relevance in the Palestinian-Israeli context where targets are often shot only to be labeled as non combatant when it is too late. Children are the first victims of these acts of belligerency. It is very difficult to make an estimate of those victims who should have benefited from Article 50.

a. Protection of Civilians, Civilian Populations, and Civilian Property The very first element of the protection of civilians is the principle of distinction: civilians, civilian populations, and civilian objects and property must be distinguished from combatants and military objectives.[8] It is forbidden to attack civilian populations, individual civilians, and civilian objects or property. Civilians should not suffer from the effects of war or be targeted by attacks (Article 13 GCIV). The presence of armed elements within the population does not deprive it of its civilian character and the protection attached (Article 50 API). The general system of protection is defined in Article 51 API; it prohibits spreading terror among civilian populations (Article 51.2 API and Article 13 APII). Attacks against civilians by way of reprisals are also prohibited (Article 51.6 API). The analysis, according to which civilians cannot be used as shields to protect military objectives or to turn places into civilian's spaces immune to attacks, is derived from Article 51 API (Article 28 GCIV and

---

[7] *See* the ICRC Commentary of Article 50 (1) of Protocol I at http://www.icrc.org/ihl.nsf/COM/470-750064?OpenDocument.

[8] *Civilians* are individuals, while *civilian population* is a collective term that includes all civilians.

Article 51.7 API).[9] Articles 52 to 56 protect civilian objects, attacks against civilian and cultural objects and property, places of worship, and objects indispensable to the survival of the civilian population. Also, work or installations containing dangerous forces that may cause damage to the natural environment and hence threaten the health or survival of the population, are prohibited (Articles 52 to 56 API and Articles 14 and 15 APII). Also protected is the right to receive assistance: civilians are entitled to receive food, medical supplies, clothing, bedding, and means of shelter. Relief actions are therefore foreseen in Articles 69–70 API. There is also an extra protection granted to the following categories: civilian populations in occupied territories (Articles 47–78 GCIV and Articles 68–71 API); civilian detainees in occupied territories (Articles 64–78 GCIV); civilians belonging to a party to the conflict (Articles 72–75 API); civilian internees (Articles 79–135 GCIV); foreigners, refugees, and stateless persons (Articles 35–46 GCIV); women and children (Articles 76–78 API); wounded and sick persons (Articles 13–26 GCIV; Articles 8–31 API); medical personnel, installations, and means of transportation, and relief and humanitarian personnel. Distinctive signs and emblems must mark civilian objects. Medical units and personnel also benefit from immunity and cannot be attacked (Article 19 GCI, Article 23 GCII, Article 18 GCIV, Article 12 API, and Article 11 APII). For example, medical units, vehicles, and others means of transportation should be marked by a distinctive emblem (Articles 12 and 21 API; Article 11 APII). The same applies to cultural objects and places of worship (Articles 53 API and Article 6 APII), as well as to objects indispensable to the survival of the civilian population (Article 54 API and Article 14 APII), natural environment (Article 55 API); works and installations containing dangerous forces (Article 56 API and Article 15 APII); nondefended localities (Article 59 API); and demilitarized zones (Article 60 API). Eventually attacks on demilitarized or neutral zones were prohibited (Article 15 GCIV and Article 60 API). Civilians and civilian objects and property are therefore protected from indiscriminate attacks (Article 51 API). The following types of attacks are prohibited: attacks that are not directed at a specific military objective; attacks employing methods of combat that cannot be directed at a specific military objective; attacks employing a method or a means whose effects cannot be limited; attacks by bombardment that target a military objective located in a city or any other concentration of civilians or civilian objects; and attacks that may be expected to cause loss of civilian lives, damage to civilian objects, and that would be excessive in relation to a direct and concrete military advantage.[10]

The principle of distinction and the protection of civilians apply in international and non international armed conflicts alike. However, Additional Protocol II does not provide a clear-cut definition of combatant; the rationale is that it is harder in non international armed conflicts for parties to the conflict to mean the criteria set up in Geneva Convention III and in Protocol I regarding combatants.

---

[9] Francoise Bouchet-Saulnier, The Practical Guide to Humanitarian Law 13 (Lanham, Md.: Rowman & Littlefield c2007).

[10] *Id.*, at 13.

Instead, Protocol II distinguishes between those who are fighting and those who are not (or those who are no longer fighting). Additionally, it is established that some people may be civilians while participating in hostilities at certain times, which is impossible in international conflicts; according to Additional Protocol II, such individuals benefit from the protection granted to civilians. This protection may be suspended only for the time they directly participate in hostilities. The whole population is considered to be civilian and is protected "unless and for such time as they take a direct part in hostilities" (Article 13.3 APII). Articles 10 to 13 APII describe the protection against military actions as well as the protection of civilian objects. The right to receive assistance (Article 18) and the additional protection for specific categories of civilians (Articles 5, 7, and 9) also appear in the APII.

b. Violations of the Principle of Distinction It is the duty of the commander to make sure that military actions do not violate the principle of distinction (Articles 57 and 58 API); a duty identified as the principle of precaution in attacks. For example, General Stanley McChrystal and his successor General David Petraeus set up very strict rules of engagement in Afghanistan in order to protect civilians.[11] Article 4 GCIII makes it an obligation for an army to have a hierarchy to support that goal. This principle is now part of customary international law.[12] Meanwhile, the International Criminal Tribunal for the Former Yugoslavia (ICTY) set forth the obligation "to do everything feasible" to make sure that the objectives to be attacked are not civilian or civilian objects, or located in a civilian area.[13]

Any attacks against the civilian populations or objects mentioned above amount to a war crime (Articles 7 and 8 of the International Criminal Court Statute). There were and are major violations of the rules stated above; the Khmer Rouge in Cambodia committed genocide by killing people because of their political affiliation, education, class origin, occupation, and ethnicity. After the fall of Mazar-e Sharif in 1998, the Taliban executed 4000 to 5000 civilians. The massacres committed in Sabra and Shatila refugee camps are also war crimes. Some crimes are being investigated, others are not; international justice can be slow and there are too many violations of humanitarian law and violations of the principle of distinction to try them all. International justice often is replaced by national legal institutions or an internal commission. For example, in the case of Sabra and Shatila, no Phalangist was prosecuted; An independent commission concluded that Israeli authorities were indirectly or directly involved. The Kahan commission, an Israeli commission, found that Israel was indirectly responsible since the Israelis had been supplying the

---

[11] Jason Motlagh, *Petraeus Toughens Afghan Rules of Engagement*, TIME, Aug. 6, 2010.

[12] ICTY, Judgment, Kupreskic et al., Jan. 14, 2000, para 524, at www.icty.org/x/cases/kupreskic/tjug/en/kup-tj000114e.pdf

[13] ICTY, *Final Report to the Prosecutor by the Committee Established to Review the NATO Bombing Campaign Against the Federal Republic of Yugoslavia*, ICTY, June 13, 2000, para 29.

Phalangists with weapons and equipment, and had provided the Phalangists transportation to the camps. Ariel Sharon, at the time the Israeli Defense Minister, was found to be indirectly responsible for not restraining the Phalangist forces in question, indirectly resulting in the massacre. Ariel Sharon was forced to resign from his post.[14] The case was later heard by the Supreme Court of Belgium; Ariel Sharon and other leaders were pursued in Belgian Courts on the basis of a Belgian law claiming universal jurisdiction for war crimes. The case was lodged by twenty-three survivors of the massacre. The diplomatic impact of this trial was easy to perceive and the law was amended in 2003 after many judicial events.[15] Ariel Sharon was never tried. One cannot help noticing that the Allies are often not tried for their war crimes and that some highly political situations are never handled; the Sabra and Shatila massacre is in that category. Sometimes it takes decades before crimes are even acknowledged. In the case of the Iraqi Kurds, who were gassed in Halabja in March 1998 by the troops of Saddam Hussein, it took until 2005 for a Dutch court to rule that the attack was a war crime,[16] despite the efforts of the Islamic Republic of Iran to attract international attention to the massacre it witnessed and endured, since some of these gases were also used on Iranian citizens by Iraqi troops during the Iran-Iraq war.[17] Halabja remains

---

[14] THE BEIRUT MASSACRE: THE COMPLETE KAHAN COMMISSION REPORT (Karz-Cohl, Princeton, NJ 1983), or http://www.mfa.gov.il/MFA/Foreign%20Relations/Israels%20Foreign%20Relations%20s ince%201947/1982-984/104%20Report%20of%20the%20Commission%20of%20Inquiry%20into %20the%20e

[15] *Ariel Sharon pourra être poursuivi*, LIBRE BELGIQUE, Feb. 13, 2003.

[16] On December 23, 2005, a Dutch court ruled in a case brought against Frans van Anraat for supplying chemicals to Iraq, that "[it] thinks and considers legally and convincingly proven that the Kurdish population meets the requirement under the genocide conventions as an ethnic group. The court has no other conclusion than that these attacks were committed with the intent to destroy the Kurdish population of Iraq, and because he supplied the chemicals before March 16, 1988, the date of the Halabja attack, he is guilty of a war crime but not guilty of complicity in genocide." Press Release, Hof veroordeelt Van Anraat tot zeventien jaar cel (May 9, 2007), http://www.nu.nl/ news/1071756/13/Hof_veroordeelt_Van_Anraat_tot_zeventien_jaar_cel.html.

[17] The feeling of impunity and the massacre of Halabja gave Iran a feeling of acquiescence by the Security Council and indifference of the international community that almost amounted to an encouragement for the "ruling regime of Iraq to continue its savage atrocities" (Letter UN, S/159August 34, 18, 1983). Iran referred to the Geneva Conventions to denounce massive and targeted killings of civilians, the use of gas, and the use of new bombs. The lack of reaction confirmed Iran in the uselessness of referring to the Geneva Conventions or international law. Clearly referring to these international documents would not end the double standard Iran was a victim of. Iran than declared: "it is now abundantly clear that the failure of the UN machinery to take the Iraqi regime to task for its genocidal use of chemical weapons in Halabja and other large-scale resorts to chemical warfare against both Iranian and Iraqi targets is at least partially responsible for the continuation and escalation of the criminal behavior shown by Iraqi aggressors." Letter Iranian representative to the Secretary General in Report of the SG to the Security Council of Nov 26, 1986, UN doc S/18480; JOOST HILTERMANN, A POISONOUS AFFAIR: AMERICA, IRAQ AND THE GASSING OF HALABJA 151–52 (New York: Cambridge University Press 2007). It appears clearly that the general antipathy against the new Iranian regime lead the United Nations to make deadly mistakes and gave clear advantages to Iraq, who understood this behavior as a green light that encouraged it to violate the Geneva Conventions. Kaiyan Homi Kaikobad, *Ius ad Bellum: Legal Implications of the Iran-Iraq*

for all a blatant example of horror,[18] and Iran claimed genocide after the Halabja massacre.[19] Eventually, Ali Hassan Abd al-Majid al-Tikriti, officially titled Secretary General of the Northern Bureau of the Ba'ath Party from March 1987 to April 1989, and adviser to Saddam Hussein, was convicted in June 2007 of war crimes and sentenced to death by an Iraqi court, along with accomplices Sultan Hashem Ahmed and Hussein Rashid Mohammed.

Civilian property, may also qualify as a cultural object. The bridge of Mostar is an example of civilian property that was used to deliver humanitarian aid in the city of Mostar. It was destroyed by Croatian Defense Council units during the Bosnian-Herzegovian War on November 9, 1993. Slobodan Praljak, the commander of the Croat forces, is on trial at the ICTY for ordering the destruction of the bridge, among other charges. Indeed, the destruction of the bridge affected the delivery of humanitarian aid, but it was also the destruction of a nonmilitary objective.

2. The Rationale

Providing a straightforward definition of who is a civilian might come at the expense of all actors evolving in the grey area between the status of civilian and combatant. It could exclude, for example, workers providing electricity to a country, private citizens, and military structures alike. It could turn a scientist working for the army while at home with his family into a legitimate target. In fact, this civilian constitutes an instance of a legitimate target only while working in the U.S. military headquarters but not when he is at home with his family. Again, this is why a negative definition is provided; defining the status of civilian might have caused a lack of flexibility that would lead to the categorization of the scientist or the electrician as a combatant even when at home, in a private setting. This seems far-fetched, but one should always keep in mind the legal attempts of the lawyers of the George W. Bush administration to turn the definition of torture on its head[20] and to develop the concept of combatant to justify the existence of the category of

War, in THE GULF WAR OF 1980–88, 51–69 at 63 (Ike Dekker and Harry H. G. Post eds., Martinus Nijhoff 1992).

[18] After Saddam Hussein gassed the city, he received the help of U.S. officials to cover-up the massacre (Andrew Cockburn, An Inconvenient Truth, THE NATION, Sept. 10, 2007). Iranians were the first in the field, crossing the borders at their own risk, to save lives and rescue survivors (Jean-Jacques Bozonnet, Treize ans après, le calvaire des Kurdes gazés par Bagdad, LE MONDE, Oct. 28, 2001). They discovered the massacre, Halabja being very close to the two countries' border. (See photos taken by Kaveh Golestan, who won the Pulitzer prizes for photos taken during the war, and died walking on an Iraqi mine in Iraq in 2003). Victims of the attacks were treated in Iran for decades (Olivier Piot, Halabja, vingt and après, MONDE DIPLOMATIQUE, http://blog.mondediplo.net/2008-03-20-Halabja-vingt-ans-apres).

[19] Letter S/198May 92, 19, 1988.

[20] PHYSICIANS FOR HUMAN RIGHTS, BREAK THEM DOWN: THE SYSTEMATIC USE OF PSYCHOLOGICAL TORTURE, MAY 2005 (Cambridge: PHRUSA May 2005), http://physiciansforhumanrights.org/library/report-2005-may.html.

"unlawful combatant." The attitude of the Bush administration is exactly what proponents of international humanitarian law fear, and this is why they prefer to keep concepts loose. The flexibility is actually a way of encompassing new and extraordinary categories of people as to provide protection to as many innocent parties as possible in times of war. International humanitarian law must keep some suppleness to adapt to new situations and be effective. The definitions of combatants and military objectives have been defined, and this gives us a better idea of how we should approach the notion of civilian: all persons and objects that are not military are civilians.

This risk of limiting a notion explains also why the concept of direct participation in the hostilities has not been defined; civilians enjoy immunity from direct attacks until they directly and actively participate in hostilities. This concept of direct participation in hostilities is derived from Article 3 common to the four Geneva Conventions, as well as 51 (3) API, but has not been defined. This is why the International Committee of the Red Cross (ICRC) and the TMC Asser Institute organized a meeting to clarify the concept. The shift from protected civilian to the case of the civilian who lost his immunity is heavy with consequences. Once the civilian loses immunity, he can be targeted, captured, and subjected to penal prosecution under the domestic law of the detaining State. The civilian can either become a fighter or a combatant; the civilian will become a combatant if he decides, for example, to join an army that answers the conditions set up in Article 4a GCIII and Articles 43 and 44 API.[21] The United States wants to see a new category of combatants for these fighters who turn into combatants but who otherwise do not fulfill any of the criteria set up in Article 4a GCIII and Articles 43 and 44 API: the "unlawful combatants." This third classification is not acceptable; people are either combatants or civilians, and if an individual does not fall under the definition of a combatant, he is consequentially a civilian. The only other acceptable category would be the in-between people "unprivileged combatants." This issue will be further analyzed in Chapter 4.

Recent conflicts illustrate the need for a carefully drawn distinction: members of the Taliban do not dissociate themselves from civilians by their clothing; the Hamas is supported throughout the territories by civilians who sometimes hide fighters; in Iraq, a child standing by the road can suddenly pull a gun; or in Colombia, farmers by day become *guerrilleros* by night. Besides, civilians are more involved with the conduct of hostilities than before, either because of an expertise that leads them to work with the army or because they play a distant role in the well-being or the installation of troops (e.g., the mailman or the truck driver delivering food or military supplies). The question is: when does a civilian participate directly in hostilities and

[21] Valentina Azarov, *Who Is a Civilian in Gaza? The Dangers in Adopting a Membership Approach to Direct Participation in Hostilities*, March 15, 2009, http://www.alternativenews.org/english/1647-who-is-a-civilian-in-gaza-the-dangers-in-adopting-a-membership-approach-to-qdirect-participation-in-hostilitiesq.html.

consequently lose his immunity? In other words, what is the yardstick to measure the degree of participation?

B. Who Is a Combatant? A Specific Definition

Defining who is a combatant is crucial since a non combatant is defined negatively by contrast to the combatant. It seems at first sight easier to define a combatant than a non combatant: a combatant is someone who takes part directly in the hostilities. Once captured, the combatant will benefit from prisoner of war status. The Third Geneva Convention is the main reference for combatants.

There is however a debate regarding combatants that has been renewed by the war in Afghanistan and the Bush administration's policy toward captured fighters. Indeed it is sometimes difficult to distinguish combatants from non combatants in Afghanistan. Therefore, lawyers of the Bush administration used an old distinction made between privileged combatants who follow the rules of armed conflicts and can be identified clearly under GCIII, and unlawful combatants, who are combatants not following and respecting GCIII and who do not clearly distinguish themselves from civilians. According to that approach, an unlawful combatant is a civilian who does not become a soldier according to Article 4a GCIII and Articles 43 and 44 API, who directly engages in armed conflict in violation of international humanitarian law and may be detained or prosecuted under the domestic law of the detaining State for such action. The term "unlawful combatant" appears in legal literature, military manuals, and case law. It was first used in U.S. municipal law in a 1942 U.S. Supreme Court decision called *ex parte Quirin*. In this case, the Supreme Court upheld the jurisdiction of a U.S. military tribunal over several German saboteurs in the United States. The concept does not appear in international humanitarian law, which has opted instead for the concept of unprivileged combatant: the latter is a civilian who has engaged in direct participation in hostilities; he will not benefit from the status of prisoner of war when captured, he can be tried under domestic law, and he benefits from fundamental guarantees under Article 75 API.

The concrete consequences for these so-called unlawful combatants can be dreadful for child soldiers, for example. In the case of the Bush administration, the outcome was that the status of war was refused to many combatants who were considered to have no rights, which initiated the torture routine.

1. Who Is a Combatant?

Not all situations are blurred or complex; most of the time, it is easy to identify a combatant thanks to Article 4 GCIII and Articles 43 and 44 API, which apply to international armed conflicts. Article 4 GCIII informs us about who can benefit from the status of prisoner of war. By doing so, it provides us with a definition of the notion of combatant. Combatants are "members of the armed forces of a Party to the conflict, as well as members of militias or volunteer corps forming part of such armed force." This excludes medical and religious personnel, but includes all people working for an armed forces, even though their tasks are not directly linked to hostile activities. A combatant is also any other person who takes a direct part in the hostilities. Being a combatant means that one is a legitimate target for attacks.

Paragraph 2 of Article 4 provides four conditions to identify a combatant. The first condition, the subordination to a responsible commander, excludes individual war or vendetta. No one in the army can be a "*franc tireur,*" and all have to obey a chain of command. Isolated actions from a lone soldier don't count. A soldier is therefore not entitled to lead his own military mission or his own private war. The three other conditions are directly linked to the principle of distinction since they help make the difference between civilians and combatants; armed forces are expected to have a fixed distinctive emblem that is recognizable from a distance. They must use it when going to official missions and meetings with the enemy and for any formal contact,[22] but they are not expected to wear it when they are either working in the backline or when they are training. They do not have to light an emblem at night since this undermines camouflage. Camouflage using the geography of a country is accepted as a military ruse; it is not accepted when the emblem is hidden to deceive the other camp; an armed force hiding a flag to look like civilians would therefore violate the condition. The emblem must appear also on vehicles. Identification is crucial because it allows for the distinction from civilians. This is also why wearing a uniform is important. The third condition, carrying arms openly, is again a way to distinguish a civilian from a combatant; combatants have to carry their arms in an open fashion, or as openly as they can be carried; it is not expected that a combatant carry a grenade in his hands. Again, as for other conditions, he must abstain from creating doubt regarding his status. The fourth condition is to behave according to customs and laws of war; one cannot expect to benefit from this body of law if he does not respect it, so the laws dealing with war must be respected by all parties to the conflict.

Yoram Dinstein identifies three other conditions in the chapeau and the text of the article:[23] (1) the obligation to be an organization, (2) the obligation to belong to a party to the conflict, and (3) the lack of duty of allegiance to the detaining power that he derives from the case law of the Geneva Conventions. The fifth condition, the obligation to be an organization, he says, strengthens the first condition; it insists upon the chain of command. It does not suffice to be commanded; there is also the need for a structure. The sixth condition, belonging to a party to the conflict, derives from a 1969 judgment by an Israeli military court in the Kassem case.[24] A group comprising persons of different Arab nationalities was part of the Popular Front for the Liberation of Palestine. They crossed the river Jordan to enter the Occupied Territories and wanted to commit sabotage. They were captured and judged;

---

[22] Howard S. Levie, *Prisoners of War in International Armed Conflicts,* 59 Int'l Legal Stud. 47, (1978).
[23] Yoram Dinstein, The Conduct of Hostilities under the Law of International Armed Conflict 36–37 (New York: Cambridge University Press 2004).
[24] Military Prosecutor v. Omar Mahmud Kassem and Others, Israel Military Court sitting in Ramallah, case 1April 09, 13, 1969.

they invoked the status of prisoners of war but since none of the governments they belonged to were at war with Israel, and since these irregular forces were even illegal in Jordan, the condition of belonging to a party to the conflict was not fulfilled, and the members could not benefit from the status of prisoners of war.[25] Members of a group acting on its own devise, without any attachment to a party to the conflict, cannot be regarded as regular combatants under Geneva Convention III; a degree of relationship is needed. Arabs were therefore judged under domestic law. The role of the court was, according to Article 5, to define the status of these prisoners. There was discontentment with this decision; Georg Schwarzenberger said the Geneva Conventions were not meant to limit the scope of the lawful combatancy under preexisting rules of international law.[26] He believes the concept of belonging can be broad and should not, for example, encompass tests such as the legality or illegality of a movement. Consequently, the fact that the group was illegal in Jordan was not sufficient to break the link of belonging with parties to the conflict. There should be "a liberal interpretation of the connection required between a belligerent and irregular armed forces."[27] The last condition Dinstein identifies is the non allegiance to the detaining power that he derives from case law. The principle is that a soldier from a State cannot fight in a war against that very State. Dinstein refers to the *Koi* jurisprudence.[28] Twelve paratroopers under the command of Indonesian officers were captured in Malaysia during a confrontation between Indonesia and Malaysia. They were convicted for possessing arms in a security zone and sentenced to death. Their defense was that they were to benefit from the status of prisoners of war and therefore were entitled to protection under Geneva Convention III. The paratroopers were Chinese Malay born or settled in Malaysia. The Geneva Convention does not say whether prisoner of war status is applicable to nationals of the captor State or to persons owing allegiance to the captor State. After a close analysis of the Third Convention, the UK Judicial Committee of the Privy Council declared that GCIII and commonly accepted rules of international law indicated that a prisoner of war cannot be a national of the detaining power. Therefore, the Chinese Malay could not benefit from the status of prisoners of war in Malaysia. The fact that the paratroopers were serving in the Indonesian military and arrived in Malaysia as part of the Indonesian army did not affect the case. They could therefore be prosecuted under domestic law for criminal offences. The lesson from this case is that prisoners of war cannot hold the citizenship of the detaining power and cannot owe it any duty of allegiance. This concretely means that the SS officers who rebelled against Hitler could not benefit from the status of prisoners of war. The rationale is that the

---

[25] Benjamin Rubin, *PLO Violence and Legitimate Competency: A Response to Professor Green*, 1989, Isr. Ybook H. R. at 185 (Tel Aviv: Published under the auspices of the Faculty of Law, Tel Aviv University).

[26] Georg Schwarzenberger, *Human Rights and Guerrilla Warfare*, 1971, 1 Isr. Ybook H. R. at 246, 252 (Tel Aviv: Published under the auspices of the Faculty of Law, Tel Aviv University).

[27] *Id.*, at 250.

[28] Public Prosecutor v. Oie Hee Koi and connected appeals, Judicial Committee of the Privy Council (U.K.), December 4, 1967, Dec. 04, 1967, A.C. 829.

sovereign State is responsible for dealing with treason and rebellion within its army, and such offences will be dealt with at the domestic level.

2. Other Categories of Combatants

The four conditions must be fulfilled together, which raises issues for many insurgent groups. These conditions were at the core of a heated debate pertaining to the Taliban captured in Afghanistan. Indeed, the Taliban does not meet several requirements of paragraph 2, Article 4.[29] Another issue deals with civilians taking part in hostilities.

a. Rebels, Terrorists, and Insurgents The four conditions—seven if one wishes to include Dinstein's analysis—make it very difficult for an irregular army to exist and to act. Indeed, a regular army meets the conditions quite easily while an irregular force's very existence and philosophy of war might go against Article 4. For example, guerrilla movements rely on the effect of surprise: therefore, its combatants do not move openly like a regular army. They might not wear a uniform so that they will not risk capture, and they might hide their weapons to catch the enemy by surprise. As stated by an expert of irregular armies, R. R. Baxter, "secrecy and surprise are the essence of guerrilla warfare."[30] In the strategy of the war of the poor that is guerrilla warfare, the whole environment changes, and some rules stated in the Geneva Conventions are this difficult to apply. This is a real challenge for humanitarian law since most conflicts today involve irregular armies.

This raises the question of partisans and any other group fighting for self-determination. The *Francs Tireurs et Partisans*, or *résistants*, in France played a crucial role not only in opposing the Nazi regime when it invaded the country but also during the liberation. It was an armed group rising against an occupying force. During World War II, these armed groups who took direct part in the hostilities were denied the status of prisoners of war and were subjected to repressive measures such as executions. They are now protected by Article 4 GCIII, provided that they are commanded by a person responsible for his subordinates, have a fixed distinctive sign recognizable at a distance, carry arms openly, and conduct their operations in accordance with the laws and customs of war. Articles 43 and 44 API complete the definition by adapting the concept of combatant to wars of self-determination. Indeed, Article 43 (1) does not speak of "armies" but rather that "the armed forces of a Party to a conflict consist of all organized armed forces, groups and units," which opens up the category of combatant to guerrilla groups. The Protocols were

[29] *See, e.g.*, Jay S. Bybee, *Status of Taliban Forces under Article 4 of the Third Geneva Convention of 1949: Memorandum of Opinion for the Counsel to the President, TALIBAN, in* THE TORTURE PAPERS: THE ROAD TO ABU GHRAIB 80 (Karen J. Greenberg & Joshua L. Dratel eds., Cambridge University Press 2005).

[30] R. R. Baxter, *So-called "Unprivileged Belligerency: Spies, Guerrillas and Saboteurs,"* 28 BYBIL 323–28 (1951).

designed to address issues raised by wars of self-determination during which the Geneva Conventions were put to the test. It was decided that further rules were needed to encourage armed groups, or guerrilla groups, fighting for self-determination to respect the laws of war. The idea was also to provide them with legal protection. The two articles combined with customary law and Article 4 GCIII result in the categorization of guerrilla movement fighters as combatants. This means they are also entitled to the prisoner of war status, as long as they fulfill the four conditions. Considering that guerrilla fighters hardly take these four conditions into account as mentioned earlier, Protocol I relaxes the obligation to wear an insignia at all times, but they must distinguish themselves from civilians at all times. The accent has been set instead on carrying arms openly during the hostilities and before the attack. If guerrilla fighters do not respect these rules, they forfeit their status as combatants: they are civilians in arms and can be prosecuted domestically.

The Taliban is only a visible illustration of an armed group not fulfilling the conditions set in Article 4, paragraph 2. Many armed groups across the globe do not wear uniforms. There seems to be at first a legal limbo for these groups: this is how the Bush administration exploited and labeled members of the Taliban unlawful combatants. The Taliban do not have an obvious and clear chain of command; uniforms do not distinguish the members from civilians in a clear fashion; sometimes, they throw away their arms upon capture; and it was argued that they did not respect the customs and laws of war. The argument was that "the Taliban have not effectively distinguished themselves from the civilian population of Afghanistan and did not the standards set in Article 4a GCIII and Articles 43 and 44 API, or even the relaxed standards of Protocol I. Moreover, they have not conducted their operations in accordance with the laws and customs of war. Instead, they have knowingly adopted and provided support to the unlawful terrorist objectives of Al Qaeda."[31] This means they cannot be considered combatants, or rather as regular combatants, which means that once captured they do not benefit from prisoner of war status. Since they are not civilians either, questions arise as to their status.

A legal limbo is very rare and in this specific case, international humanitarian law provides protection to all those standing in between categories: Article 75 API, which is also a customary rule of international law, grants an ad minima protection to the ones called unprivileged combatants. It grants fundamental guarantees to those who do not "benefit from more favorable treatment under the Conventions." It guarantees humane treatment with no "distinction based upon race, color, sex, language, religion or belief, political or other opinion, national or social origin, wealth, birth or other status, or on any other similar criteria." Several acts are prohibited: "violence to the life, health, or physical or mental well-being of persons, in particular: murder; torture of all kinds, whether physical or mental; corporal punishment; and mutilation" but also "outrages upon personal dignity, in particular

---

[31] Press Releases 2002, United States Mission–Geneva, Statement by White House Press Secretary Ari Fleischer (Feb. 7, 2002), www.state.gov/s/l/38727.htm

humiliating and degrading treatment, enforced prostitution and any form of indecent assault; the taking of hostages; collective punishments; and threats to commit any of the foregoing acts." Since the people captured do not benefit from the status of prisoner of war, a conviction must be pronounced by an impartial court, and principles of law must be respected. A court will decide upon the status of the captured. This protection afforded to the unprivileged combatant is the outcome of the philosophy of humanitarian law as illustrated by the Martens Clause: Combatants who do not fulfill these conditions but remain at all times "under the protection and authority of the principles of international law derived from established custom, from the principles of humanity and from the dictates of public conscience."

b. Civilians Who Take Part in Hostilities Therefore Article 4 (a) (2) helps make the distinction between combatants and civilians. In addition, paragraph 4 of Article 4 says that people accompanying armed forces without being members of the army—like journalists, contractors, civilians working for the army, and others—must be provided with an identity card that identifies them as civilians. Paragraph 6 says that "inhabitants of a non-occupied territory, who on the approach of the enemy spontaneously take up arms to resist the invading forces, without having had time to form themselves into regular armed units, provided they carry arms openly and respect the laws and customs of war," qualify for POW status. This refers to mass uprising, *levée en masse*, in an event of an invasion, and the capacity of the people to organize in military units. In general, the conditions set in Article 4 (a) (6) are relaxed when it comes to the phenomenon of "*levee en massé*," during which people may temporarily take up arms to resist invading forces: there is no need to meet all four conditions in a cumulative fashion. Two conditions remain cumulative: carrying arms openly and respect for the laws of war. The two other conditions, the subordination to a responsible commander and the use of a fixed distinctive emblem, are not obligatory.

Civilians who take part in hostilities will be considered unprivileged combatants if their participation is direct. According to the ICRC, the concept of direct participation implies that there are indirect forms of participation; this should be a more explicit guideline. For example, the electrician mentioned above provides indirect support to the military by providing energy to the entire country; consequently, he takes no direct participation in hostilities and is a protected civilian. The interpretation of the concept should be narrow, in order to provide an extended protection to civilians and uphold the principle of distinction. If anyone who brings help to the army loses immunity, the concept of civilian and the principle of distinction will be reduced to almost nothing. In many countries, taxes support the military. It does not mean that all citizens from that country lose their civilian status.

The commentary to Additional Protocol I explains that the behavior of the civilian must constitute a direct and immediate military threat to be considered a direct participation in hostilities. This raises crucial questions examined later in the book: are supporters of Hamas who have never touched a weapon but support violence combatants or civilians? In practice, there are attempts to broaden the concept of combatants. For example, some support the membership approach to define direct participation to the hostilities; the argument under this approach is that anyone who is affiliated with a party to the conflict is not a civilian. This would mean that anyone belonging to Hamas in the Gaza Strip directly takes part in hostilities and is a legitimate target.[32] Article 51 (3) API and the sentence "unless and for such time as they take a direct part in hostilities" are at the core of the debate; the language of Article 51 (3) is vague. It explains that when a person takes a direct part in the hostilities, he becomes for such time a legitimate target. This means that he can recover his status of civilian if he ceases his direct participation. This approach is being contradicted by the supporters of the membership approach, who understand that when a civilian supports a group like Hamas, he becomes affiliated with it and loses the status of civilian for good. Thanks to the membership approach, people close to Hamas can be targeted at any time, even if they are not in arms. This is problematic because it means they could be targeted anywhere at anytime, even in a private family setting; a Hamas collaborator could be partying at a wedding while a legitimate target. This raises questions regarding the targeting of the man, but also the security of the people around him. There is additionally a moral problem; how can an army target an unarmed man? This sets dangerous precedents for the extension of the concept of direct participation in hostilities; would it mean that political parties deriving from such groups would also constitute legitimate targets? Indeed, whether it is Hamas or Hezbollah, they have a political branch with unarmed politicians.[33] This is an overly permissive interpretation of the concept, which demonstrates why the membership argument is so dangerous.[34] There are intense debates regarding the concept, and the privatization of armed forces has complicated the matter further. This is why there are ongoing efforts to clarify the concept of direct participation in hostilities, with some trying to broaden it, and others trying to restrict it. The issue will be further analyzed in Chapter 4.

c. Mercenaries and Spies Mercenaries are defined in Protocol I; Article 47 states that a mercenary is hired either locally or abroad to fight in an armed conflict. Therefore, the mercenary directly participates in hostilities. A mercenary is neither a national of one of the parties to the conflict nor does he belong to the States' troops elsewhere. His motivation is financial: he is being paid for his participation in the conflict. Foreigners who take up arms to join on a voluntary basis organized groups linked to the conflict or to armed forces are consequently

[32] Press Release, B'Tselem, B'Tselem to Attorney General Mazuz: Concern over Israel Targeting Civilian Objects in the Gaza Strip (Dec. 31, 2008), http://www.btselem.org/English/Gaza_Strip/20081231_Gaza_Letter_to_Mazuz.asp.
[33] ANISSEH VAN ENGELAND & RACHAEL RUDOLPH, FROM TERRORISM TO POLITICS (Aldershot, England/Burlington, VT: Ashgate 2008).
[34] Jean-Francois Quéguiner, Direct Participation in Hostilities under International Humanitarian Law, Nov. 2003, working paper Program on Humanitarian Policy and Conflict Research at Harvard University, www.icrc.org/Web/ara/siteara0.nsf/htmlall/particpation-hostilities-ihl-/311205/SFile/Direct_participation_in_hostilities_Sept_2003_eng.pdf

not mercenaries. For example, al Qaeda's volunteers who fought in Bosnia and Afghanistan.[35] Mercenaries are not entitled to the status of combatant and prisoner of war or any of the categories of protected persons under the Geneva Conventions unless they are wounded or sick. They are unprivileged combatants and must always benefit from ad minima rights and protection granted by customary law: they must be treated with humanity. Article 45 (3) API that states: "Any person who has taken part in hostilities, who is not entitled to prisoner-of-war status and who does not benefit from more favourable treatment in accordance with the Fourth Convention shall have the right at all times to the protection of Article 75 of this Protocol." They are therefore treated as non combatants who have taken part in hostilities.[36] They will be criminally responsible if they commit war crimes or grave breaches of humanitarian law and can be tried in domestic courts.[37]

When caught, a spy is like a saboteur; he cannot benefit from the status of prisoner of war. He benefits, however, from fundamental guarantees granted by customary international law, as explained above. Spying is not prohibited.[38] There is a difference between espionage and intelligence activities: during intelligence activities, data are collected by members of armed forces wearing uniforms. Intelligence officers gather information, analyze it, and assess the enemy's situation. The collection of information by combatants wearing uniforms is done openly. This will not be considered espionage if the agent works in uniform. By comparison, the secret methods used by spies are not always lawful.[39] The spy will therefore be the one who gathers information in a clandestine fashion or under false pretext. A spy caught in the act will not benefit from the status of prisoner of war but must be treated with humanity and has a right to a fair trial (Article 5 GCIII and Article 5 GCIV). The weak point of Article 5 GCIII regarding spies is that it is difficult to define what type of activity is hostile to the security of the State. There is a secrecy issue when a party arrests a spy since it does not wish this information to be public; the key is to reconcile the rights of the spy with the needs of war. For example, how does the spy held in custody benefit from his right to communicate with the outside world? The Convention takes this into account, and Article 136 gives two weeks for the authorities to give the name of a person kept in custody. Article 25 guarantees the right to communicate with family, but that does not mean the message cannot be censored. The rights the person holds under Article 5 are limited; the detainee benefits from the right to correspond, to receive individual or

---

[35] This could be discussed since they were often offered a home and a wife for their participation to war, so for some they do qualify as mercenaries since they received financial help to settle in life.

[36] Katherine Fallah, *Corporate Actors: The Legal Status of Mercenaries in Armed Conflict*, 88:863 I.R.R.C 599–611 (September 2006).

[37] Leslie C. Green, *The Status of Mercenaries in International Laws*, 1978, Isr. Ybook H. R. at 9–62 (Tel Aviv: Published under the auspices of the Faculty of Law, Tel Aviv University).

[38] A. P. V. Rogers, *Unequal Combat and the Law of War*, 2004, Isr. Ybook H. R. at 21, 3–23 (Tel Aviv: Published under the auspices of the Faculty of Law, Tel Aviv University).

[39] Baxter, *supra* note 30, at 323.

collective relief, to receive spiritual assistance from ministers of his faith, and to receive visits from representatives of the Protecting Power and the International Committee of the Red Cross. The detainees have to be treated humanely, which is reaffirmed in Articles 37 and 38 of the Fourth Convention. Torture is prohibited. Article 136 guarantees that the name of those kept in custody will be released within two weeks.

d. Prisoners of War According to the Third Geneva Convention, a combatant who is captured by an adverse party to the conflict during an international armed conflict will be granted the status of prisoner of war. Additional Protocol I enumerates the categories of persons who must be granted the status of prisoner of war when captured by an adverse party. If the combatant is *hors de combat* because he surrenders or because he is sick, wounded, or shipwrecked, and is captured by enemy forces, he is entitled to the status of prisoner of war (POW). If a doubt arises, the individual will continue to benefit from the status of POW and will be protected by GCIII until a competent, independent, and impartial tribunal determines the status of the individual according to the rule of law (Article 5 GCIII and Article 45 API). This demonstrates that the concept of unlawful combatant does not exist in humanitarian law; the tribunal will decide whether the individual is a combatant. If he is, he will be a POW. If he is not a combatant, he is a civilian and will then be tried under domestic law.

He can be detained and must be treated according to GCIII in the case of an international armed conflict and according to Common Article 3 in the case of a non international armed conflict. This deprivation of liberty is not a punishment for a crime committed during hostilities; it is a way to neutralize a combatant, to make sure he doesn't take part in the hostilities anymore. He cannot be prosecuted for taking part in hostilities.[40] The Conventions and Protocols regulate the conditions of detention regarding housing, food, supplies, hygiene, medical care, and other fundamental guarantees. Prisoners of war can be interrogated but cannot be coerced or tortured. If a prisoner of war has violated international humanitarian law, he will not lose his status but can be prosecuted according to the rule of law and judicial guarantees. In non international armed conflicts, there are provisions and guarantees for the treatment of persons detained for reasons related to a conflict in Article 5 APII.

The Third Geneva Convention regulates the treatment of prisoners of war. Article 44 API enumerates the categories of persons who will benefit from the status of prisoners of war. Prisoners of war are combatants, but POW status can be extended to civilians who are members of armed resistance groups or who participate in uprisings (Article 45 API). The combatant must meet all the conditions laid out in Article 4 GCIII, as well as Articles 43 and 44 API to be entitled to the status of POW.

---

[40] ALLAN ROSAS, THE LEGAL STATUS OF PRISONERS OF WAR: STUDY IN INTERNATIONAL HUMANITARIAN LAW APPLICABLE TO ARMED CONFLICTS 82 (Annales Academiae Scientiarum Fennicae. Dissertationes humanarum litterarum 1976).

The four conditions set in Article 44 to identify a combatant actually find their source in Article 1 of the Regulations Respecting the Laws and Customs of War on land, annexed to the Hague Convention (II) of 1899 and the Hague Convention (IV) of 1907. These four cumulative conditions—subordination to a responsible command; a fixed distinctive emblem; arms carried openly; and respect of international humanitarian law—are therefore to be found in GCIII, and only a combatant who meets all the criteria will be granted POW status. Article 44 API loosened the conditions, and therefore members of guerrilla groups also qualify as combatants, and if captured are also granted the status of POW. In addition, Protocol I loosened the conditions needed in order to be considered a combatant in order to take into consideration the evolving notion of a combatant tied to the next military technology and strategy. Under this new definition, provided in Article 44, guerrilla fighters and civilians can in some circumstances benefit from the status of combatant, and if captured, will be prisoners of war. The definitions of combatant and POW are therefore expanded by API.[41] The criteria for evaluating whether someone is a combatant or not became objective with API: the criteria are based upon the direct participation in hostilities rather than membership in armed forces. Consequently, combatants for guerrillas, partisans, and resistance movements also benefit from the status of prisoners of war. This is extremely important, since nowadays there are less international armed conflicts and most conflicts are either transnational with an armed group opposing a State or several States, or are of a non-international nature, with local groups opposing one another or the State. For example, Colombia is composed of several of these irregular forces opposing one another while also opposing the regular Colombian army. The conditions set forth in Article 44 API therefore apply to these irregular forces as well. It loosens Article 4 GCIII standards; for example, the uniform condition is loosened since most of these groups do not don a uniform; wearing a bandana might be enough to qualify as wearing a uniform.[42] API expanded the definition of prisoners of war to match the loosened standards of Article 44.

In addition to the members of the armed forces fulfilling these relaxed criteria, the Third Geneva Convention adds two extra categories of people who should be treated as prisoners of war: members of armed forces who have been released from detention in an occupied territory and are then re-interned, and members of armed forces or belligerents who reach neutral territory and have to be interned there under international law. The first case pertains to occupied territories, and the second to neutral countries. Inhabitants of non occupied territories who take up arms to resist invading forces through a levee en masse are also granted the status of prisoners of war (paragraph 6 of Article 4 (a)).

POW status is therefore granted to members of armed forces who meet the criteria of Article 4 (a) of Geneva Convention III. The conditions are cumulative. Meanwhile, case law has demonstrated that it is not enough to establish that

[41] Analyzed in Chapter 4.
[42] Commentary III Geneva Conventions 60.

someone belongs to an armed force for him to achieve POW status. A soldier who dresses in civilian clothes to commit an act of sabotage loses his entitlement to such status. In the *ex parte Quirin* judgment, members of the German armed forces who took off their uniforms to commit an act of sabotage could not be afforded POW status.[43] This rule was reaffirmed in the Mohamed Ali case in 1968. Indonesian soldiers had planted explosives in a Singapore building that then belonged to Malaysia. They had done so dressed as civilians. They also lost their entitlement to POW status since at the moment of the action, they did not wear the uniform.[44]

The criterion of combatancy is the direct participation in the conflict rather than the former legal criterion of formally belonging to armed forces. An armed group that violates humanitarian law cannot be deprived of its right to have its members benefit from POW status, even if they violate international law (Article 44.2 API), but only if the members distinguish themselves from civilians during the attack or before the attack and as long as the members fulfilled one criteria: carrying arms in the open "during each military engagement, and during such time as he is visible to the adversary while he is engaged in a military deployment preceding the launching of an attack in which he is to participate" (Article 44.3). A combatant who belongs to such an armed group and who does not meet this requirement will be stripped of his right to be a prisoner of war but will benefit from protection stated in the Geneva Conventions, the Protocols, and customary law for unprivileged combatants. This clearly applies to members of the Taliban, who are unprivileged combatants benefiting from the ad minima rights existing in the aforementioned documents. The concept of unlawful combatant has therefore no legal grounding in international humanitarian law: regular combatants meeting the criteria set forth in Article 4 GCIV and Articles 43 and 44 API will be regular POWS; fighters who are members of armed groups will also be combatants under Articles 43 and 44 API as long as they meet the conditions set forth (either the four conditions or the lose conditions set forth in API) and will therefore be regular POWS. If they do not fulfill the criteria, as explained above, they become unprivileged combatants protected by Article 75 API, which is part of customary law. Civilians who directly take part in hostilities are not entitled to POW status but are considered as unprivileged combatants and are protected by Article 75 API. All articles are carefully laid down so as to avoid any possibility for the detaining party to use discretionary power. If there is a doubt as to whether someone is entitled or not to the status of prisoner of war, the status will be determined by a competent tribunal (Article 5 GCIII and Article 45.1 API). If a person has been captured, is not held as a prisoner of war, and is being tried for an offense related to hostilities, he has the right to claim his entitlement to the status before a judicial tribunal that will decided whether he can benefit from the status (see the *Kassem* and *Koi* jurisprudence described above).

[43] Ex Parte Quirin et al., at 35–36.
[44] Mohamed Ali et al. v. Public Prosecutor, 1968, AC 430, 449.

When possible, the tribunal judging the offence will also decide the POW status question (Article 45.2 API).

The principle of distinction is so entrenched in humanitarian law that the combatant who fails to distinguish himself from civilians and who is captured will forfeit his right to be a prisoner of war (Article 44.4 API). Despite the forfeiture of his right to benefit from POW status when he does not fulfill the conditions, the prisoner has rights: international humanitarian law affords protection ad minima. Additionally, mercenaries and spies will not benefit from the status of POW (Articles 46 and 47 API). Both categories, mercenaries and spies, benefit from ad minima rights called fundamental guarantees. Fundamental guarantees granted to spies, saboteurs, mercenaries, civilians, children, and combatants who have failed to distinguish themselves from civilians are ad minima rights: when captured and detained, they do not benefit from the status of POW, which does not leave them without protection. During international armed conflicts, they will benefit from the fundamental guarantees described in Article 75 API. During non international armed conflicts, Protocol II—which does not refer to the definition of POW—will protect them: they will benefit from Common Article 3, which is a mini-convention in itself, and from customary law, Article 75 API being considered as part of customary law. International humanitarian law has a special protection for child combatants: they remain protected by the provisions set up in the Geneva Conventions and the Protocols, whether or not they are prisoners of war (Article 77 API). No one falls outside the scope of international humanitarian law.

e. The Sick, the Wounded, and the *Hors de Combat* The wounded and the sick are *hors de combat* (they are kept out of combat) not because they lowered their weapons or they were captured, but because their health situation does not permit them to keep participating in hostilities; they are in need of medical care and can play no role in hostilities (Article 8 API). In these situations, the status of the wounded or sick takes over the status of combatant. This lasts as long as the disease or the wound keeps the individual *hors de combat*. Once the combatant has recovered, he is again involved in hostilities. If he is in the hands of the enemy, he is then captured and becomes a prisoner of war.

The sick and the wounded must be treated humanely at all times, and they must receive medical treatment with no delay, and to the fullest extent possible. There are medical ethics; doctors are expected to take care of the wounded and the sick from all sides, including their enemies. This is why U.S. military doctors treat Taliban hurt in combat.[45] Medical installations are also protected from attacks (Article 18 GCIV, Article 12 API, and Article 11 APII) and requisitions (Article 57 GCIV and Article 14 API). Medical supplies must pass freely, even in besieged areas (Article 23 GCIV).

---

[45] Daniel Hennan, *We Should Treat the Taliban Wounded as We Treat Our Own*, THE TELEGRAPH, Jan. 22, 2009.

Humanitarian law obliges armies to search, collect, and care for the wounded and the sick (Common Article 3, Article 16 GCIV, and Article 8 APII). To carry out those tasks, medical personnel benefit from a special protection.

C. Legitimate Military Targets

The principle of distinction also means that there are lawful targets and illegal targets; it is prohibited to target civilian properties, while it is legal to target military objectives. There is no definition of civilian property in international humanitarian law: instead one has to look at the definition of military targets to know what is civilian. Article 52-2 API gives a definition of military objectives: "military objects are limited to those objects which by their nature, location, purpose or use make an effective contribution to military action and whose total or partial destruction, capture or neutralization offers a definite military advantage." There are two criteria to identify a military target:

- The nature, the place, the purpose, or the use of the object must effectively contribute to military action.
- The destruction of the object, its capture, or its neutralization is an effective contribution to military action.

There is a non exhaustive list of civilian objects in API (Article 52-2) and an open list of examples of civilian objects (Article 52-3 API). In case of doubt about whether an object is civilian or military, and if the object is usually used for civilian purposes, parties should assume it is civilian and it cannot be targeted (Article 52.3 API). If a party decides to attack, it must be a legitimate attack: the party must prove that the object or property was used for military purposes and that destruction remains proportional. There are additional rules and guidelines: military commanders have the obligation to take precautions during the attacks to protect civilians (Article 57 API). An attack might fulfill the criteria above but still be illegal if excessive.[46]

Collateral damage is damage that is unintended or incidental. Jamie Shea, the spokesperson of NATO, was criticized for his blunt description of the war going on in Former Yugoslavia, and in particular shocked the world with his repetitive use of the concept of collateral damage to describe deaths of civilians.[47] International humanitarian law sets forth a principle that works hand in hand with the distinction between combatants and non combatants: the principle of proportionality. According to this principle, "the effect produced by the means

[46] Marco Sassoli, Legitimate Targets on Attacks under International Humanitarian Law, Background paper, Harvard Program on Humanitarian Policy and Conflict Research, www.oejc.or.at/recht/Session11.pdf

[47] Robert Fisk, *War in the Balkans: "Collateral Damage" Lies Dying in a Shattered Belgrade Hospital,* THE INDEPENDENT, Apr. 14, 1999.

and methods of warfare used in a given situation must not be disproportionate to the military advantage sought."[48] International humanitarian law does not prohibit collateral damage as such, but indiscriminate attacks are prohibited under Article 57 of the 1977 Additional Protocol I to the 1949 Geneva Conventions. This article states that during an international conflict, there should be constant care for the civilian population, civilians, and civilian objects. Article 57 is clear in the sense that it prohibits some types of attacks with uncontrollable effects. In non international armed conflicts, Protocol II grants a seemingly lesser protection since it states only that civilians "shall enjoy general protection against the dangers arising from military operations" and "shall not be the object of attack." Protocol II also prohibits an act or threat of violence, the primary purpose of which is "to spread terror among the civilian population." Coupled with the principle of proportionality, this provision makes clear that there is a positive obligation for the military to respect the difference between combatants and non combatants. There is room for military judgment that must be exercised carefully; Michael Walzer refers to the example of aerial bombing by the Free French Air Forces during World War II against German military infrastructure.[49] The difficulty for the pilots was to destroy the infrastructure without hurting the farms spread around. There were deaths, because killing some people along the way was inevitable, but these deaths remained limited. Pilots used their skill to fly as low as they could to avoid detection. During an aerial bombing, it is sometimes difficult for a pilot to fly as low as possible to target the military object in view, and some civilians might be the victims of the attack. War reality catches up with humanitarian law, and that is why international humanitarian law has created the concept of proportionality; if the attack brings a serious military advantage and causes limited civilian suffering, the attack is legitimate. This is a very different situation from a direct attack, when for example, Bosnian males were rounded up by the Serbs and shot in Srebrenica. The act is expected to fulfill some criteria that Walzer defines this way: the purpose of the attack, the direct effect, the intention, and the impact must compensate for the evil.[50] This is in brief the principle of proportionality. The major problem is to measure the actor's intent. For example, if a young soldier who put a bomb upside down and, once released, it does not hit its intended object but instead destroys a bridge with thousands of refugees on it, can we say that his intent his evil? One usually speaks of "collateral damage" in that type of situation. Evil was not intended but fulfilled altogether. The way the military approaches this concept is through the concept of intent. The U.S. Air Force Intelligence Targeting Guide defines the concept as follows: it is "[the] unintentional damage or incidental damage affecting facilities, equipment, or personnel, occurring as a result of military actions directed against targeted enemy forces or facilities.

[48] BOUCHET, *supra* note 9, 331.
[49] MICHAEL WALZER, JUST AND UNJUST WARS 157 (New York: Basic Books 1977).
[50] *Id.*, at 153.

Such damage can occur to friendly, neutral, and even enemy forces."[51] For the U.S. Department of Defense, collateral damage is an "unintentional or incidental injury or damage to persons or objects that would not be lawful military targets in the circumstances ruling at the time. Such damage is not unlawful so long as it is not excessive in light of the overall military advantage anticipated from the attack."[52] Intent is consequently the key element in understanding the military definition as it relates to its target. Walzer turns the argument upside down in his study devoted to the double effect.[53] He says: "[s]imply not to intend the death of civilians is too easy; most often, under battle conditions, the intentions of soldiers are focused narrowly on the enemy. What we look for in such cases in some sign of a positive commitment to save civilians' lives [...] and if saving civilians' lives means risking soldiers' lives, the risk must be accepted." Basically, it is not enough "not to try to kill civilians: you have to try not to kill them."[54]

The concept of collateral damage is in itself shocking, and Amnesty International makes a point to denounce what lurks behind the wording of collateral damage; it said about the attack of Lebanon in the summer of 2006:

The Israeli Air Force launched more than 7,000 air attacks on about 7,000 targets in Lebanon between 12 July and 14 August, while the Navy conducted an additional 2,500 bombardments. The attacks, though widespread, particularly concentrated on certain areas. In addition to the human toll an estimated 1,183 fatalities, about one third of whom have been children, 4,054 people injured and 970,000 Lebanese people displaced [...] the civilian infrastructure was severely damaged.

The Israeli Air Force said that it was targeting Hezbollah's positions and infrastructure and that resulting destruction of civilian infrastructure and the civilian death toll was incidental or was the result of the use of the "human shield" by Hezbollah. However, the intensity of the attack, as well as the number of civilian casualties, begs the question of whether this concept of collateral damage has not become an excuse to explain deliberate targeting of civilians. In this situation, one could rather argue that these are unlawful killings under the disguise of a well-rounded principle. This concept allows the army to demonstrate that the

---

[51] USAF Intelligence Targeting Guide—Air Force Pamphlet 14-210 Intelligence, at 180, 1998, http://www.fas.org/irp/doddir/usaf/afpam14-210/part20.htm#page180.

[52] U.S. Department of Defense, Joint Publication 3-60.

[53] The doctrine (or principle) of double effect is often invoked to explain the permissibility of an action that causes a serious harm, such as the death of a human being, as a side effect of promoting some good end. It is claimed that sometimes it is permissible to cause such a harm as a side effect (or "double effect") of bringing about a good result even though it would not be permissible to cause such a harm as a means to bringing about the same good end. This reasoning is summarized with the claim that sometimes it is permissible to bring about as a merely foreseen side effect a harmful event that it would be impermissible to bring about intentionally. STANFORD ENCYCLOPEDIA OF PHILOSOPHY, http://plato.stanford.edu/entries/double-effect.

[54] Judith Lichtenberg, *The Ethics of Retaliation, in* WAR AFTER SEPTEMBER 11 at 18, 11–20 (Verna V. Gehring ed., Lanham, Md.: Rowman & Littlefield Publishers 2003).

attack was accidental and regrettable,.[55] In a time when technology is so advanced that some speak of a bomb that can disintegrate human beings without affecting infrastructure, it is legitimate to wonder if the amount of collateral damage in Former Yugoslavia committed by NATO was not the outcome of carelessness and disregard for the principle of distinction. Accepting arguments regarding the reality of war seems almost like an insult considering the technology at hand. There are certainly accidents that occur during a war, but there should not have been as many as occurred in Lebanon in 2006.

The drafters of Article 52-2 API tried to present a narrow interpretation of what constitutes a military objective. Both criteria mentioned above are cumulative. It is each attack that is weighed and checked, not the entire war. The rules, although clear, have given birth to several borderline situations. When NATO attacked a Belgrade radio station, Radio Televizija Srbija (RTS), used by the military and killed civilians, it argued that the military use of the radio had transformed a civilian building into a military target.[56] The problem was rather that NATO destroyed the radio because it emitted propaganda; this gave birth to a debate[57] as to whether radio or TV stations emitting programs inciting to war crimes and genocide like the Radio des Mille Collines in Rwanda are or not legitimate military targets.[58] One could consider that freedom of expression is curbed. It seems that international law is going toward the criminalization of hate and genocide propaganda[59] based upon the Nuremberg Trials and the decision of the International Criminal Tribunal for Rwanda in the Radio des Mille Collines case.[60] However this does not turn a civilian radio into a legitimate target.

The war in the Former Yugoslavia is full of examples of attacks in which civilian objects were targeted as if they were considered legitimate military objects. Some targets were used for both civilian and military purposes (bridges, railways, radio stations, and others); for some, since roads were used for armies to move around and radio used to propagate propaganda, and since both prolong war, they were legitimate military objectives.[61] For others, the damage inflicted on civilians when targeted were too high and disproportionate. Precautionary measures

---

[55] Horst Fischer, Collateral Damage, http://www.crimesofwar.org/thebook/collateral-damage.html.

[56] U.S. Secretary of Defense William S. Cohen and Chairman of the Joint Chiefs of Staff Gen. Henri H. Shelton, Joint Statement on the Kosovo After Action Review (Oct. 14 1999) http://armed-services.senate.gov/statemnt/1999/991014wc.pdf.

[57] For more about the debate, see Sassoli, *supra* note 46.

[58] *See, e.g.,* cited in Sassoli's piece, in William J. Fenrick, *Targeting and Proportionality During the NATO Bombing Campaign Against Yugoslavia,* 12 E.J.I.L. 497, 489–502 (2001); George Aldrich, *Yugoslavia's Television Studios as Military Objectives* 1:3 INT'L L. FORUM 150, 149–50 (1999).

[59] Wibke Kirstin Timmermann, *The Relationship Between Hate Propaganda and Incitement to Genocide: A New Trend in International Law Towards Criminalization of Hate Propaganda?,* 18:2 L.J.I.L 257–282 (2005).

[60] See the summary of the judgment, at http://liveunictr.altmansolutions.com/Portals/0/Case/English/Nahimana/judgement/Summary-Media.pdf.

[61] James A. Burger, *International Humanitarian Law and the Kosovo Crisis: Lessons Learned or to Be Learned,* 837 I.R.C.C. 131–32, 129–45 (2000).

were often not taken. Besides, the concept of concrete and direct military advantage is rather vague. The ICTY was entrusted with the mission of deciding whether some of these targets were indeed legitimate military targets.[62] Obviously, the Allies who participated in the creation of the ICTY at the United Nations did not expect the tribunal to judge its actions harshly: what was really expected from the tribunal was to judge crimes committed by Serbs, Croats, and other communities in the Former Yugoslavia.[63] Therefore, NATO felt itself virtually untouchable and additionally felt justified and entitled in most of its targeting; even when it targeted a radio station and when it targeted a bridge, hitting instead a train, the ICTY justified the attacks. So-called international justice appears therefore rather to be the justice of the victorious and lose credibility in the eyes of many. The unacceptable is justified, such as the targeting of buildings with dual use full of civilians at the time of the bombing (120 civilians were working in the Belgrade radio station when it was hit), the double targeting of a train (the Grdelica train during which the pilot hit a train instead of a bridge and then hit it again to complete his mission), or the attack on the refugee Djakovica Convoy that NATO initially denied.[64] These attacks were disproportionate and demonstrated how little civilian lives were worth: the destruction of the TV station and the bridge in the Grdelica gorge were objects of dual use (the station was used to transmit Serb military propaganda and the train to transport the military) and indeed contributed to the war effort. However, their destruction did not give a "definite military advantage" within the meaning of Article 52-2 API, as demonstrated later by the author. Instead the death of civilians was approached under Article 51-5 (b) as collateral damage, damage which would not be "excessive in relation to the concrete and direct military advantage anticipated." Was the radio-station destruction that killed so many civilians justified in relation to the concrete and direct military advantage anticipated, considering that the station was not diffusing hate speech but propaganda? This led Robert Fisk to declare "Once you kill people because you

---

[62] A committee was set up by the Prosecutor on May 14, 1999, to investigate whether NATO committed war crimes. The report issued by the committee was an advice to the prosecutor, who had complete control over the committee since no rules of procedure speaks of the creation of such a committee: it was the prosecutor's creation. In most cases, the committee decided that no war crimes had been committed; for other cases, it invoked the difficulty to obtain sufficient evidence to sustain an indictment. Therefore, the committee recommended that no investigation should be commenced regarding the NATO bombing campaign, and the prosecutor followed that advice. The final report can be read online at www.icty.org/sid/7846. The ICRC harshly criticized the results of the committee. ICRC, cited in Pierre Hazan, Justice in a Time of War: The True Story Behind the International Criminal Tribunal for the Former Yugoslavia 135–36 (James Thomas Snyder trans., College Station: Texas A & M University Press 2004).

[63] A very interesting analysis on the topic can be found here: Natalino Ronzitti, *Is the Non Liquet of the Final Report by the Committee Established to Review the NATO Bombing Campaign Against the Federal Republic of Yugoslavia Acceptable?*, 840 I.R.C.C. 1017–1028 (2000).

[64] Albanian refugees traveling in a convoy were repeatedly bombed in April 1999 by NATO, who thus killed seventy-three civilians. NATO first denied this, before arguing that it was sure the convoy was accompanied by Serb military vehicles. Investigations carried out by Human Rights Watch found no basis for that claim.

don't like what they say, you change the rules of war."[65] This said, the director of RTS was condemned in 2002 to ten years of imprisonment for ordering some of the staff to remain in the building, although he knew there might be an attack. This example demonstrates that identifying a legitimate military target, especially those of dual uses, is very difficult. It also shows that rules of international humanitarian law, whether the principle of distinction or the one of doubt benefiting civilians and civilian property, are often disregarded.

II. THE DISTINCTION IN CUSTOMARY INTERNATIONAL LAW

The distinction therefore exists in law. However, although the Geneva Conventions have been ratified by most countries, it is different for the Protocols. Protocol I, which grants more protection to civilians during international armed conflicts but also to fighters engaged in self determination struggles, has not been ratified by major countries such as the United States, Israel, Iran, or Pakistan. The United States, Iran, and Pakistan signed it on December 12, 1977, with the intention of ratifying it. For many, Protocol I has become customary law, although the United States disagrees and considers that since it has not ratified the Protocol, it is not applicable to U.S. citizens. The main objection of the United States is the protection of combatants engaged guerrilla actions. Indeed Protocol I extends or rather loosens the conditions set forth in Article 4 GCIII and Article 44 API: fighters who do not wear uniforms to distinguish themselves from the civilian population are combatants. President Ronald Reagan argued that this would protect terrorist or so-called unlawful combatants.[66] The debate regarding international customary law is so intense that the ICRC conducted major research on the topic.[67]

A. What Are Customary Rules of Humanitarian Law?

Customary international humanitarian law is a source of international humanitarian law, just like treaties or conventions. By ratifying a treaty or a convention, like the Geneva Conventions and the Protocols, a State expresses its consent to be bound by them. There are however rules binding States even though they have expressed no formal consent to respect them: these are rules of customary international humanitarian law.

---

[65] Robert Fisk, THE INDEPENDENT, Apr. 23, 1999.

[66] George H. *Aldrich, Prospects for United States Ratification of Additional Protocol I*, 85 A.J.I.L. 1–20 (1991).

[67] JEAN-MARIE HENCKAERTS & LOUISE DOSWALD-BECK, CUSTOMARY INTERNATIONAL HUMANITARIAN LAW 5 (Cambridge, UK/New York, NY, USA: Cambridge University Press 2005).

Customary law is a body of unwritten rules that derives from "a general practice accepted as law,"[68] and therefore does not require any ratification process. Practice remains the main element to prove whether a rule is customary or not. Practice relates to official States' activities. This practice must be "widespread, representative and virtually uniform"[69] according to the case law of the International Court of Justice. Therefore, one has be certain that a rule of international law is widely and uniformly applied and reflected in legal opinion before determining whether it is a custom or not. While treaty law is codified and written, customary rules are not written.

Customary law was the first form taken by international humanitarian law and international law in general until the Hague law. For example, in 1899, Fyodor Martens laid down the following principle: "civilians and combatants remain under the protection and authority of the principles of international law derived from established custom, from the principles of humanity and from the dictates of public conscience."[70] This was the Martens Clause and was a customary rule of conduct.[71] It was later incorporated in the Hague body of law, and the modern version is in Article 1-2 API. The process of codifying international humanitarian law started in the middle of the nineteenth century, and developed throughout the twentieth century with the Hague and the Geneva bodies of law. Even though there are today numerous conventions on international humanitarian law, customary law has an important role to play as it fill in the gaps to avoid legal loopholes. Customary rules are often the main source of law in today's conflicts, especially since most of which are non international, and those conflicts are covered solely by Common Article 3 and APII. The body of law governing international armed conflicts is more developed that the one dealing with non international armed conflicts. Therefore, rules of customary law are a helpful additional source of law. For example, this body of law details the rules pertaining to the conduct of hostilities. Common Article 3 of the Conventions and Protocol II do not expressly prohibit attacks against civilian objects in non international armed conflicts. Customary international law does.

Furthermore, most States have ratified the Geneva Conventions rather than Additional Protocol I. When an international armed conflict occurs in a country that has not ratified Protocol I, customary law applies, and States are bound by norms and principles that are detailed in Additional Protocol I even if they have not ratified the document. Article 75 API is an illustration: it conveys rights that are ad minima and that apply in all situations other than the ones covered by the Geneva Conventions and the Protocols. If someone is captured and is neither a combatant

---

[68] Article 38(1)(b) in the Statute of the International Court of Justice.

[69] *See, e.g.,* North Sea Continental Shelf Cases (Fed. Rep of Germany v. Netherlands), I.C.J. (February 1969, 20).

[70] Article 1-2 API.

[71] Theodor Meron, *The Martens Clause, Principles of Humanity, and Dictates of Public Conscience,* 94:1 A.J.I.L. 78–90 (January 2000).

nor a civilian *stricto sensu*, he will be an unprivileged combatant in the sense that he will not benefit from GCIII's protection but from Article 75 API, which guarantees fundamental rights detailed in that article. For example, Article 75-2 (a) prohibits "violence to life, health, or physical or mental well-being of persons, in particular murder; torture of all kinds, whether physical or mental; corporal punishment; and mutilation." This has a direct impact on the distinction between civilians and combatants: if a person falls in between categories, he still benefits from an ad minima protection detailed in Article 75, which is also reflected in customary law. The fact that this article is considered to be a customary rule of humanitarian law allows for broader and better enforcement of humanitarian law, as well as a complete protection of all individuals in all situations. States cannot argue that since they have not ratified Protocol I, Article 75 API is not applicable to them. Consequently, in situations where treaties are not applicable or show gaps, customary law can take over. This is relevant when a State is not a party to a treaty or when a non state actor considers itself not a party. For example, the United States has not yet ratified the first Additional Protocols to the Geneva Conventions. This non-ratification was determinant when the country captured Taliban and al Qaeda fighters in Afghanistan: the U.S. government argued that they were neither civilians nor combatants, and were unlawful combatants. It relied on Article 4 GCIII to explain that al Qaeda and Taliban fighters did not meet the conditions to be considered as combatants and were therefore unlawful combatants. The United States then felt entitled to ignore Article 75 API, which grants these ad minima rights, since the country has not ratified the Protocol. This is how their prisoners became so-called unlawful combatants, losing all protection, which paved the path to abuses. Meanwhile, the United States violated customary humanitarian law; there is no legal limbo in humanitarian law. Article 75 is considered to be a rule of customary international humanitarian law,[72] and therefore, the United States violated its obligations under customary international humanitarian law by not respecting the standards set by Article 75 API. The United States has assumed this position for decades as it considers Protocol I gives recognition and legitimacy to insurgent and terrorist groups.

Customary law therefore completes international humanitarian law and gives it a much-needed flexibility, as shown above with Article 75 API. Looking at customs helps bridge the gaps between, for example, the invention of a new military weapon and the ratification of a treaty. Besides, looking at customary law is extremely

---

[72] Michael J. Matheson, Remarks on the United States Position on the Relation of Customary International Law to the 1977 Protocols Additional to the 1949 Geneva Conventions, reprinted in *The Sixth Annual American Red Cross-Washington College of Law Conference on International Humanitarian Law: A Workshop on Customary International Laws and the 1977 Protocols Additional to the Geneva Conventions*, 2 AM. U. J. INT'L. L. & POL'Y 415, 425–26 (1987); *see for further discussion*, *e.g.*, JAMES R. SILKENAT & MARK R. SHULMAN, THE IMPERIAL PRESIDENCY AND THE CONSEQUENCES OF 9/11: LAWYERS REACT TO THE GLOBAL WAR ON TERRORISM (Westport, Conn.: Praeger Security International 2007); KAREN J. GREENBERG & JOSHUA L. DRATEL, THE TORTURE PAPERS: THE ROAD TO ABU GHRAIB (Cambridge/New York: Cambridge University Press 2005).

useful to complete the existing codified law. Customs also arise from needs in the field, which means that they often reflect the needs and expectations of the people better than treaties would. Customary law can be very useful for clarifying a law. For example, the ICRC relied on customary rules of humanitarian law to challenge the U.S. administration's interpretation of the Geneva Conventions regarding the treatment of detainees at Guantanamo Bay and other bases. Rather than prepare a new treaty, which is time consuming, one can refer to custom until such a treaty is adopted and ratified.[73] This is why the ICRC spent years working on a project to set forth customary rules of humanitarian law.

B. The ICRC Study

This body of law is so crucial that the International Committee for the Red Cross (ICRC) developed a study to gather and analyze customary rules of international humanitarian law in both international and non international armed conflicts. The outcome of the study is the publication of two volumes of customary international humanitarian law. The ICRC has identified 161 rules of customary humanitarian law ("c.h.1.") in order clarify this body of unwritten rules. Amid these rules are rules relating to the distinction between civilians and combatants. Rule 1 states: "the parties to the conflict must at all times distinguish between civilians and combatants. Attacks may only be directed against combatants. Attacks must not be directed against civilians." This applies in both types of conflict. Regarding international armed conflicts, Rule 2 says: "Acts or threats of violence the primary purpose of which is to spread terror among the civilian population are prohibited." The negative definition of civilians as non combatants is in rule 5. Rule 6 explains that civilians are protected against attacks until they take part in hostilities. The wording of that rule is important because it says that if a civilian takes part directly in hostilities, he will lose his immunity for the time of his participation. Even though the principle of distinction is set and described in the treaties, there is still a need to emphasize it in customs. Indeed, even though the distinction between civilians and combatants seems easy to understand, there is a lack of clarity in practice.

The principle of distinction is clearly defined in international armed conflicts but seems to be more ambiguous in non international armed conflict. For example, are members of armed opposition groups civilians or combatants? This lack of clarity is reflected in Additional Protocol II, which does not define civilian or civilian population (see Additional Protocol II, Articles 13–15 and 17–18). The problem is

---

[73] François Bugnion, *The International Committee of the Red Cross and the Development of International Humanitarian Law*, 5 CHI. J. INT'L L., 191–211 (2004).

that subsequent treaties refer to the distinction in non international armed conflicts and the concept of civilian and combatant without defining them.[74] The conclusion of the ICRC is that many of the rules applicable to non-international armed conflicts are the same as the rules applicable to international armed conflicts. Regarding civilians, the rules stated in Article 3 common to the four Geneva Conventions apply in both types of war. Therefore, the legal qualification of a conflict as being international or non international loses much of its relevance for the application of customary international humanitarian law; the same rules must be respected in any armed conflict. International humanitarian law acts as rights ad minimum; it affords the basic minimal protection. The distinction between civilians and combatants does not change according to the type of conflict. This is how customary rules complete and clarify the law. There are also customary rules that are similar or identical to those laid down in treaty law. Customary law goes even further than Protocol II; practice has created other rules that are more detailed and that fill gaps. For example, Additional Protocol II contains meager rules regarding the conduct of hostilities; Article 13 states that "the civilian population as such, as well as individual civilians, shall not be the object of attack... unless and for such time as they take a direct part in hostilities." Customary law fills those gaps.

The list drawn by the ICRC study is somewhat of a reminder of the Conventions, except that these rules are customary, so they do not require States' signatures or ratification. The principle of distinction is listed as a rule of customary international law. The process of codification was crucial, but customary law remains essential: it is often the main source of law in today's conflicts since most conflicts are non international. The principle of distinction between combatants and civilians is not new; it existed prior to the Conventions. It is also a principle of customary international humanitarian law.

Amnesty International has relied on the rules of customary international humanitarian law laid out by the ICRC to condemn the suicide bomb attacks carried out in Sri Lanka. Amnesty International reminded the world and the attackers that targeting civilians or attacking indiscriminately violates international humanitarian law and customary rules.[75] The attacks in Sri Lanka involved armed opposition groups which were not parties to international treaties, but were bound to respect Common Article 3 applying to non international armed conflict. Amnesty International also said the attackers were compelled to respect customary rules of humanitarian law. Therefore, the principle of distinction exists in law and in customary law; civilians and combatants must be distinguished. Both benefit from such protection, as analyzed in Chapter Three.

---

[74] *See, e.g.*, Amended Protocol II to the Convention on Certain Conventional Weapons, Article 3(7)–(11); Protocol III to the Convention on Certain Conventional Weapons, Article 2; Ottawa Convention on the Prohibition of Anti-personnel Mines, preamble; Statute of the International Criminal Court, Article 8(2)(e)(i), (iii), and (viii).

[75] Amnesty International, Sri Lanka: Mounting Civilian Casualties as Conflict Persists, AI Index: ASA 37/017/2008, Apr. 9, 2008.

III. CONCLUSION

There is an interest for everyone in sparing civilians. First, the war will be led among parties to the conflict, without making unnecessary and unwilling victims. Second, sparing citizens allows the army to have an economy of force; bombing cities is expensive and takes time. It is also counterproductive to destroy places that ones wishes to conquer after the war (which explains why the Bosnian Serbs used snipers to spread terror in the streets of Sarajevo rather than bombing the cities to ashes, although this campaign of terror was coupled with a few bombings, such as the bombing of the library of Sarajevo); eventually, the sparing of property also means that after the war, there will be less to rebuild or repay. This pragmatism, which is reflected in regular military strategies, coupled with a process of humanization of war via the Hague and Geneva laws is, however, often put to the test, as demonstrated in the next chapters.

3 Protection Afforded to Civilians and Rights of Combatants

International humanitarian law does not prevent war, because war is a reality. It mitigates war's effects on all actors, and establishes limits to avoid total destructive war. The distinction between civilian and combatant is made to grant each actor in hostilities a specific protection; civilians are immune from the effects of war while combatants benefit from protection when captured. This chapter analyzes the protection resulting from the principle of distinction.

I. ANALYSIS OF THE PROTECTION AFFORDED TO CIVILIANS

Civilians benefit from immunity. They are protected from the effects or war and cannot be targeted. This is a direct outcome of the distinction. The Geneva Conventions, and later the Additional Protocols, focused on the protection of civilians, while previous laws, such as the Hague body of law, focused instead on the conduct of hostilities. The humanization of conflict through the Geneva law is therefore a major improvement.

A. The Aim of Geneva Convention IV and the Additional Protocols

The Fourth Geneva Convention is relative to the Protection of Civilian Persons in Time of War. The Convention was ratified on August 12, 1949, at the end of a conference held in Geneva from April 21 to August 12. The Convention entered into force on October 21, 1950. It is now part of customary international law.[1] Common Article 3 protects civilians during non international armed conflicts. This article, which is common to the four Geneva Conventions, is a mini-treaty itself. Two Additional Protocols complete the existing Geneva Conventions. There is Protocol Additional I (API), which relates to the Protection of Victims of International Armed Conflict; it was adopted on June 8, 1977, and entered into force on December 7, 1979. Additional Protocol II (APII) relates to the protection of victims of non international armed conflicts. According to Professor Julius Stone, the protection of civilians in the Geneva Conventions "is a desire to seek a new starting point for the modern movement to protect human rights."[2] How do the Conventions and Protocols concretely protect civilians, civilian populations, and civilian properties?

1. Protection of Civilians as a Principle

The Fourth Geneva Convention (GCIV) explains how combatants should behave toward non combatants and sets up prohibited belligerent actions against civilians. The Convention is applicable in times of international armed conflicts and when there is partial or total occupation of the territory of a Contracting Party. It has a wide scope, as it applies to almost all situations. Additional Protocols I and customary law complete the Convention in cases of international armed conflicts. Civilians in non-international armed conflicts are protected by Common Article 3, Additional Protocol II, and customary rules of international humanitarian law.

With the emergence of the Geneva Conventions, we witnessed the division of the modern law of war into two categories: *jus in bello* and *jus ad bellum*. The *jus in bello* tells combatants how they have to act once war has begun, while *jus ad bellum* is a set of criteria that have to be consulted before engaging into a war to determine whether the war is justifiable. The principle of distinction is at the root of the *jus in bello*;[3] the *jus in bello* distinguishes between acceptable and unacceptable conduct of war, and targeting civilians in not acceptable. As noted by the International Court of Justice in its 1996 Advisory Opinion, *Legality of the Threat or Use of Nuclear Weapons*, the principle of distinction is fundamental and intransgressible.[4] From the principle of distinction comes the protection granted to civilians.

[1] In 1993, the UN Security Council adopted a report from the Secretary General and a Commission of Experts which concluded beyond doubt that the Geneva Conventions had passed into the body of customary international law that is binding on non signatory parties whenever they engage in armed conflicts. See Report of the Secretary General Pursuant to Paragraph 2 of Security Council Resolution 808 (1993), presented May 3, 1993, (S/25704), www.icty.org/x/file/Legal%20Library/Statute/statute_re808_1993_en.pdf

[2] JULIUS STONE, LEGAL CONTROLS OF INTERNATIONAL CONFLICT: A TREATISE ON THE DYNAMIC OF DISPUTE 684 (New York, Rinehart 1954).

[3] Yoram Dinstein, *Legitimate Military Objectives under the Current Jus in Bello*, 2002 ISR. YBOOK on H.R. 31, 1–34.

[4] Advisory Opinion on the Legality of the Use of Threat or the Use of Nuclear Weapons, I.C.J., 1996, Rep. 226, 257.

The Fourth Geneva Convention protecting civilians applies in international armed conflict (Article 2 of the Convention). Article 4 provides us with a definition of protected persons in a conflict, analyzed in Chapter 2. The Convention is applicable to the following civilians:

Persons protected by the Convention are those who, at a given moment and in any manner whatsoever, find themselves, in case of a conflict or occupation, in the hands of a Party to the conflict or Occupying Power of which they are not nationals. Nationals of a State which is not bound by the Convention are not protected by it.

When enforcing the protection granted to civilians, there should be no discrimination; "the whole of the populations of the countries in conflict, without any adverse distinction based, in particular, on race, nationality, religion or political opinion, and are intended to alleviate the sufferings caused by war." (Article 13 GCIV). Consequently, the principle of distinction entails the immunity of civilians, the civilian population, and civilian property.

2. Illustrations of Protection from Effects of War and from Attacks: Articles 31–34 GCIV

The goal of the Convention is to protect civilians from the effects of war as mentioned in Article 14 GCIV. This means that parties to the conflict have positive obligations when it comes to civilians' immunity. Examples of immunity and humanization of warfare include, for example, Articles 31, 32, and 33 GCIV; these three articles protect the civilian population from torture (Article 31) and from physical extermination (Article 32). Article 31 states that no physical or moral coercion can be exercised against civilians to obtain information. It is therefore prohibited to torture civilians to extract information about, for example, the whereabouts of the opponent, a scenario that does occur. For example, the Sri Lankan government has reportedly tortured civilians to extract information about the guerrilla organization the Tamil Tigers, in full violation of the Convention.[5] This article is completed by Article 32; it details what is prohibited, and the broad definition of torture encompasses corporal punishment or any form of physical abuse, which enlarges the definition given in the 1984 Convention against Torture. Article 32 says that the parties must refrain from taking actions that could "cause the physical suffering or extermination of protected persons in their hands. The prohibition applies not only to murder, torture, corporal punishments, mutilation and medical or scientific experiments not necessitated by the medical treatment of a protected person." The text of the article clearly refers to war atrocities, such as

---

[5] Randeep Ramesh, *Sri Lankan Government accused of Torture*, THE GUARDIAN, Oct. 30, 2007. To read more about the use of torture on civilians, see DARIUS REJALI, TORTURE AND DEMOCRACY (Princeton, NJ: Princeton, University Press 2007); MARNIA LAZREG, TORTURE AND THE TWILIGHT OF EMPIRE: FROM ALGIERS TO BAGHDAD (Princeton, NJ: Princeton, University Press 2008).

the conduct of German SS Officer Josef Mengele, who performed human experiments on camp inmates during World War II. The end of the article speaks about "any other measures of brutality whether applied by a civilian or military agents". Article 33 prevents the use of collective punishment against the civilian population, such as measures of intimidation, measures of terrorism, pillage, and reprisals. Collective punishments are considered to be a war crime under the Geneva Conventions. Art. 33 addresses, for example, collective punishment that occurred during World War II, and in particular, the crimes committed by the Germans upon defeat; for example, 124 villagers were slaughtered by departing Nazis on August 1944, in Maille, France. In the French village of Oradour-sur-Glane, 642 inhabitants were killed as retaliation for Resistance acts carried out by the FFI (Forces Françaises Intérieurs, an umbrella group for all movements resisting the German occupation).[6] Additionally, Article 34 prohibits the taking of hostages. It prevents the use of civilian shields like the ones Saddam Hussein used in Iraq in 1991 or the ones used in Palestinian territories.[7] These few examples demonstrate how important Geneva Convention IV is regarding the humanization of war, the principle of distinction, and the protection of non combatants; it seeks to learn from the history of warfare to improve civilians' protection at war.

3. Illustrations of Civilian Protection Granted by Additional Protocol I

Additional Protocol I completes GCIV in times of international armed conflicts. It addresses a series of important issues that were overlooked, hardly appeared, or needed clarification in the Fourth Geneva Convention. The Protocol contains much more detailed protection and solves issues raised by the enforcement of the Geneva Conventions in the field. This is explained by the fact that the Geneva Conventions were drafted after World War II; the world underwent major changes with the Iron Curtain and then decolonization, phenomena that affected humanitarian law. It was therefore necessary to "update" the Conventions with Protocols covering new issues such as the behavior of self-determination fighters. Improvements include the clear layout of the principle of distinction in Article 48 API. Civilians, the civilian population, and civilian property are protected against the general effects of hostilities (Article 51 API). They cannot be targeted by combatants, which is the direct outcome of the distinction. The weapon race and the rapid technological developments led to Article 35 API, which stresses that "in any armed conflict, the right of the parties to the conflict to choose methods or means of warfare is not unlimited." This means that weapons that are far-reaching or that lack precision cannot be used since they put the civilian population at risk of an indiscriminate attack. Article 36 compels a contracting party to determine whether the employment

---

[6] SARAH FARMER, ORADOUR—10 JUIN 1944: ARRET SUR MEMOIRE (Paris, Perrin 2007).

[7] Al Mezan Center for Human Rights, *Hiding Behind Civilians—The Continued Use of Palestinian Civilians as Human Shields by the Israeli Occupation Forces*, April 2008, Gaza: al Mezan.

of a "study, development, acquisition or adoption of new weapons, means or method of warfare" would be prohibited under the Protocol or any rules of international law. These articles show that a lesson was learned from World War II when the Allies dropped the nuclear bomb on Japan. That lesson did not, however, prevent NATO from bombarding the Former Yugoslavia, causing massive "collateral damages," although new technology has entitled armies to speak of surgical strikes.[8] The Protocol also deals with the issue of wars of national liberation, which was not addressed directly by the Geneva Conventions. Decolonization took place right after the war and most of the process was violent. This is why wars of national liberation are addressed in Article 1 API. They are considered to be international armed conflicts.

In addition to the new rules that try to cover most of the changes that occurred since 1949, the Protocol details the protection civilians benefit from. Article 49 defines attacks while Article 51 describes the protection of civilians from attacks. Article 51-1 API could not be clearer: "The civilian population and individual civilians shall enjoy general protection against dangers arising from military operations." And so does Article 51-2: "The civilian population as such, as well as individual civilians, shall not be the object of attack." Article 56-1 protects works and installations containing dangerous forces (e.g., dams, dikes, and nuclear stations) from attacks. During the Iran-Iraq War, the Iraqis bombarded a civil nuclear power station in violation of Article 56-1 API, to which neither Iran nor Iraq is a party, causing major damage to the environment and for civilians.[9] The second paragraph of this article allows for exceptions when these installations are used as "regular, significant and direct support of military operations." In 1981, the Osirak Iraqi nuclear reactor was bombarded by Israel. The aim of the attack was to slow the progress in weapons-grade plutonium that might have been later used for nuclear or military purposes by the regime of Saddam Hussein. This could justify the attacks under Article 56-2; all measures were taken to protect the civilian population from suffering the effects of the attacks although a French engineer died in the attack. It remains that the attack was led in an anticipatory fashion, a factor which gave rise to much debate.[10] The operation was condemned by the United States (which later destroyed completely the facility during the 1991 Gulf War) and the UN Security Council unanimously passed UN Resolution 487 that "strongly condemns the military attack by Israel in clear violation of the Charter of the

---

[8] DAVID R. METS, THE LONG SEARCH FOR SURGICAL STRIKE: PRECISION MUNITIONS AND THE REVOLUTION IN MILITARY AFFAIRS (Maxwell Air Force Base, AL: Air University Press 2001).

[9] Fritz Kalshoven, *Prohibitions or Restrictions on the Use of Methods and Means of Warfare, in* THE GULF WAR OF 1980–88: THE IRAN-IRAQ WAR IN INTERNATIONAL LEGAL PERSPECTIVE 106 (Ike Dekker & Harry H. G. Post eds., Dordrecht: Martinus Nijhoff 1992).

[10] *See, e.g.,* Uri Shoham, *The Israeli Aerial Raid upon the Iraqi Nuclear Reactor and the Right to Self Defense,* 109, MIL. LR 191, 206 (1985); W. Thomas Mallison & Sally V. Mallison, *The Israeli Aerial Attack of June 7, 1981, Upon the Iraqi Nuclear Reactor: Aggression or Self-Defense?,* 15 VAND. J. TRANSNAT'L. L. 417, 435–37 (1982); STANIMIR A. ALEXANDROV, SELF-DEFENSE AGAINST THE USE OF FORCE IN INTERNATIONAL LAW (The Hague/Boston: Kluwer Law International 1996).

United Nations and the norms of international conduct"[11] because of the use of force in violation of Article 2 (4) of the UN Chapter and the violation of the territorial integrity of Iraq.

API is also a major step forward regarding principles other than distinction and protection. The principles of proportionality and precaution are laid down respectively in Article 51-5 and Article 57. Paragraph 5 of Article 51 API states that "an attack by bombardment by any methods or means which treats as a single military objective a number of clearly separated and distinct military objectives located in a city, town, village or other area containing a similar concentration of civilians or civilian objects" is considered indiscriminate; and "an attack which may be expected to cause incidental loss of civilian life, injury to civilians, damage to civilian objects, or a combination thereof, which would be excessive in relation to the concrete and direct military advantage anticipated" is also indiscriminate The principle of proportionality states that the effect produced by an attack must not be disproportionate to the military advantage sought. Article 57 lays down the principle of precaution: armies should take all precautionary measures during attacks to avoid civilian casualties. This means that attacks have to be carefully planned so that neither civilians nor civilian objects will be victims of the hostilities. In case of a doubt about an objective, the attack should be suspended. Attacks from the air or the sea have to be in conformity with the rights and duties under international law, and all precautionary measures to avoid civilian casualties must be taken. Article 58 extends the precautionary principle to the effects of the attacks. This means that the parties should avoid targeting military objectives that are close to densely populated areas. These articles are now part of customary law.

Another interesting addition in Protocol I is that it addresses terrorism in Articles 49, 51, and 52. Acts of terrorism during international armed conflicts, such as attacks against civilians or civilian objects, are prohibited. The treaty also explicitly prohibits acts or threats of violence, the primary purpose of which is to spread terror among the civilian population. Anyone carrying out such actions will be liable for criminal prosecution. The Protocol has reinforced the prohibition of attacks that might cause large, durable, and grave damage to the environment (Article 55-1). Therefore, API tries to draw the lessons of warfare's evolution since 1949.

4. Illustrations of Civilian Protection in Non International Armed Conflicts

We have analyzed so far the principle of distinction and the protection of civilians in situations of international armed conflicts. In non international armed conflicts, Protocol II applies in addition to Article 3, common to the four Geneva Conventions. Article 3 is a mini-convention and is considered to be customary international law; even if a country has not ratified the Convention, it will have to respect the rules

---

[11] UN Resolution, S-RES-487 (1981) Security Council Resolution 487 (1981) http://www. undemocracy.com/S-RES-487.

laid down in Article 3. That article guarantees ad minima standards for civilians and those who no longer take part in hostilities; to benefit from the protection of Article 3, one should either be a civilian or someone who is "taking no active part in the hostilities, including members of armed forces who laid down their arms and those placed *hors de combat* by sickness, wounds, detention, or by any other cause." This article allows for the enforcement of the main provisions of the Geneva Conventions' principles in cases that are not expressly covered by the Conventions. It lists a series of prohibited acts:

(a) violence to life and person, in particular murder of all kinds, mutilation, cruel treatment, and torture;

(b) taking of hostages;

(c) outrages upon personal dignity, in particular humiliating and degrading treatment;

(d) the passing of sentences and the carrying out of executions without previous judgment pronounced by a regularly constituted court, affording all the judicial guarantees which are recognized as indispensable by civilized peoples.

These acts are absolutely prohibited in all times and circumstances. Therefore Article 3 provides ad minima rights, the minimum level of protection, for civilians in non international armed conflicts, as well as to those who no longer take part in hostilities. Additionally, Article 3 exists to provide relief to civilians in cases of civil war or insurrections, during which the government tends to view almost anyone as a common criminal.[12] The International Committee of the Red Cross (ICRC) can also provide services to a government during internal disturbances and tensions. The reason why the ICRC does not interfere and leaves it to the States to decide whether they wish to have the assistance of the organization is that there was fear that rebels or common brigands would form organizations to benefit from the Geneva Conventions when they should be judged under national criminal law.[13] The ICRC could also be used by more established rebel groups to gain popularity, or at least more legitimacy. Article 3 has limits of enforcement; the notion of armed conflict does not, for example, apply to cases of rebellion. The commentary of the Fourth Geneva Convention by the ICRC gives a list of criteria for the enforcement of this Article.[14] These criteria are supposed to help distinguish an armed conflict from banditry. Meanwhile, the ICRC is in favor of the widest understanding possible to permit the enforcement of Article 3. Since most armed conflicts today are non international, Common Article 3 is very important. Even though useful, this article is not complete when it comes to civilians. First, it says nothing about indiscriminate attacks. Then, it intends to protect civilians as individuals rather than the civilian population as a whole.

---

[12] ICRC Commentary of Article 3, http://www.icrc.org/ihl.nsf/COM/380-600006?OpenDocument.
[13] *Id.*
[14] *Id.*

Later, provisions of Article 3 were strengthened in Additional Protocol II, which provides detailed obligations (for example, Article 13-1). Additional Protocol II is innovative; it is the first real effort of codification of the protection of civilians in non international armed conflict. The drafting of this document corresponds to another need: the one of protecting civilians during internal conflicts. It completes and develops Article 3 common to the four Geneva Conventions. The application of Additional Protocol II is actually more limited than the scope of Article 3: the application of the treaty is limited to situations where a dissident group controls a portion of the territory of the government it is challenging. The drafters of the treaty, however, acknowledged that Common Article 3 applied to a broader category of non-international armed conflicts; the Commentary indicates "the Protocol only applies to conflicts of a certain degree of intensity and does not have exactly the same field of application as common Article 3, *which applies in all situations of non-international armed conflict.*" Additional Protocol II also includes fundamental guarantees for people who will face trial (Article 6). The protection afforded in this protocol strongly resembles Article 75 API.

Articles 27, 31, 34, and 64 to 77 of the Protocol define in detail parts of Article 3. The conditions of application of Protocol II are stricter than those provided in Article 3. In non international armed conflicts, Article 3 will apply. Protocol II prohibits attacks on the civilian population and individual civilians (Article 13) and objects indispensable to the survival of the civilian population (Article 14). It also regulates the forced movement of civilians (Article 17). Shelters can also be designated as stock cultural objects. Forced movements of the population are prohibited (Article 17). In addition to protecting civilians, civil populations, and civilian buildings from attacks, special protections can also be afforded, for example, to cultural objects or places of worship to avoid the destruction of buildings and the looting of cultural objects. This rule is probably the outcome of the looting of museums during World War II, as well as the raids of Dresden and the numerous castles that were used by military forces throughout Europe (for example, the Royal Castle at Warsaw and the summer palace of the Tsars at Tsarskoe Selo, both occupied by the Germans). Paris was also targeted when the Nazis placed bombs under all major monuments upon departure. In the end, none of them was activated.

The aim of the documents that are only a part of humanitarian law is to help distinguish civilians from combatants and to grant protection to civilians and combatants. The documents are therefore focused on distinguishing civilians from combatants and on protecting civilians by granting them immunity during hostilities. A civilian will lose the immunity granted by international humanitarian law if he directly participates in hostilities.

5. Rights and Fundamental Guarantees

International humanitarian law protects civilians from attacks and effects of war, but also takes positive steps by granting them effective fundamental guarantees. This is another major contribution made by the Geneva law. These fundamental guarantees grant protection to civilians in all circumstances; they are ad minima rights for all. First, civilians benefit from the protection granted by human rights in situations of international disturbances and tensions. Indeed, international humanitarian law applies in times of war, while human rights are to be enforced in times of peace, which includes internal disturbances. During a state of emergency or events such as a siege, human rights could be restricted. However, there are core human rights that cannot be derogated from at any time. These rights are listed in Articles 6, 7, 8.1 and 8.2, 11, 15, 16, and 18 of the International Covenant on Civil and Political Rights (ICCPR): the right to life, the prohibition of torture, the prohibition of slavery, the respect of the law, and freedom of conscience. Additionally, Common Article 3, an article common to the four Geneva Conventions, can be invoked during internal disturbances, by humanitarian organizations, a procedure in line with the ICRC's role as an intermediary during troubles and internal strife.[15] Protocol II is not applicable.

During armed conflicts, inalienable human rights are applicable, as well as fundamental guarantees set out in international humanitarian law. Common Article 3 is applicable in times of international as well as non international armed conflicts. It is a mini-convention in itself, and is part of customary law. It establishes the most fundamental rules for civilians and combatants, such as the prohibition of torture, outrages upon personal dignity, and non-respect of a fair trial. Each Geneva Convention addresses a different category of actor in war and therefore provides tailored protection. Common Article 3 appears as ad minima standards, the minimum granted to all actors.

Protocol I applies to civilians in international armed conflicts and reinforces Common Article 3 and other fundamental guarantees set up in GCIV for civilians during international armed conflicts. For example, it broadens the definition of torture by including mental torture and sexual offences. It also details judicial guarantees of due process. Article 75 is probably one of the most important and the most cited article of the Protocol; it allows for the protection of every human being and sets fundamental rights for any civilian who would be detained during the hostilities. It is considered to be part of international customary law. There are also several measures for the protection of refugees (Article 73) women (Article 76), children (Articles 77–78), and journalists (Article 79).

Protocol II applies in times of non-international armed conflicts and completes Common Article 3. Article 4 APII describes the fundamental guarantees applicable. It reinforces children's rights, as well as gender protection and protection against slavery. Article 5 grants ad minima rights to civilian detainees and those interned. The protection of the civilian population is then detailed in Articles 13 to 18. Judicial guarantees are set out in Article 6. These fundamental guarantees are applicable in all circumstances and are part of customary international law.

---

[15] Djamchid Momtaz, *The Minimum Humanitarian Rules Applicable in Periods of Internal Tension and Strife*, 324 I.R.R.C. 455–62 (1998).

B. Protection of Civilian Property

International humanitarian law extends the distinction and the immunity to objects and property: attacks, reprisals, and acts of violence are prohibited against them. Protocol I protects civilian objects (Articles 48 and 52). There is a negative definition of civilian property: civilian objects are non military objects. Some civilian property must be identified by an emblem, for example, medical units and vehicles (Articles 12 and 21 API; Article 11 APII); cultural objects and places of worship (Article 53 API; Article 16 APII); protection of objects indispensable to the survival of the civilian population (Article 54 API; Article 14 APII); and the natural environment (Article 55 API), which is why starvation is prohibited as well as the destruction of food stuffs, crops, livestock, and so on as described in paragraph 2 of Article 54; works and installations containing dangerous forces (Article 56 API; Article 15 APII); nondefended localities (Article 59 API); and demilitarized zones (Article 60 API). If there is a doubt as to whether an object is of civilian use or not, the parties to the conflict must presume that the object is civilian (Article 52 API). There are dual-use objects, objects that have both civilian and military purposes, such as bridges or a dam. Attacks on dual-use objects or property must respect the principle of proportionality, according to which the effects produced by an attack should not be disproportionate to the military advantage sought. The principle seeks to limit damages, and a military operation must be necessary and unavoidable. Military commanders must take precautionary measures to limit the effects of such attacks on civilians objects and populations (Articles 57–58 API).

Cultural objects and places of worship are protected and must be marked with a distinctive emblem. The war in Iraq has put this rule of protection of cultural objects and places of worship to the test;[16] several U.S. soldiers and Iraqis looted museums. There was an international outcry, and although conventions affording protection to cultural objects and property were emphasized, little seemed to be done.[17] This is why one can easily find Iraqi valuable objects for sale online. Additionally, the U.S. army used the archeological zone of Babylon as a base between 2003 and 2004, parking massive tanks and destroying mosaics, and causing important damage by "digging, cutting, scraping and leveling"; key structures harmed "include the Ishtar Gate and the Processional Way."[18] The situation was such that the UN Educational, Scientific, and Cultural Organization (UNESCO) held an emergency meeting, and a team of restoration experts from the British Museum were sent immediately to Iraq while millions were raised.[19] The United States had then no other choice but to

---

[16] LAWRENCE ROTHFIELD, THE RAPE OF MESOPOTAMIA: BEHIND THE LOOTING OF THE IRAQ MUSEUM (Chicago: University of Chicago Press 2009).

[17] Matthew D. Thurlow, *Protecting Cultural Property in Iraq: How American Military Policy Comports with International Law*, 8 YALE HUMAN RIGHTS & DEVELOPMENT L. J. 153–87 (2005).

[18] British Museum Report on Meeting at Babylon, 2005, http://www.britishmuseum.org/the_museum/news_and_press_releases/latest_news/meeting_at_babylon.aspx.

[19] Press Release, New UNESCO Report Consolidates and Updates Assessment of Babylon Archaeological Site, UNESCO, 2009.

collaborate;[20] Congress put forward House Resolution 2497 and Senate Bill 1291 to "[t]o provide for the recovery, restitution, and protection of the cultural heritage of Iraq." Mosaics and other cultural properties have been repaired, but the semi-destruction of Babylon remains a case study for many when it comes to the protection of civilian objects, in particular cultural objects. Other examples include direct attacks against cultural objects such as the Buddha of Bamyan bombed by the Taliban[21] and attacks on Shiite shrines in Iraq. The destruction of the golden dome of Al 'Askarī Mosque in Iraq, one of the most important Shia mosques in the world, caused violent retaliations and violence between communities.[22] The dome was rebuilt in April 2009.[23] In addition to the protection received under API, cultural objects are also protected by a wide set of international conventions, and one of UNESCO's missions is to monitor armed conflicts to make sure the prohibition on targeting cultural objects is respected.

What occurs if there are combatants in a civilian building? Does it become a military target? Paragraph 3 of Article 50 API says it does not; it is expected in war that military or armed elements will mingle with civilians to run away, to hide, or to use civilians as shields. Soldiers might also be in a civilian building because they are visiting their family. Their presence does not turn the civilian population into a legitimate target; the civilian population and the civilian object retain immunity under Article 50-3 API. Article 58 completes the picture by explaining that military structures should not be established in civilian vicinity, and that all civilian elements should be removed.

II. CONCRETE EXAMPLES OF PROTECTION TO CIVILIANS

International humanitarian law provides concrete protection to civilians and combatants. We have analyzed fundamental guarantees and protection of civilian objects, but there is much more to civilian immunity and to combatants' protection. Some of the immunity granted to civilians has given rise to debates and is sometimes difficult to enforce, such as in neutralized zones. Other types of immunity demonstrate the novelty of the Geneva Conventions, such as special protection afforded to the category of civilians. The following brief study provides us with an overview that a thorough reading of GCIV, API, and APII will illustrate.

[20] Speech Colin Powell, Powell Says Meetings on Iraq's Future Will Be Forum for All IraqisApr. 13, 2003, http://www.globalsecurity.org/wmd/library/news/iraq/2003/iraq-030414-usia03.htm.
[21] Patty Gerstenblith, *From Bamiyan to Baghdad: Warfare and the Preservation of Cultural Heritage at the Beginning of the 21st Century*, 37:2 GA. J. INT'L. L. 245–351 (Winter 2006).
[22] Damien Cave & Graham Bowley, *Shiite Leaders Appeal for Calm after New Shrine Attack*, N.Y.TIMES, June 13, 2007.
[23] *Bombed Iraq Shrine Reopens to Visitors*, TEHRAN TIMES, Apr. 18, 2009.

A. Safe Zones

Providing protection to civilians in safe areas is a controversial but useful strategy, in particular for internally displaced person during a conflict.[24] These safe areas are called safe havens, security zones, safety zones, or zones of refuge. The development of aerial warfare explains in part the development of the concept of safety zones in international humanitarian law. In these protected areas and zones, populations will be safe, and no fighting will take place. The first attempts to create zones of refuge occurred during Word War II but were useless; there were projects and attempts to have zones of refuge with conventions to establish safety zones or protect hospitals. There were drafts but no final agreement was reached, and aerial bombings caused heavy casualties among civilians as an outcome. Zones were created under the auspices of the ICRC when the Israeli-Palestinian conflict broke out. There were three zones at the time, and the Red Cross emblem was used to delimit the zones. Women, children, and the aged were hosted temporarily in the zones during fighting.

Safe havens and zones of special protection are provided for by the GCIV and API. There are four types of zones, two in the Convention and two in the Protocol: non-defended localities, hospital zones and localities, neutralized zones, and demilitarized zones. The United Nations has added the concept of a safe haven, secure humanitarian areas where civilians are to be protected. Srebrenica is an example. On April 16, 1993, the UN Security Council passed Resolution 819, which demanded that "all parties and others concerned treat Srebrenica and its surroundings as a safe area which should be free from any armed attack or any other hostile act."[25] UN Protection Force (UNPROFOR) troops arrived in Srebrenica to protect the city. The creation of the zone did not prevent the largest massacre since World War II in July 1995, despite the presence of 400 armed Dutch peacekeepers.[26]

Article 14 GCIV creates hospital and safety zones and localities to protect a special category of civilians from the effects of war. When hostilities begin, or even later during the conflict, parties can create mutually recognized zones and localities. Protecting powers as well as the ICRC are in charge of these zones whose aim is to protect the sick, wounded, the eldest, children under fifteen, pregnant women, and mothers with children under the age of seven. The First and the Fourth Geneva Conventions suggest the creation of such zones, even in times of peace. An annex to the Convention is a draft agreement to set up the zones during conflicts. The ICRC can be invited to help, and the localities must be marked by a distinctive emblem that must clearly be seen. Failure to produce the emblem can be interpreted as a perfidy and is a grave breach of humanitarian law, amounting therefore to a war crime (Article 85 API). An example of a hospital and safety zone was the

---

[24] CATHERINE PHUONG, THE INTERNATIONAL PROTECTION OF INTERNALLY DISPLACED PEOPLE 136 (Cambridge: Cambridge University Press 2004).

[25] Security Council, Resolution 819, United Nations, Apr. 16 1993, para. #1.

[26] ICTY, *Prosecutor v. Krstic, Judgment*, Case No. IT-98-33, United Nations, Aug. 2, 2001, paragraphs 18 and 26; Udo Ludwig & Ansgar Mertin, *Srebrenica Massacre Survivors Sue Netherlands, United Nations*, DER SPIEGEL, June 5, 2007.

one set up in a Phnom Penh Hotel in Cambodia in 1975, but it failed in its mission to protect civilians.[27] Another one was opened in 1992 in Osijek, Croatia. The city was at the heart of the war zone and the hospital was constantly bombed. Another example of a failure is the bombing of a hospital located in such a zone, in Sri Lanka in 2009, when the government sought to destroy the Tamil Tigers.

Article 15 GCIV creates neutralized zones to shelter civilians from the effects of war. These zones can be created directly or through a neutral State or a humanitarian organization by any party to the conflict. The people who can be sheltered are the wounded and the sick combatants or non combatants, and civilian persons who take no direct part in the hostilities. If they reside within the zones, they cannot work for the military; civilians who do not participate in hostilities are also protected, as long as the do not engage in military actions in these zones. Details regarding the location, duration, administration, and supervision are up to the parties to the conflict to decide. In 1992 the parties to the conflict in Croatia, with the assistance of the International Committee of the Red Cross, established two neutral zones in Dubrovnik, one in a hospital and the other in a monastery.[28]

Article 59 API creates non–defended localities; no fighting can take place in these areas. Distinctive marks must be used to designate them (Article 59-5 to 59-7). There are strict conditions to meet; all combatants, weapons, and military equipment, at least the mobile ones, must be evacuated; no use of fixed military installations can be made; no acts of hostility can be committed by the population; and no activities in support of military operations can be undertaken. Article 59-1 of Protocol I states that all the inhabited areas close to the zones or inside them can be declared non-defended localities, as long as no military material is stored in them. If one of these conditions is not respected, the localities will lose the status of protected zones and they could become a legitimate military target. The concept of non defended localities is not new but was given a clear shape with Protocol I. The aim is to limit damage to civilians and civilian objects.

Demilitarized zones are created by Article 60 API; no military operations can be carried out in these zones, and they cannot be used for the conduct of military hostilities. These areas are granted the title of demilitarized zones after an agreement between the parties to the conflict. The agreement can be obtained either expressly, verbally, or by writing, or through the meditation of a Protecting Power or an impartial humanitarian organization. The same conditions as above must be met; the area must be weapon-free as well as combatant-free. There should be no military equipment in the zones. No acts of hostility should be carried out by the authorities or the civilian population. If there are police forces within the zone, their only role is to maintain law and order. None of the parties can use the zone, even if the fighting is quite close to it. If one of the parties violates the agreement, the other party

[27] Karin Landgreen, *Safety Zones and International Protection: A Dark Grey Area*, 7: 3 INT'L J. REFUGEE L. 436–58 (1995).

[28] HIKARU YAMASHITA, HUMANITARIAN SPACE AND INTERNATIONAL POLITICS: THE CREATION OF SAFE AREAS 18 (Ashgate 2004).

will be freed from any obligation, and the zone will lose its status, although civilians will still be protected by the Protocol.

These provisions have been used in practice in Bosnia in 1993 and in Rwanda in 1994. The UN Security Council established six safe areas in Bosnia Herzegovina in 1993 (the cities of Sarajevo, Tuzla, Bihaj, Gorazde, Zepa, and Srebrenica) to protect civilian populations from Bosnian Serb forces. The UNPROFOR was in charge of securing these zones and defending the civilians against attacks. The zones were vague and the mandate was unclear, with deadly results;[29] Srebrenica was invaded by the Serbian militias of General Ratko Mladic that committed the massacre. They killed Muslim civilians in July 1995 while the Dutch soldiers of the UNPROFOR stood by and watched, limited by their unclear mandate. Sarajevo was bombed and besieged for months, making it the site of the longest siege in the twentieth century.[30] The two leaders of the Bosnian Serbs, Radovan Karadzic (who was arrested in July 2008), and Ratko Mladic (who is on the run but lives in Serbia), await their trials before the International Criminal Tribunal for Former Yugoslavia (ICTY) for the crimes they have committed against the civilian populations in the security zones of Sarajevo and Srebrenica between April 1992 and July 1995. In July 1995, UN troops stood by again as the genocide in Rwanda unfurled.[31] A force led by France created a refuge zone that was later used by the genocidaires, when the French retired.[32] Safety zones have received bad press because of these examples. They remain, however, necessary in war, and the difficulty is to protect them from external assault. The complexity of protecting civilians in a city that could become a safe heaven is illustrated by the case of Paris. During World War II, Paris was declared an "open city," consequently announcing that all defensive efforts had been abandoned, because of the Germans' advance in 1940. There was no realistic way to protect the city while ensuring the protection of civilians. Declaring it an "open city" was the best option to protect civilians. Fighting would have served no purpose. The challenge is to ensure that civilians in an open city or any safe zone will be safe in reality, a problem that relates back to the principle of distinction.

Some countries also created very controversial no-fly zones. After the 1991 Gulf War, France, the United States, and the United Kingdom created such zones in the Kurdish and Shiite areas of Iraq. The humanitarian aim was to protect the people

---

[29] For a discussion regarding the role of the U.N in the protection of civilians, see, e.g., LINDA POLMAN, WE DID NOTHING: WHY THE TRUTH DOESN'T ALWAYS COME OUT WHEN THE UN GOES IN (London: Viking 2003).

[30] JOYCE P. KAUFMAN, NATO AND THE FORMER YUGOSLAVIA: CRISIS, CONFLICT AND THE ATLANTIC ALLIANCE (Lanham: Rowman & Littlefield c2002).

[31] To know more about safety zones in Rwanda and the failure to protect civilians, see e.g., ROMEO DALLAIRE, SHAKE HANDS WITH THE DEVIL: THE FAILURE OF HUMANITY IN RWANDA (New York: [Berkeley, Calif.]: Carroll & Graf; Distributed by Publishers Group West 2005); PHILIPP GOUREVITCH, WE WISH TO INFORM YOU THAT TOMORROW WE WILL BE KILLED WITH OUR FAMILIES (New York: Farrar, Straus, and Giroux 1998); POLMAN, supra note 29.

[32] Jerry Gray, Rwandans' Exodus from Safe Zone Swells, N.Y. TIMES, Aug. 20, 1994.

from President Saddam Hussein's attempts to decimate them.[33] The system remained operative until 2002, based upon Resolution 688 of the UN Security Council, which stated that civilian populations of Iraq needed protection.[34] However, the resolution did not mention the creation of no-fly zones, and Secretary General Boutros Boutros Ghali even called no-fly zones illegal.[35]

Another option, also much debated, is the creation of a humanitarian corridor, which allows people to flee to safety or stranded civilians to receive food and medical supplies. It is also a way for humanitarian organizations to reach out to supply relief. In practice, these corridors are extremely difficult to set up and they can actually increase fighting in the territories are not included in such a corridor.[36] It can also be used to bribe or blackmail humanitarians and civilians. In Rwanda, genocidaires tried to condition the evacuation of children; they wanted to use children's convoys arranged by the United Nations to reach the airport safely and bring reinforcement to their groups located in that part of the city.[37] Bernard Kouchner proposed such a zone for Darfur near Chad when he became France's minister of foreign affairs,[38] but Chad rejected the idea.[39]

B. Extra Protection Afforded to Civilians

1. Protection

Besides the regular protection, some elements of the civilian population can benefit from extra protection. The only discrimination that is allowed must be reasonable and help civilians in trouble; it would then be acceptable to distinguish an old man or a pregnant woman from the rest of the civilian population because of their health and specific needs. It concretely means that these civilians benefiting from specific care will benefit from special treatment (Articles 38.5 and 50 GCIV) and will have the priority during the distribution of relief supplies (Article 70.1 API). As an illustration, essential supplies such as food, clothing, and medications intended for children and pregnant women must have free passage in besieged areas or Occupied Territories (Article 23 GCIV). The protection granted to civilians is also extended to the search for wounded and sick (Article 16.2 GCIV), evacuation of these special

---

[33] *No-Fly Zones: The Legal Position*, BBC, Feb. 19, 2001, http://news.bbc.co.uk/2/hi/middle_east/1175950.stm.

[34] Security Council, Resolution 688 (1991), S/RES/0688.

[35] Interview with John Pilger, Aug. 7, 2000, http://www.johnpilger.com/page.asp?partid=307.

[36] *Le CICR et les Personne Déplacées Internes*, http://www.icrc.org/web/fre/sitefre0.nsf/html/5FZFS9.

[37] Jacques Morel & Georges Kapler, *Concordances humanitaires et génocidaires, Bernard Kouchner au Rwanda*, Mar. 22, 2007, http://www.france-rwanda-tribune.over-blog.com/pages/Concordances_humanitaires_et_genocidaires_Bernard_Kouchner_au_Rwanda_JMorel_GKapler-1013195.html.

[38] Appel, Bernard Kouchner, *Nous Sommes Attendus au Darfour*, March 2007, http://www.aidh.org/darfur/appel01.htm.

[39] Habibou Bangré, *Darfour: Bernard Kouchner fait marche arrière*, AFRIK.COM, June 7, 2007, http://www.afrik.com/article11879.html.

civilians from besieged and encircled areas (Article 17 GCIV), the protection of civilian hospitals and their staff (Articles 18 to 20 GCIV), medical transport (Articles 21 and 22 GCIV), and the consignment of medical supplies and equipment (Article 23 GCIV).

Article 16 GCIV specifies protection of those who are weak or sick: the wounded, the infirm, children, and pregnant women. They benefit from "special protection," which means that extra care and attention should be paid to this sub category of civilians.[40] It applies to all parties and means that every action possible to search, bring in, protect, and to remove all these wounded and sick civilians from the war zones should be taken. If civilians cannot be removed, they have to be protected from all effects of war.

Articles 18 and 19 grant protection to civilian hospitals. The definition of a hospital is broad and encompasses all possible options, including day care for elderly people. This also means that maternity and civil hospitals must be protected. The immunity given to the hospital will not cease except if harmful acts are committed against the enemy. That would not immediately lift the protection; a warning must be given, as well as a reasonable time limit (Article 19 GCIV). The problem is that the 1949 Conference did not provide a concrete definition of what acts are harmful to the enemy. An obvious example is the use of a hospital to hide armed combatants or to store ammunition. The presence of sick or wounded members of armed forces carrying light weapons will not be seen as acts harmful to the enemy. NATO violated the Geneva Convention during the war in Former Yugoslavia; Belgrade's Dragisa Misovic Hospital was hit by cluster bombs. Patients were killed and women in labor in the maternity ward were injured. The bombs destroyed the hospital's maternity ward and its center for children with lung diseases, the only such facility in the western Balkans. NATO spoke of an accident since a bomb had overshot its target, which is common with these "smart" bombs; there is only a 50 percent chance that one will hit its target. NATO did not explain why it was using cluster bombs in a densely populated city. Israel also hit Gaza hospitals during the siege of the zone in the winter of 2008–09,[41] including the January 2009 bombing of the UN Relief and Works Agency (UNRWA) in Gaza City, where humanitarian goods were stored, and where a hospital was hit. In February 2009, the Sri Lanka Air Force dropped cluster bombs on Ponnampalam Memorial hospital in Puthukkudiyiruppu, which provided medical help to an entire district.[42] This violates both Article 14 and Article 19 of GCIV.

[40] *See* the ICRC Commentary of Article 16, Geneva Convention IV, http://www.icrc.org/ihl.nsf/ COM/380-600020?OpenDocument.

[41] AFP, *UN Chief Leads Protests as Israel Hits Gaza Hospital*, AFP Jan. 15, 2009.

[42] Neha Madhiwalla & Nobhojit Roy, *Bombing Medical Facilities: A Violation of International Humanitarian Law*, 6(2) Indian J. Med. Ethics 64–65 (2009).

Women benefit from an extra protection set in Article 76 API which grants them a special respect and protects them against rape, forced prostitution, and any form of indecent assault. The Protocol is very innovative regarding rape during war, but one had to wait for the 1990s to see a concrete turning point in the field; indeed rape was used as a war crime or a weapon for ethnic cleansing in the Former Yugoslavia and in Rwanda.[43] Crimes of sexual violence are now prosecuted under international criminal law as war crimes.[44] Article 76 also protects pregnant women and mothers of young children arrested or detained, who are given "the utmost priority." Pregnant women are indeed considered to be "wounded persons" because their current status calls for specific medical attention, and so they benefit from the same protection as all wounded and sick under Article 8 API. The third paragraph of Article 76 identifies the death penalty of pregnant women and women with young infants as an offence related to armed conflict. This extra protection has been criticized as encouraging a gendered approach to humanitarian law; indeed, international humanitarian law tends to describe women as victims and not as perpetrators.[45] Events have shown that women can also be genocidaires, as in Rwanda,[46] or torturers, as in the Iraqi prison of Abu Ghraib.[47] Additionally, men have also been victims because of their gender;[48] the Serbs separated men from women and shot the men. Children were first targets in Rwanda—in particular, little boys, to extinguish changes of reproduction in an ethnic group. This targeting is often associated with ethnic cleansing; men should be eradicated and women should be raped so that a whole ethnic group can be erased through death or the dilution and purification of blood when raped women would give birth to bi-ethnic children. Men can also be victims of sexual abuse, especially as a means of torture.[49] The same question applies to homosexuals, who can also become targets in a war.[50]

---

[43] Janet Fleischman & Binaifer Nowrojee, *In Rwanda, Too, Rape Was a War Crime and Must Be Punished*, N.Y. TIMES, July 25, 1996.

[44] ANNE-MARIE L. M. DE BROUWER, SUPRANATIONAL CRIMINAL PROSECUTION OF SEXUAL VIOLENCE: THE ICC AND THE PRACTICE OF THE ICTY AND THE ICTR (Antwerpen: Intersentia 2005); UNIFEM, *Preventing Wartime Rape from Becoming a Peacetime Reality*, New York: UNIFEM, June 2009; WAR'S DIRTY SECRET: RAPE, PROSTITUTION, AND OTHER CRIMES AGAINST WOMEN (Anne Llewellyn ed., Cleveland, Ohio: Pilgrim Press 2000).

[45] TSEARD BOUTA ET AL., GENDER, CONFLICT AND DEVELOPMENT 83 (Washington, D.C.: World Bank 2005).

[46] AFRICAN RIGHTS, RWANDA, NOT SO INNOCENT: WHEN WOMEN BECOME KILLERS (London: African Rights 1995).

[47] *Woman Soldiers Admit Iraq Abuse*, BBC, May 2, 2005.

[48] R. Charli Carpenter, *Recognizing Gender-Based Violence Against Civilian Men and Boys in Conflict Situations*, 37:1 SECURITY DIALOGUE 83–103 (2006).

[49] LIBBY TATA ARCEL, WAR, VIOLENCE, TRAUMA AND THE COPING PROCESS: ARMED CONFLICTS IN EUROPE AND SURVIVOR RESPONSE (Copenhagen: Institute of clinical Psychology 1998).

[50] RICHARD PLANT, THE PINK TRIANGLE: THE NAZI WAR AGAINST HOMOSEXUALS (New York: H. Holt 1986).

3. Extra Protection for Children

Extra protection is also granted to children. Orphans or children separated from their families and under the age of fifteen benefit from extra protection because of their vulnerability. GCIV has several articles addressing children's immunity. Article 38 speaks of a preferential treatment for children at war. Article 14 states that safety zones may in particular protect children under fifteen. Article 17 provides for the evacuation of civilians from besieged areas and includes children. Article 23 deals with the free passage of relief aid addressed to the weakest segments of the population and children under fifteen are included in these categories. Article 24 deals with orphans and children under fifteen separated from their families. It sets a positive obligation for the parties to the conflict to take care of these children. There is also an obligation to identify children under the age of twelve. Article 50 speaks of children in Occupied Territories: the Occupying Power must facilitate the mission and the proper functioning of institutions devoted to children. If there are no institutions or if they are not functioning, the Occupying Power must make arrangements for the care and education of orphans and children separated from their parents. It cannot alter their personal status (by having them adopted, for example) or enlist them in an organization. Article 51 prohibits the use of children under eighteen for compulsory work. The authorities should also work toward family reunification; family life has to be protected and family reunification is encouraged (Article 24 GCIV). Article 82 GCIV does not prevent the internment of children but explains that internees should be grouped by family so that parents and children stay together. In the case of transfers, evacuation, or deportation, authorities have to do their best to keep families together (Article 49 GCIV).

Article 77 API reinforces the protection of children as civilians. Article 77-1 API states that children are the object of special respect and must be protected against "any form of indecent assault." In addition, the parties to the conflict have to make sure that children below the age of fifteen will not be enrolled in combat (Article 77-2). The Geneva Conventions do not address directly the issue of child combatants; this is why Article 77.2 API is important, especially coupled with Article 38.3 of the Convention of Children (CRC), which prohibits the use of children in war if they are below the age of fifteen. Prosecuting children for war crimes is extremely complicated from many viewpoints.[51] International law does not prohibit the prosecution of children who commit war crimes. The only limit set in Article 37 CRC is that the child cannot be punished by capital punishment or life imprisonment. The Paris principles state that children who participated in hostilities

who are accused of crimes under international law allegedly committed while they were associated with armed forces or armed groups should be considered primarily as victims of offences against international law; not only as perpetrators. They must be

---

[51] *Child Soldiers and War Crimes*, MEDICAL NEWS TODAY, Oct. 29, 2006, http://www.medical-newstoday.com/articles/55047.php.

treated in accordance with international law in a framework of restorative justice and social rehabilitation, consistent with international law which offers children special protection through numerous agreements and principles.[52]

This principle is repeated in Article 7 of the Special Court for Sierra Leone (SCSL) statute, which does not rule out prosecution, but emphasizes rehabilitation and reintegration. The Chief Prosecutor of the SCSL, David Crane, interpreted this article in a crucial fashion, choosing to focus on the recruitment of child soldiers as a crime rather than the prosecution of child soldiers themselves. Indeed, children are victims rather than perpetrators. However, in the Omar Khadr case, the United States has chosen another path; it has prosecuted a young man who at the time of his capture in Afghanistan was fifteen years old.[53] There is therefore a heated debate to know whether a child who has lost everything and was the victim of war before becoming a war criminal himself should be judged or considered a victim. For some, children should not be judged at the international level;[54] for others, they are perpetrators who should be judged, especially when children enlisted willingly, which raises the issue of how a child can volunteer to become a soldier.[55] They have killed, looted, or raped. The statute of the ICC takes another approach, saying that enlisting children under the age of fifteen as combatants is a war crime, and the Court has under some conditions jurisdiction to prosecute the perpetrators of such crimes (Article 8.2.e. VII). The trial of Thomas Lubanga is major step in that regard; he is the first person to be prosecuted before the ICC on such charges. He is accused of committing war crimes in the Democratic Republic of Congo (DRC) and of having enrolled children in his armed opposition group, the Union of Congolese Patriots.[56] His army was even nicknamed "the army of children."[57] In 2007, the SCSL convicted four persons of recruiting child soldiers. The ICC also has brought similar charges against commanders from the DRC and Uganda, like Joseph Kony, leader of the

[52] The Paris Principles and Guidelines on Children associated with armed forces or armed groups, Section "Treatment of children accused of crimes under international law," at Feb. 9, 2007. The Paris Principles were defined during the first International Workshop on National Institutions for the Promotion and Protection of Human Rights in Paris on October 7–9, 1991, and adopted by United Nations Human Rights Commission Resolution 1992/54 of 1992 and General Assembly Resolution 48/134 of 1993. The Paris Principles relate to the status and functioning of national institutions for protection and promotion of human rights.

[53] Lauren McCollough, *The Military Trial of Omar Khadr: Child Soldiers and the Law*, Crimes of War project, Mar. 10, 2008, http://www.crimesofwar.org/onnews/News-Khadr.html.

[54] Nienke Grossman, *Rehabilitation or Revenge: Prosecuting Child Soldiers for Human Rights Violations*, 38 GEO. J. INT'L L. 325 (2007).

[55] REDRESS, VICTIMS, PERPETRATORS OR HEROES: CHILD SOLDIERS BEFORE THE INTERNATIONAL CRIMINAL COURT 18 (London: Redress 2006).

[56] Catherine Philipp & Frances Gibb, *Thomas Lubanga Becomes First to Stand Trial for War Crimes at the ICC*, TIMES ONLINE, Jan. 26, 2009.

[57] Interview with Jonathan Sukulu, by Susan Schulman, GUARDIAN WEEKLY, Jan. 28, 2009, http://www.guardianweekly.co.uk/?page=editorial&id=888&catID=2.

Lord's Army Resistance in Northern Uganda.[58] It is also a major issue in Charles Taylor's trial. Therefore parties have to refrain from recruiting children under the age of fifteen. What happens when voluntary children fight in wars of national liberation? The ICRC commentary addresses this issue when detailing Article 77 of Protocol I, which states that authorities should prevent a child under the age of fifteen from being a volunteer by encouraging him to continue his education.[59] Another issue is the use of very young children in hostilities as soldiers to carrying weapons or messages.[60] If a child of six is compelled to bring food to an armed group, does that amount to a direct participation in the hostilities? Does that mean the child is a combatant under GCIII? The ICRC considers that such involvement of a child is prohibited, and this is why the organization suggests that the concept of "direct" participation should be dropped when it comes to children under fifteen; they should never, either directly or indirectly, participate in hostilities.[61] A child over fifteen who is a combatant will be covered by GCIII; he is a combatant and will be treated as a prisoner of war if captured. Article 16 GCIII speaks of a privileged treatment because of age; if a child over fifteen is captured, he will benefit from a special treatment. If a child under fifteen participates in the hostilities and is captured, he will keep his immunity, as stated in paragraph 3 of Article 77 API, whether or not he is granted POW status. Children benefit from fundamental guarantees as well. When arrested or detained, paragraph 4 of Article 77 states that children should be kept in separate quarters from adults, except if the adults are family members; this is why family units should be provided to detainees. They retain priority during the distribution of relief when they are detained (Articles 23 and 50 GCIV and Article 70 API). Eventually, and in agreement with the International Covenant on Civil and Political Rights (ICCPR), the death penalty cannot be enforced upon a child who is under eighteen years old or who was not yet eighteen when the offence was committed.

Article 78 of the same Protocol deals with the evacuation of children. If a city is besieged or encircled, children must be removed. For example, during the siege of Sarajevo, the Serbs occupying the hills around the city violated API by not evacuating children. UN Children's Emergency Fund (UNICEF) reported that 65,000 to 80,000 children were stranded in the city during the siege, and that 40 percent of them had been directly shot at by snipers; 51 percent had seen someone killed; 39 percent had seen one or more family member killed; 19 percent had witnessed a massacre; 48 percent had their home occupied by someone else; 73 percent had their home

---

[58] Jo Becker, *Paying for Sending Children to War*, THE GUARDIAN, Jan. 27, 2009, http://www.guardian.co.uk/commentisfree/2009/jan/27/warcrimes-humanrights.

[59] ICRC, Commentary Article 77 API: http://www.icrc.org/ihl.nsf/COM/470-750099?OpenDocument.

[60] GERALDINE VAN BUEREN, THE INTERNATIONAL LAW ON THE RIGHTS OF THE CHILD 334 (Dordrecht/Boston: Kluwer Academic Publishers c1995).

[61] O.R.XV.465.CDDH/407/Rev.1, para. 63.

attacked or shelled; and 89 percent lived in an underground shelter.[62] An estimated 1,525 children were killed or missing in Sarajevo, out of 10,000 persons. Out of 56,000 people, 14,538 children were wounded.[63] A monument has been erected to the memory of the Sarajevo children victims of the siege.[64] International humanitarian law insists on the importance of keeping family ties, on finding parents, and on avoiding evacuation to another country. Each child should have a card with a photograph if the child is interned or deported. The Central Tracing Agency located within the ICRC is the organization that works on reuniting families.

Protocol II, which applies in non international armed conflicts, also provides protection to children in its Article 4, paragraph 3. It explains that children must be taken care of, especially if they are separated from their parents. All steps should be taken toward family reunification. It stresses that children under the age of fifteen cannot take part in the hostilities and cannot be recruited by armed forces.

C. Refugees and Internally Displaced People

Wars are bound to create massive movements of people, whether within a country (internally displaced persons or IDPs) or across borders (refugees). The protection afforded to civilians on the move is not different from the protection granted to regular civilians. There is no category within the category.

1. Internally Displaced Persons: IDPs

People fleeing violence or persecutions during conflict do not always cross borders. Actually, there has been a recent increase of internally displaced persons (IDPs), especially in a conflict like Iraq; rather than fleeing to neighboring countries, Iraqis have since 2003 moved within the country. IDPs are protected by national laws and human rights in times of peace and by humanitarian law, as civilians, in times of war. Sometimes, movements of a population within a country might be at the core of a policy or a military action; people or certain communities are forced to move for ethnic cleansing purposes. This is why there are specific rules to protect IDPs; humanitarian law prohibits forced population displacement (Article 49 GCIV); prohibits methods of warfare that intend to spread terror among the civilian population (Article 51.2 API); regulates the conduct of hostilities to prevent military

---

[62] STEVE POWELL & ELVIRA DURAKOVIC-BELKO, SARAJEVO 2000: THE PSYCHOLOGICAL CONSEQUENCES OF WAR (Sarajevo: Sarajevo 2000, 2002).

[63] The casualty reports contained in this table are based on the B&H Institute for Public Health Bulletins beginning on June 26, 1992 and ending on September 27, 1993. *See also* the *Study of the battle and siege of Sarajevo: Final report of the United Nations Commission of Experts established pursuant to security council resolution 780 (1992) Annex VI—part 1*, "Study of the battle and siege of Sarajevo," Under the Direction of M. Cherif Bassiouni Chairman and Rapporteur on the Gathering and Analysis of the Facts, Commission of Experts Established Pursuant to Security Council Resolution 780 (1992).

[64] *Sarajevo Remembers Child Victims of Bosnian War*, AFP, May 9, 2009.

harassment of populations or communities that might cause exodus or forced migrations; facilitates the delivery of humanitarian aid to civilians so that they don't have to flee and wander in the country; and establishes fundamental guarantees to protect IDPs such as the right to international assistance and the right to protection. In these scenarios, humanitarian organizations have an important role to play in monitoring situations: reminding parties to the conflict about humanitarian rules or delivering humanitarian aid. The presence of the ICRC or other organizations is therefore mandatory.

The conflict in Bosnia and Herzegovina provides an example of the difficulty in dealing with an internal displacement during war: the creation of safe areas encouraged migrations. In a sense, humanitarian law helped ethnic cleansing as people from the same ethnic background and who were attacked moved to the safe areas.[65]

2. Refugees

Unlike IDPs, refugees do cross borders. They benefit from a wide range of protection in times of peace. In times of war, the rules applicable are the same as the rules for IDPs, since the causes for mass movements are similar. Article 17 AP II, Article 85.4 (a) API, and the Rome Statute of the International Criminal Court also protect refugees. They benefit from the civilian immunity (Article 73 API), and this protection extends to stateless people. Articles 44, 45.4, and 49 GCIV deal with deportations, transfers, and evacuations, which also apply to IDPs. Article 49 GCIV draws attention; it prohibits forced migrations and deportations and also prohibits compelling civilians to leave their places of residence absent a security reason or an imperative military reason. In theory, there should be no displacement of civilians, but if there is, people will be protected. Refugees benefit first and foremost from the protection from refugee law and from the mandate of the Office of the UN High Commissioner for Refugees (UNHCR). If refugees are in a State involved in an armed conflict, they will also benefit from international humanitarian law. It will amount to a double protection in I.H.L. The reason refugees benefit from several layers of protection is to be found in their vulnerability and in the absence of protection by their State of nationality. How do these multiple layers concretely work? The ICRC only helps the refugees covered by GCIV, while the UNHCR covers all other situations. They also work hand in hand when the situation is unclear or in a grey zone. For example, in the Balkans, both the ICRC and the UNHCR brought humanitarian aid to civilian victims.

[65] Yves Sandoz, *The Establishment of Safety Zones for Persons Displaced within their Country of Origin*, in INTERNATIONAL LEGAL ISSUES ARISING UNDER THE UNITED NATIONS DECADE OF INTERNATIONAL LAW (Najeeb M. Al-Nauimi & Richard Meese eds., The Hague: Kluwer Law International 1995).

These rules are very important in avoiding further trauma. Refugees and IDPs are harshly affected by the conflict at several levels. Civilians on the move are easy targets, as demonstrated in the DRC conflict or in Somalia. In the latter, cities have become so insecure that people had to flee to live in camps established on the main roads leading to cities. During the genocide in Rwanda, the refugees fleeing to Congo (Zaire) were attacked on the way by genocidaires who were hidden among the ranks of the refugees, or by genocidaires who had followed them. The genocidaires even attacked refugee camps, a blunt violation of the principle of distinction. The situation was extremely complex.[66] Hutus led an open and direct warfare aimed at civilians through the genocide and attacked refugee camps, while Tutsi also attacked Hutu refugee camps.[67] This is why that period of the genocide is called the war on refugees.[68] The outcome was the dismantlement of the camps. Attacks on refugees and IDPs are a grave matter of concern; camps can be attacked but can also be the target of a war between two opponents, refugees being the hostages of the conflict. The 2007 fighting in the Palestinian refugee camp of Nahr al-Bared, in Lebanon, is an illustration; refugees living in the camps were caught between the Fatah al-Islam and the Lebanese army.[69] Refugees were caught between the intense shelling of the zones by the Lebanese army and the attacks by the Fatah al-Islam, with heavy casualties among civilians. The armed group was also accused of using human shields.[70] There is no doubt that such intense fighting in highly populated zones, with civilians restricted in their movements, could only have ended in a blood bath. The principles of distinction and proportionality were not only violated; regarding the specific context, they were hardly taken into account. Another sadly infamous event is the attacks of the Sabra and Shatila refugee camps. Managing a camp and protecting refugees during an armed conflict is extremely difficult; in 2001, when Kabul fell, Afghan warlords armed refugee camps to fill the power vacuum and to protect their drug traffic and human smuggling.[71] In Morocco, the front Polisario uses a refugee camp in southwest Algeria, in Tindouf province, as military headquarters and a detention center for their prisoners of war. These examples explain why refugees and IDPs need extra protection and why their camps also need to be protected from hostilities.

---

[66] Elly-Elikunda Mtango, *Military and Armed Attacks on Refugee Camps*, *in* REFUGEES AND INTERNATIONAL RELATIONS (Gill Loescher & Leila Monahan eds., Oxford/New York: Oxford University Press 1989).

[67] *Situation in Refugee Camps called Dangerous*, UN CHRONICLE, June 1995.

[68] James Turner Johnson, *Protection of Non-Combatants*, 37: 4 J. PEACE RESEARCH 421–48, 437 (July 2000).

[69] Press Release, Human Rights Watch, Fighting at Refugee Camp Kills Civilians (May 23, 2007).

[70] *Id.*

[71] Andrew Bushell, *Warlords Arm Afghans in Refugee Camps*, WASH. TIMES, Jan. 24, 2002.

D. Journalists

Statistically, journalists are ten times more likely to be killed in Iraq than American and British soldiers present.[72] The war in Iraq is the biggest killer, with 177 to 207 journalists and media workers killed since the beginning of the war.[73] There was a sharp increase in journalists' deaths in 1994, when 103 journalists were killed in Rwanda, Algeria, and the Former Yugoslavia, but it does not compare to the war in Iraq, in which more than 200 journalists and media workers have been killed.[74] The number of journalists killed has risen 244 percent in the past five years.[75] Others have complained about the difficulty of working freelance in a field where embedded journalists have prime access to news, while others have denounced the difficulty of working with civilians rejecting them in fear of being targeted.[76] What exactly is the protection provided by international humanitarian law for reporters in war zones?

1. Journalists Are Civilians

Journalists' jobs have become increasingly dangerous, especially since journalists have become the targets for ransom or political motives in Iraq, Chechnya, and Afghanistan. The captors sometimes ignore the fact that they hold civilians, or rather they hardly take notice of it. Few combatants are aware that journalists benefit from a special protection. This is why it is often recommended to journalists to have a copy of the Geneva Conventions in their pockets. To remind potential captors and combatants that embedded journalists are civilians within the meaning of Article 50-1 API, Article 79-1 API suggests that accredited journalists should be provided with an identity card issued by a government or the medium employing the journalist. Training journalists to know their rights under international humanitarian law is vital. Problems arise when such documents and status are wrongly granted. In the summer of 2009, two French intelligence officers were abducted in Somalia by Islamist rebels after they pretended to be journalists.[77] The misuse of the status of journalist is dangerous and threatens any French journalist who would now wish to travel to Somalia.

The targeting of journalists during armed conflicts is a violation of the Geneva Conventions; indeed journalists are civilians under Article 50-1 API and benefit from the immunity. This is applicable in international and non international armed conflicts. Article 79 API details the protection from which they benefit. A journalist

---

[72] EMBEDDED: THE MEDIA AT WAR IN IRAQ, AN ORAL HISTORY at xi (Bill Katovsky & Bill Katovsky eds., 2003).

[73] Committee to Protect Journalists, *Journalists Killed: Statistics and Background*, CPR, http://www.cpj.org/deadly/index.html.

[74] *Id.*

[75] Reporters Without Borders, Jan. 2 2008, http://www.rsf.org/article.php3?id_article=24909.

[76] *Control Room*, documentary, directed by Jehane Noujaim (2004; Noujaim Films).

[77] *French Security Agents Now Held by Islamist Rebels*, FRANCE July 24, 16, 2009.

working in a war zone does not lose this immunity because of his profession, even if he accompanies armed forces. The category of journalist is broad and includes war reporters as well as all people working for the press and the media, but there is no definition as such. War correspondents are "people who follow armed forces without actually being members thereof."[78] The ICRC commentary suggests looking at Article 2 (a) of the International Convention for the Protection of Journalists engaged in Dangerous Missions in Areas of Armed Conflict as a guide for the interpretation of Article 79: "The word 'journalist' shall mean any correspondent, reporter, photographer, and their technical film, radio and television assistants who are ordinarily engaged in any of these activities as their principal occupation [...]." Thus, journalists benefit from the same protection as other civilians. This protection does not mean that journalists are free to act as they wish; if they act in any way that involves them in the conflict as a warring party, they will lose the protection. Any direct participation in hostilities would put an end to this immunity, just as with other civilians. A journalist loses his immunity if he is armed or dressed like a militant and works as an embedded journalist. The fact that journalists benefit from civilian immunity does not grant them the right to seek or obtain information. Article 79 API grants them only a right under international humanitarian law, which is the right to be protected from the effects of war. In addition, if a journalist participates in an armed conflict and commits offences, he can be tried in a civilian court for violation of domestic law. It does not have to be a violent crime; entering a country without a visa suffices. Embedded journalists will be treated as prisoners of war if they are caught, because although they are not members of the armed forces, they are civilians associated with the war effort.[79]

Despite all these rules, journalists are increasingly taken as targets; journalists are arrested, tortured, abducted, or killed. Since reporters are civilians, it means that any attacks against them are war crimes. In 2001, Colombia's Ejército Nacional de Liberacion (National Liberation Army, ELN) issued a press release declaring journalists Guillermo Aguilar Moreno and Carlos Enrique Aristizabal "military targets." The policy of the Colombian group since 1999 has been to declare as military targets all journalists suspected of serving as "circulation channels" for the paramilitaries (journalists who diffuse information about paramilitaries or interview them). As an outcome, seven journalists were abducted by this guerrilla group in 2000.[80] In April 2008, a young Palestinian journalist working as a cameraman for Reuters was killed by a flechette shell fired by an Israeli tank. He stood 1.5 km away from the tank but

---

[78] Art. 4.A (4) of the Third Geneva Convention relative to the Treatment of Prisoners of War of 12 August 1949 (hereinafter Third Geneva Convention, or GCIII).

[79] Id.

[80] Diana Calderón Fernández, *Colombia's Truth Held Captive*, GLOBAL JOURNALIST, July 1, 2003, http://www.globaljournalist.org/stories/2003/07/01/colombias-truth-held-captive/; IFEX, Two Journalists Declared "Military Targets" by Guerrillas, IFEX, http://www.ifex.org/colombia/2001/04/18/two_journalists_declared_military/.

was identified by his press coat as well as by his press vehicle.[81] Several organizations denounced his death as a war crime.[82] In the war in Iraq, both sides, the United States and the insurgency, have been accused of war crimes against journalists. Indeed, organizations like Reporters Without Borders (RSF) claim that there are violations of international humanitarian law and that war correspondents are intentionally being fired at. In Iraq, on April 3, 2008, an American tank fired at the Palestine Hotel, which mainly host foreign journalists. A journalist and a cameraman died. On May 27, 2003, the Committee to Protect Journalists (CPJ) published a report of their investigation into the tank shelling; the report said that the attack on journalists, although not deliberate, was avoidable; the tank's officer thought he was targeting an enemy, but the military knew the hotel was full of journalists.[83] A Spanish journalist was killed in the shelling and a Spanish judge indicted three U.S. soldiers in the killings: Sergeant Shawn Gibson, Captain Philip Wolford, and Lieutenant Colonel Philip DeCamp. The three men were charged with homicide and committing a crime against the international community. The procedure was suspended twice with a final stop in July 2009 for lack of evidence.[84] Additionally, it seemed that the three soldiers ignored the fact that the hotel was full of civilians.[85] The debate is still vivid: former military intelligence linguist, Army Sergeant Adrienne Kinne, revealed that she saw secret U.S. military documents that listed the Hotel Palestine as a potential target although it was full of civilians.[86] There are also reports that the U.S. tank took a sure aim at the hotel and that it was not in retaliation to any attacks since the area was quiet at the time. This version reported by journalists of France 3 who were present in the hotel does not match the U.S. army report's claim that they were in a self-defense scenario.[87]

The UN Security Council has condemned the attacks against journalists during hostilities.[88] There were even talks at the United Nations of creating a specific status for journalists. There was a debate regarding the creation of such a status when Protocol I was drafted; it was then decided that a special status for journalists would

---

[81] To know more, read the beautiful piece, by Tim Butcher, *A Portrait of Life and Death in Gaza*, TELEGRAPH, Apr. 23, 2008.

[82] Press Release, Human Rights Watch, Israel: Investigate the Death of Gaza Civilians: Evidence Suggests Soldiers Targeted Reuters Journalist (Apr. 18, 2008).

[83] Joel Campagna & Rhonda Roumani, Report: *Permission to Fire?*, New York: Committee to Protect Journalists, May 27, 2003, http://cpj.org/reports/2003/05/palestine-hotel.php.

[84] Press Release, Reporters Sans Frontières, Spanish Court Rules that Investigation into Cameraman's Death to Stay Closed (July 15, 2009).

[85] Jean-Paul Mari, Deux Meurtres pour un mensonge Reporters Sans Frontières, Jan. 2004, http://www.rsf.org/Deux-meurtres-pour-un-mensonge.html.

[86] Video, *Fmr. Military Intelligence Sgt. Reveals US Listed Palestine Hotel in Baghdad as Target Prior to Killing of Two Journalists in 2003*, DEMOCRACY Now, http://www.democracynow.org/2008/5/13/fmr_military_intelligence_officer_reveals_us.

[87] Campagna, *supra* note 83.

[88] Department of Public Information, News and Media Division, Security Council, "Security Council Condemns Attacks Against Journalists in Conflict Situations," Resolution 1738, 2006, 5613th meeting, http://www.un.org/News/Press/docs/2006/sc8929.doc.htm.

be a bad idea because "any increase in the number of persons with a special status, necessarily accompanied by an increase of protective signs, tends to weaken the protective value of each protected status already accepted [...]."[89] The identity card mentioned in paragraph 3 of Article 79 does not create a special status, and the possession of the card is not a prerequisite to be considered a civilian. There is actually no need to grant journalists a special status as long as journalists are clearly identifiable, and they are thanks to Protocol I. As stressed in the Randal case by the ICTY Appeals Chamber, journalists working in war zones serve a "public interest" since they "play a vital role in bringing to the attention of the international community the horrors and reality of conflict."[90] This public perception does not include seeing war reporters as having a special status; they are civilians working for the international civil society. Despite the protection afforded, there are calls to increase it and to grant journalists a special status due to the demands of the profession that bring journalists in the line of fire.

2. Embedded Journalists

Another issue is embedded journalists, who are war reporters working alongside an army party to the conflict. During World War II, embedded journalists had to wear uniforms and sometimes were compelled to carry weapons.[91] They were clearly identified as combatants and were therefore legitimate targets. Journalists could even be considered spies and as such ran the risk of being executed. The phenomenon of embedded journalists has only increased, and rules have changed. First the war in Vietnam and then the war in Iraq are examples of the phenomenon.[92] Journalists have come to play a unique role in the war zone in the sense that they report what is happening at high costs. The term embedded journalist is quite recent and does not appear in the Geneva law.

The Geneva Conventions have improved the status of the journalists, although as stressed above, combatants often ignore the fact that journalists are civilians. During the 2003 war in Iraq, correspondents were embedded with military units. They agreed to follow certain rules to ensure their protection; therefore, they became war correspondents within the meaning of the Third Geneva Convention. When accredited by and when accompanying an army, journalists are legally part of that military group, whether they see themselves that way or not. If captured, they will be treated as prisoners of war. As an illustration, the media guidelines

---

[89] Yves Sandoz et al., Commentary on the Additional Protocols of June 8, 1977 to the Geneva Conventions of August 12, 1949, para. 3265 (ICRC/Martinus Nijhoff Publishers, Geneva 1987).

[90] The Randal Case: Prosecutor v. Radoslav Brdjanin & Momir Talic, ICTY, Dec. 11, 2002, JL/P.I.S./715-e.

[91] Joel Simon, *Journalists Are Owed Protection in Wartime*, Newsday, Mar. 31, 2003.

[92] *Too Close for Comfort? The Role of Embedded Reporting During the 2003 Iraq War: Summary Report*, prepared by a team of researchers from the Cardiff School of Journalism for the BBC, November 2003.

issues by the British Ministry of Defence[93] states that embedded journalists are to be granted the status of prisoner of war if captured.[94] They are non uniformed civilians participating in a military enterprise. They do not play a role in the hostilities, but embedded correspondents still officially perform a role in an organized army force. They are not to be treated as spies, but as civilians working for an army. They can be detained for "imperative reasons of security" and can be held with the same legal protections as a prisoner of war. This includes the right not to respond to interrogation, which of course echoes the right to protect sources in times of peace. However, notebooks and film may legally be confiscated by military personnel (Articles 17 and 18 GCIII).[95]

3. Freelance Journalists

By comparison, a freelance journalist who works without accreditation takes higher risks, and if captured, he will be a civilian protected under the Fourth Convention and Protocol I. A Dutch freelance journalist Sander Thoenes was killed in Dili, East Timor, in 1999; he was arrested by men wearing Indonesian uniforms and was shot.[96] This illustrates the little protection freelance journalists have. This is an important issue since many journalists work freelance, because there is less formal support in the business than before; they are therefore easy targets for arrests and convictions. The fragility of the status explains the increase of arrests and imprisonment of freelance journalists. This is a worrisome factor, especially since the U.S. and U.K. armies in Iraq developed a new practice of facilitating the access to information for embedded journalists, while independent and freelance journalists have a more difficult time accessing information and do not benefit from extra security. They need to take extra risks to gather information. There is therefore the fear that the number of journalists killed might actually lead to an increase of embedded journalists, which would give some control to the armies to the conflict over the content of information.[97] Those who will want to remain neutral will have to take higher risks to have access to information. It is in that atmosphere that the "Declaration on the safety of journalists and media personnel in situations involving armed conflict" was drafted in 2003 and was drafted by the organization Reporters Sans Frontières. The document underlines that "journalists have a right to identical protection regardless of their professional status (freelance journalists or those who belong to an agency or to other media), of their nationality, and of whether or not

---

[93] *Id.*

[94] *Id.*

[95] Alexandre Balguy-Gallois, *Protection des journalistes et des médias en période de conflit armé*, 853 I.R.C.C. 37–67 (March 2004).

[96] *Journalist Killed in East Timor: A Dutch Journalist Working for a British Newspaper Has Been Killed in East Timor*, BBC News, Sept. 22, 1999.

[97] Press Release, Coalition Accused of Showing "Contempt" for Journalists Covering the War in Iraq, Channel Canada, Mar. 31, 2003; Press Release, Reporters Without Borders Calls on the US to Guarantee that the Media Can Work Freely and in Safety, RSF (Mar. 19, 2003).

they are taken off into an accompaniment system." A practice is developing whereby embedded journalists are protected by GCIII while regular war correspondents either attached to a channel or freelance take all the risks and are perceived as weaker by the warring parties. The document goes on to explain why a freelance journalist deciding to hire armed bodyguards is a developing practice. For example, a British journalist working in Somalia explained that once he arrived at the airport, his first act was to hire bodyguards.[98] Training for journalists has developed to help them deal with violence and kidnappings.[99] This has a negative impact on journalism as it directly impacts their status: an armed journalist or a journalist who has armed bodyguards could forfeit his status as a civilian and be considered as directly taking part in hostilities.

4. Military Journalists

There are no issues with military journalists, who are civilians or military working for the internal and external army press support. Indeed armies usually have their own press organs. Additionally, the U.S. military has trained communicators, military, and civilians, who work in all fields of journalism. The task of these people is to provide news about military activities.[100] They can also, for example, assist an embedded journalist in his coverage of the news. Since they clearly work for the military, they are legitimate targets.

5. Debates Regarding Journalism at War

The question of armed journalists or journalists hiring bodyguards for their protection is crucial.[101] Some journalists do not shy away from revealing that they cannot work safely without bodyguards. The risk is to have a driver/bodyguard betray you, which happened to a French journalist in Somalia (the journalist kept filming and the video was broadcasted on French television).[102] Another risk is illustrated by the CNN team who traveled to Tikrit, Northern Iraq, on April 13, 2003, accompanied by an agent of a private security company, who fired several times at an insugent after a shot was heard.[103] The BBC had to change its policy after the shooting of a cameraman in Saudi Arabia in 2004 and has allowed armed

---

[98] *Canadian Journalist Reported Abducted in Somalia*, CBC News, Aug. 23, 2008.

[99] *Somali Journalists Trained to Report Safely in Africa's Most Dangerous Country*, INSI, June 26, 2008.

[100] Jane Morse, *U.S. Military Journalists Strive for Truth, Trust, Credibility*, May 1, 2008, http://www.america.gov/st/democracyhr-english/2008/May/20080501153255ajesrom6.510562e-02.html.

[101] Jeffrey Gettleman, *The Most Dangerous Place in the World*, Foreign Policy, March/April 2009.

[102] Abdiqani Hassan, *Un journaliste français enlevé au Puntland en Somalie*, Capital, December 16, 2007.

[103] Press Release, Reporters Sans Frontières, CNN Crew's Bodyguard Fires Back with Automatic Weapon When Crew Comes Under Fire (Apr. 13, 2003).

bodyguards to protect BBC crews.[104] This raises questions as to journalistic ethics and as to journalists' forfeiture of the status of civilians. The issue is also affecting some non-governmental organizations or international organizations that are recruiting armed bodyguards or requesting the help of the army to protect them. Robert Ménard, Secretary-General of Reporters Without Borders, says

[s]uch a practice sets a dangerous precedent that could jeopardize all other journalists covering this war as well as others in the future [. . .] There is a real risk that combatants will henceforth assume that all press vehicles are armed [. . .] Journalists can and must try to protect themselves by such methods as travelling in bulletproof vehicles and wearing bulletproof vests, but employing private security firms that do hesitate to use their firearms just increases the confusion between reporters and combatants.[105]

After the killing of a journalist in Iraq, a colleague asked President Jalal Talibani whether it would be possible to allow journalists to carry weapons for self-defense.[106] The President agreed with the request.[107] This prompted a debate, and the International News Safety Institute urged journalists to avoid carrying weapons since they would lose their status as neutral observers. It would also have endangered them, as they would forfeit their civilian immunity. The question it raised is also the one of a civilian who wishes to defend himself. If a man decides to have weapons at home to protect his family during a war and fires it when his house is under attack, does that make him a criminal under national law, or a combatant under Geneva Convention III? Article 13 APII, which details Common Article 3, says that civilians enjoy protection unless they take direct part in the hostilities. The question raised here is to know what a direct participation in hostilities means. The Inter-American Commission on Human Rights has pointed out that "It is generally understood in humanitarian law that the phrase 'direct participation in hostilities' means acts which, by their nature or purpose, are intended to cause actual harm to enemy personnel and material. Such participation also suggests a 'direct causal relationship between the activity engaged in and harm done to the enemy at the time and place where the activity takes place.'"[108] Therefore, a journalist's carrying of a weapon or hiring armed bodyguards might not technically amount to direct participation in war; warring parties might however interpret such behavior as participation in war: why would a journalist whose mission it is to gather information carry a gun? By carrying a gun or having bodyguards, the journalist undermines his position as a civilian and becomes a potential threat to an armed force. Lines between combatants and journalists as civilians should not be blurred. If a journalist decided

---

[104] *Journalist Shootings Force BBC to Use Armed Guards*, REUTERS, June 8, 2004.

[105] RSF, *supra* note 75.

[106] Julia Day, *Journalists "Must Resist Call to Carry Arms,"* THE GUARDIAN, Feb. 24, 2006.

[107] Post by Kevin Jon Heller, *Journalists and Self-Defence in Iraq*, Opinio Juris, March 1, 2006, http://lawofnations.blogspot.com/2006/03/journalists-and-self-defense-in-iraq.html.

[108] Inter-American Commission on Human Rights, Third report on human rights in Colombia, Doc. OEA/Ser.L/V/II.102 Doc. 9 rev. 1, Feb. 26, 1999, Chapter IV, §§ 53 and 56.

to protect himself by carrying weapons, his immunity could be challenged, as stated in paragraph 2 of Article 79 API. The work of journalism (meetings, interviews, photos, and the like) has clearly been established as civilian in nature, but the moment the journalist carries a weapon, the protection could be suspended. Once the journalist stops participating in hostilities by yielding his gun, for example, he will recover his civilian immunity. If he is captured while participating in the hostilities, Article 45 API will be applicable to him; he will be judged according to national laws. He can also be interned under GCIV. Eventually, journalists can be charged for perfidy under Article 37.1 (c) API.

Media equipment also benefits from civilian objects' protection. Media equipment and facilities that are not used for military purposes and that do not meet the conditions set out in Article 52 (2) (see below) fall into the category of civilian objects, which "[...] shall not be the object of attack or reprisals [...]." In case of a doubt, and according to Article 52 (3) of Protocol I, journalists will be considered civilians, and their equipment civilian property. The objects will cease being protected if media equipment is used for hostile purposes; it indeed amounts to a direct participation in the conflict. So if a civilian radio transmitter is used by a party to the conflict, as occurred in the Former Yugoslavia, he is a legitimate target, as the ICTY reminds us.[109] There is also the danger in having a media station used for both military and civilian purposes. The U.S. Army Field Manual considers a dual-use radio transmitter a legitimate military target.[110] After the attack on the Palestine Hotel, where the foreign press was gathered, a spokesman for the U.S. Defense Department said that the hotel had become a legitimate target within the last forty-eight hours because there had been a meeting between Iraqi officials inside.[111] This demonstrates how humanitarian rules that all believe to be clear and firm can be manipulated to justify what clearly is an attack against civilians and what could therefore amount to a war crime. The issue is not yet settled and is complicated by decisions such as the decision of the ICTY regarding NATO's air campaign. In April 1999, a radio station, Radio Televizija Srbija (RTS) was bombarded because it emitted civilian programs but was also part of the C3 network (the Serbian Army Command) and broadcasted aggressive war propaganda. The ICTY considered in its final report that this double use qualified as a military objective.[112] The coldness of this reasoning leaves little place for doubt; there were civilians working in this station, and no one knew for sure whether they agreed with Serbian policies. Several workers had resigned early on, but it cannot be assumed that all of those who stayed supported Milosevic. Some might even have been opposed to him but had no other choice than to comply with official policies. Besides, political ideas should not be taken

---

[109] *Final Report to the Prosecutor by the Committee Established to Review the NATO Bombing Campaign Against the Federal Republic of Yugoslavia*, ICTY, June 8, 2000, paras. 55, 75, and 76,

[110] U.S. Army Field Manual, para. 40 (c).

[111] Mari, *supra* note 85.

[112] Final Report to the Prosecutor by the Committee Established to Review the NATO Bombing Campaign Against the Federal Republic of Yugoslavia paras. 55, 75, and 76.

into account: a civilian is to be protected. These types of attacks are justified in the name of military necessity; yet, one can question the urgency of bringing down a radio station that emits propaganda where civilians work. The issue of proportionality is therefore raised; is it worth killing or hurting scores of civilians to destroy one radio station that solely distributes propaganda—propaganda that will be distributed in another fashion once the station is destroyed? It seems hardly rational to think so. In the case of the Belgrade station, the transmitters were repaired and were working again a few hours after the attack; so lives were lost for no gain. One has to be reminded that a journalist cannot be punished for publishing propaganda; a journalist spreading propaganda is not considered to participate directly in hostilities unless he spreads hate messages.[113] It seems, rather, that targeting the Serbian station emitting propaganda[114] or the attack against al Jazeera's offices in Kabul[115] goes against freedom of the press. One might disagree with the idea that the Serbs or al Qaeda propagates, but no one is entitled to kill to silence these voices. The offices of al Jazeera in Kabul were bombed, while the United Press and BBC offices nearby were also almost destroyed (a BBC correspondent had to duck under his desk to survive), on the grounds that the offices belonged to the Taliban and al Qaeda. This assimilation between an independent Muslim news station and the Taliban demonstrates that a propaganda war takes place during conflicts, and that journalists are the direct victims of this war. Additionally, a strict and rational reading of Article 52 API indicates that propaganda cannot be the sole justification for a military attack since there is no definite advantage in destroying the civilian objects that broadcast propaganda. The ICTY mitigates this reading by saying that any propaganda encouraging genocide or grave breaches of international humanitarian law turns the media into a legitimate target.[116] This approach is clarified by a reading of the case law of the Radio-Télévision Libre des Mille Collines case in Rwanda: the direct participation of three media workers at the radio station made no doubt of the genocide.[117] Hate media can therefore be a legitimate target. The reasoning is that journalists

[113] Stuart D. Stein, Nuremberg Judgment: Streicher, Jan. 18 1999, http://www.ess.uwe.ac.uk/genocide/Streicher2.htm.
[114] *Nato Challenged over Belgrade Bombing*, BBC, Oct. 24, 2001.
[115] *Al-Jazeera Kabul Offices Hit in US Raid*, BBC, Nov. 13, 2001.
[116] ICTY, *supra* 109, paras 47, 55, 74, and 76.
[117] Three media workers were brought before the International Criminal Tribunal for Rwanda (ICTR) on charges of direct and public incitement to genocide and other offences. Ferdinand Nahimana was found guilty of inciting genocide for broadcasting on Radio Rwanda the contents of a false document that led to the killing of hundreds of Tutsi civilians (*The Prosecutor v. Ferdinand Nahimana, Jean-Bosco Barayagwiza, Hassan Ngeze*, Case No. ICTR-99-52-T, December 3, 2003); Jean-Bosco Barayagwiza founded the station. He was found guilty of inciting genocide in 2003. The decision was reversed on appeal in 2007 because he could not be proved to have effective control over the radio station a day before the genocide began (*Summary of Judgment: Nahimana et al. v. The Prosecutor*, Case No. ICTR-99-52-A, November 28, 2007.) However, he remained convicted on other grounds, including distribution of arms to the local people to kill Tutsis and chanting "Let's exterminate them" at demonstrations. Hassan Ngeze, editor of the newspaper *Kangura*, distributed weapons and supervised the identification and targeting of Tutsis at roadblocks to kill them.

working for those media, although civilians, clearly demonstrate a desire to be there and to propagate hate speech to cause deaths. There is therefore no doubt as to their direct involvement in hostilities. In the case of the RTS in Belgrade, it is clear that the radio and television stations broadcast anti-NATO and anti-Western propaganda.[118] It broadcasted the patriotic tune of "We love you, our fatherland," played between programs.[119] Televised programs depicted the NATO symbol turning into a swastika and a montage of Madeleine Albright growing Dracula teeth in front of a burning building. RTS never reported on Albanian refugees who spoke of executions and ethnic cleansing in Kosovo. However, journalists played no direct role in military efforts, and the station was not used as a military command center. The propaganda, although quite aggressive, did not encourage people to commit genocide, unlike Radio Mille Collines. The journalists and other media people working in the building did not therefore participate directly in hostilities. Even if there was a doubt about their activities, Article 50.1 API, states: "in case of doubt whether a person is a civilian, that person shall be considered to be a civilian." Yet apparently for the ICTY, the fact that RTS employees were not legitimate targets does not in itself make the bombing illegal.

The question is then to know whether the radio station constitutes a legitimate target. The ICRC actually included TV stations in a list of possible military objectives: "installations of broadcasting and television stations; telephone and telegraph exchanges of fundamental military importance."[120] All these targets must still satisfy the two criteria laid out in Article 52 to make them valid military targets. According to the ICTY committee, disrupting the "propaganda machinery" of Milosevic's regime was secondary to NATO's primary goal, which was to disrupt the Serbian military command, control, and communications system, which is a legitimate military objective.[121] Considering that after the destruction of the RTS, programs resumed within three hours, one can say that the bombardment was *useless*, or rather brought no advantage .[122] Another argument was the lack of proportionality in the attack. States approach the concept of proportionality not during a single event. The ICTY considered that the death of sixteen civilians in Yugoslavia was not disproportionate in regard to the expected outcome. The ICTY committee suggested, in its final report, that the yardstick to measure the loss of lives and the military gains should be the determination of a "reasonable military commander."[123] This means that the very ones who are acting in the conflict and have interest in its outcomes should weigh whether an attack respects the principle of proportionality.

---

[118] Nicholas J. Cull, Propaganda and Mass Persuasion: A Historical Encyclopedia, 1500 To Present 36 (Santa Barbara, Calif.: ABC-CLIO 2003).

[119] Media Focus, *Medienhilfe Ex-Jugoslawien*, Media Focus 9: Monitoring Period February 11–February 24 http://archiv.medienhilfe.ch/Projekte/SER/MediaReports/MediaFocus/iwpfrfy.09.htm.

[120] Sandoz, *supra* note 89, at 632.

[121] ICTY, *supra* note 109, para 76.

[122] Cindy Gierhart, *Targeting Media: The Legal Restrictions on States Attacking Media in Times of War*, ExpressO, 2008, http://works.bepress.com/cindy_gierhart/1.

[123] ICTY, *supra* note 109, para. 50.

The ICTY believes that since the responsibility of the commander will be engaged under Article 85.3 (b) API and Article 8.2 (b) of the Rome Statute, he will be careful. Therefore, the issue seems to lie with instruments used to measure proportionality. The reality is that international humanitarian law has a negative approach to the protection of civilians; the main idea is to limit damages in the war zones rather than take positive extra measures to enforce immunity as a principle. This raises a debate as to whether the focus of international humanitarian law should not be more idealistic. A pragmatic response is that States will never accept such positive laws and prefer to see international humanitarian law limited in the battlefield rather than setting rules. Meanwhile, the George W. Bush administration's era has demonstrated how dangerous such passive and conservative positions are, since they give way to leeway. Having no optimism or utopia in the field of humanitarian law does not serve civilians' interests. Principles such as military necessity and proportionality also fail to take into account the fact that ethics at war is changing. Humanitarian law should therefore now adopt a more aggressive stance rather than its currently defensive one.

E. Occupied Territories

Occupied Territories are under the authority of a hostile army, without the consent of the domestic government. Humanitarian law sets forth rights and duties, as well as rules for administration for the occupying forces. It also establishes rights, duties, and rules for civilians living in the Occupied Territories. The Fourth Geneva Convention addresses the issue of Occupied Territories from Article 47 to 78, and Additional Protocol I addresses the topic in its Articles 63, 69, and 72 to 79. The 1907 Hague regulations also lay down laws of occupation, and have the status of international customary law. Basically, the duty of the Occupying Power is to maintain law and order.[124] Armed resistance against the occupying forces is legal when it targets military objectives solely.

Civilians are protected when they live in Occupied Territories (Article 47). The 1907 Hague law was deemed an insufficient protection for civilians. After the two world wars, it was decided that this text did not provide enough protection. The Fourth Geneva Convention is more detailed and completes the 1907 law. It explains the rights and duties of the occupying power. A key article is Article 49 GCIV, which states that there should be no transfer, deportation, or displacement, even partial, of the population. Article 53 GCIV prohibits the destruction of civilian objects unless it is necessary for military operations. This article is often invoked because of Israel's destruction of Palestinian houses, which has become a counterinsurgency military tactic of the Israeli Defense Forces: the houses of Palestinian suicide bombers' relatives are destroyed by the army. Other cases of destruction include houses where

---

[124] FRANCOISE BOUCHET-SAULNIER, THE PRACTICAL GUIDE TO HUMANITARIAN LAW 293 (Lanham, Md.: Rowman & Littlefield c2007).

the resistance is said to gather.[125] This destruction is controversial since it violates Article 53 GCIV; there is no absolute necessity for such military operations. Furthermore, the destruction also constitutes a form of collective punishment; the community is punished for the deeds of few, which is the definition of collective punishment under Article 33 GCIV.[126] An illustration is the destruction of a building from which a rocket that killed four Israeli soldiers in Rafah was sent.[127] Additionally, this destruction can be seen as a way to increase land property for the expansion of Israeli settlements.[128] The topic is highly controversial, with some Israelis harshly criticizing the methods used.[129]

The Occupying Power has the duty to ensure that adequate food, medical supplies, and objects of religious worship is provided to the civilian population (Article 55 GCIV and Article 69 API). The Occupying Power must also allow for the presence of the Protecting Power, the ICRC, or any other organizations. The latter will monitor the situation (Articles 30, 55, and 143 GCIV); the ICRC is therefore a presence in Palestinian territories. A large number of humanitarian organizations are also present. They organize the delivery of humanitarian aid to the civilians. Relief and aid must benefit from easy and rapid access. There have been numerous violations of this principle; for example, in 2008, the Israeli navy blocked an aid ship with Gaza as a final destination.[130] The duty to allow access to the humanitarian organizations does not affect the positive obligation for the Occupying Power to supply food and other things necessary to the survival of civilians (Articles 59–62 GCIV, 108–111 GCIV, and 69–71 API). Another illustration of the violation of the aforementioned articles is the blockade that Gaza has had to endure since 2007, which aims at preventing weapons from entering the territory but also to putting an end to attacks by Hamas. Gisha, an Israeli human rights group, has brought a case to force the authorities to disclose a list of what is prohibited to import into the territories. The government has indeed never produced a list, an absence that paves the way to abuses. Some food or medications are prohibited, just as some crucial material to build houses and schools. It is reported that even wheelchairs are prohibited. The seizure and the attack of the ship carrying humanitarian aid in international waters in May 2010 that resulted in the deaths of nine militants also violated humanitarian law. None of the circumstances under international law justifying an approach from Israelis were present. Israel claimed that the vessel had entered its sovereign waters near the coastline and represented a threat to the country. The Israeli authorities,

[125] Fred Abrahams et al., *Report—Razing Rafah: Mass Demolitions in the Gaza Strip* (Washington DC: Human Rights Watch 2004).

[126] Press Release, Amnesty International, Israel and the Occupied Territories: Under the Rubble: House Demolition and Destruction of Land and Property (May 17, 2004) MDE 15/033/2004.

[127] Yael Stein et al., *Report—Policy of Destruction: House Demolition and Destruction of Agricultural Land in the Gaza Strip*, JERUSALEM: B'TSELEM, February 2002.

[128] *EU Criticizes Israeli Demolition of Arab Homes in East Jerusalem*, M.E. NEWS, Nov 10, 2008.

[129] Gideon Levy, *The Silence of the Jurists*, HA'ARETZ, Feb. 1, 2009; Amos Harel, *IDF Probe: Cannot Defend Destruction of Gaza Homes*, HA'ARETZ, Feb. 15, 2009.

[130] Rory McCarthy, *Israel Navy Blocks Gaza Aid Ship*, THE GUARDIAN, Dec. 1, 2008.

however, had difficulty explaining the disproportionate use of force against civilians. The various reports released so far have not solved the issue. Not only did the country violate international law, but it also violated the law according to which the Occupying Power must facilitate passage of humanitarian aid.[131]

Under international law, the personal status of children must not be changed, and all institutions devoted to the work of care and educational institutions must be allowed to function. The Occupying Power cannot enlist children in organizations (Article 50 GCIV). It cannot compel people to serve in its armed forces, or to undertake any work involving them in military operations (Article 51 GCIV). Justice must respect judicial guarantees established in Articles 47, 54, and 64–75 GCIV. Detention and internment of civilians in Occupied Territories is also addressed in the Convention; protected persons who commit an offense intended to harm the Occupying Power shall be liable to internment or simple imprisonment. The duration of such internment or imprisonment must be proportionate to the offense committed. The courts provided for under Article 66 GCIV may, at their discretion, convert a sentence of imprisonment to one of internment for the same period. Therefore, humanitarian law guarantees during occupation that civilians will be well treated when free or when detained, and that combatants belonging to guerrilla movements will be granted the status of prisoners of war. They will be considered as combatants as long as they meet the criteria set up in Article 4.2 GCIV. If a combatant does not meet these criteria, he will be an unprivileged prisoner, and will be entitled to protection (Articles 44.4 and 75 API). A competent tribunal will decide whether someone is a prisoner of war (Article 45 API). Civilians can also take part in hostilities without belonging to armed forces; for example, when there is a *levée en masse*, it becomes difficult to distinguish between combatants and civilians, but civilians are still protected as such, except when they directly take part in hostilities (Article 51.3 API and Article 13.3 APII). If there is a doubt as to whether a person is a civilian, the doubt will benefit the civilian (Article 50 API). In this regard, the extension of the combatant status on a membership basis is extremely dangerous; it suggests extending the status of combatant to all supporters of a resistance movement. This would probably mean that 99 percent of the population of the Palestinian Occupied Territories would become legitimate targets!

The applicability and the observance of the Fourth Convention have been discussed in relation to the Israeli occupation of Gaza and the West Bank. Israel does not consider itself to be occupying the Palestinian territories; the Israeli argument is that since the end of the Ottoman Empire, the territories of the West Bank and Gaza Strip have not been recognized as sovereign territories.[132] Therefore, the Israeli position is that its administration could not be categorized as the occupation of the sovereign territory of another State since the Palestinian territories were never

[131] In May 2010, the Israeli Defence Forces attacked a ship carrying humanitarian aid. Nine volunteers on board were killed.
[132] Robbie Sabel, *The Problematic Fourth Geneva Convention: Rethinking the International Law of Occupation*, THE JURIST, July 16, 2003, http://www.mefacts.com/cached.asp?x_id=10357.

a State as such. However, and although Israel unilaterally disengaged from Gaza in September 2005, it has held the territory under an embargo at various times since June 2007 and is considered the occupying power in the Gaza Strip, the Golan Heights, and the West Bank (including East Jerusalem) by the United Nations, as well as by several countries and other organizations. The UN Security Council passed Resolution 446, Resolution 465, and Resolution 484, to cite the few that qualify the situation as an occupation and call for the enforcement of the Fourth Geneva Convention. The ICRC also deems Israel's activity an occupation of the Palestinian territories. The ICRC has declared that the Fourth Geneva Convention is applicable.[133] In its advisory opinion on the wall, the Israeli West Bank Barrier, the International Court of Justice described the West Bank, Gaza Strip, and East Jerusalem as occupied, without pondering whether there is indeed an occupation; it appears as a fact.[134] Israel also says it applies the rules of international law pertaining to Occupied Territories; it states that it applies "humanitarian provisions" but never declared it would enforce the Fourth Geneva Convention. The reason why Israel refuses to enforce the Convention is because there is no Palestinian State; instead Israel speaks of "humanitarian provisions," which permits the protection of the civilian population without protecting the right of a sovereign State.[135] The problem is that this type of legal reasoning resting on historical arguments deprives the Palestinian people from the protection granted by the Convention. The Convention should apply to the situation in order to protect civilians but also to uphold the humanitarian spirit of international humanitarian.[136] The Israeli Supreme Court of Justice had to address these issues. The argument of the government of Israel, argued before the Supreme Court, is that its authority in the territories is based upon the international law of "belligerent occupation," in particular the Hague Conventions. The Court agreed with this approach; instead of confronting the historical and legal arguments of Israel, according to which Geneva Convention IV cannot apply since the Palestinian territories are not and never were a sovereign State; it ruled in favor of the enforcement of customary law by looking at the Hague body of law.[137] For example, in 1979, the Court referred to the Hague law by ruling that Article 52 of the

---

[133] ICRC, Implementation of the Fourth Geneva Convention in the occupied Palestinian territories: history of a multilateral process (1997–2001), Annexe 2—Conference of High Contracting Parties to the Fourth Geneva Convention: statement by the International Committee of the Red Cross, Geneva, Dec. 5, 2001, http://www.icrc.org/Web/Eng/siteeng0.nsf/iwpList247/D86C9E662022D64E41256C6800366D55#2.

[134] Legal Consequences of the Construction of a Wall in the Occupied Palestinian Territory, I.C.J. Advisory Opinion of July 9, 2004, Summary 2004/2.

[135] Sabel, *supra* note 132.

[136] W. THOMAS MALLISON & SALLY V. MALLISON, THE PALESTINE PROBLEM IN INTERNATIONAL LAW AND WORLD ORDER (Burnt Mill, Harlow, Essex, England: Longman 1986).

[137] Michael M. Karayanni, Choice of Law under Occupation: How Israeli Law Came to Serve Palestinian Plaintiffs, working papers series, Aug. 28, 2008, http://papers.ssrn.com/sol3/papers.cfm?abstract_id=1299541.

regulations annexed to the Hague IV Convention had not been respected.[138] But the Court also ruled that the Fourth Geneva Convention is not applicable because it is only "contractual" international law: it would require specific Israeli legislation before the courts can take cognizance of it, while the Hague Convention of 1907 is part of customary international law, and therefore can be applied by domestic courts without specific legislation.[139] The same year, in the Elon Moreh case, the Israeli Supreme Court held the same position in respect to the Fourth Geneva Convention although, in his separate judgment, Justice Witkon commented: "It is a mistake to think… that the Geneva Convention does not apply to Judea and Samaria. It applies even though it is not justiciable in this court." Therefore the court has not addressed Israel's argument on the merits.[140] The Court has upheld this line, for example in its 2004[141] and 2005[142] rulings on the separation wall. Every year, the UN General Assembly adopts a resolution in which it encourages Israel to acknowledge the *de jure* enforcement of Geneva IV in the Palestinian Occupied Territories. This example demonstrates how complicated it is to enforce international humanitarian law when political interests are at stake.

In Iraq, the U.S. government has not openly acknowledged that the situation pertains to occupation, and that the Fourth Geneva Convention should be applicable, although there have been recommendations in that sense.[143] In their joint letter to the UN Security Council of May 8, 2003, the United States and the United Kingdom affirmed that they "will strictly abide by their obligations under international law including those relating to the essential humanitarian needs of the people of Iraq.[144]" The same month, in the resolution introduced by the Security Council on May 22, 1993, the United States and the United Kingdom were labeled as "occupying powers." The resolution called for "all concerned to comply fully with their obligations under international law including in particular the Geneva Conventions of 1949 and the Hague Regulations of 1907."[145] The reason why the United States avoided declaring that Iraq was an occupied territory was to pursue its

---

[138] Israel: Supreme Court Judgment with respect to the Elon Moreh Settlement in the Occupied West Bank (Oct. 22, 1979), 19 I.L.M. 148 (1980).

[139] Israeli Supreme Court sitting as a High Court of Justice, on March 13, 1979 in the Beth El/Bekaoth cases concerning Israeli settlements in the occupied territories.

[140] DAVID KRETZMER, THE OCCUPATION OF JUSTICE: THE SUPREME COURT OF ISRAEL AND THE OCCUPIED TERRITORIES 38 (Albany: State University of New York Press 2002).

[141] Beit Sourik Village Council v. The Government of Israel, The Supreme Court Sitting as the High Court of Justice, HCJ 2056/February 04, 29, 2004; Jason Litwack, *Disproportionate Ruling for All the Right Reasons:* Beit Sourik Village Council v. The Government of Israel, 31:3 BROOK. J. INT'L L. 858–96 (2006).

[142] International Legality of the Security Fence and Sections near Alfei Menashe, Israel High Court Ruling Docket H.C.J. 7957/04, September 15, 2005.

[143] J. Goldsmith, Memorandum Opinion for the Counsel to the President: Protected Person Status in Occupied Iraq under the Fourth Geneva Convention, March 18, 2004, http://www.usdoj.gov/olc/2004/gc4mar18.pdf.

[144] UN Doc. S/2003/538, May 8, 2003.

[145] UN Security Council Resolution 1483 (2003) of May 22, 2003, UN Doc.S/RES/1483 (2003), preamble and operative para. 5.

own political project without having the Security Council as a supervisor. It would have been best if a Security Council mandate explicitly requiring the enforcement of humanitarian law pertaining to Occupied Territories had been issued.[146]

III. CONCLUSION

Each category (civilians and combatants) benefits therefore from a specific protection; once civilians are distinguished from combatants, civilians are protected by GCIV, and combatants by GCIII. No one can wear both hats; an individual is either a civilian or a combatant. International humanitarian law protects those who seem to be in between categories, so no one falls outside the scope of international humanitarian law.

[146] David Scheffer, *The Security Council and International Law on Military Occupations*, in The United Nations Security Council and War: The Evolution of Thought and Practice Since 1945 597 (Vaughan Lowe et al., Oxford/New York: Oxford University Press 2008).

4 The Shift between Categories

In addition to the evolution of warfare, there has also been an evolution of the notion of civilians and combatants. Civilians sometimes play a crucial role in hostilities; a civilian can, for instance, be an expert in computers working for the Pentagon in the United States. This raises questions as to his status: is an IT expert controlling a drone a civilian or a combatant? Concomitantly, there is a resurgence of political violence and terrorist violence carried out by transnational armed groups in armed conflicts. Individuals who commit terrorist actions claim the benefit of the status of combatants. The principle of distinction seems to be blurred as an outcome of this evolution. Some of the evolutions were addressed by international humanitarian law through the 1977 Additional Protocols that took into account new technologies and the role of resistance groups. Since the 1977 Protocols, there has been no new humanitarian international document to amend or complete the Geneva Conventions and the Additional Protocols (despite the existence of several new conventions that address humanitarian issues). Recent evolutions therefore have to be addressed while relying on those documents.

What is witnessed in our current era is a change in the status of civilians and combatants; the two categories seem permeable in situations in which a civilian seems to participate directly in hostilities at work but is clearly a civilian while at home. Since in humanitarian law, one is either a civilian or a combatant, this issue has to be addressed. It is the shift from one category to the other that raises questions. Additionally, there is a resurgence of violence by transnational armed groups during armed conflicts, and Article 44 Additional Protocol I (API), which includes these groups in the category of combatant fighters from various movements, raises multiple questions in the current post-9/11 environment. The existence of the Guantanamo Bay detention center has also prompted a debate regarding the status of combatants and the potential existence of a category of combatant not covered by international humanitarian law.

I. FROM CIVILIAN TO COMBATANT

The debate revolves around the applicability of the Geneva Conventions and the Protocols in some situations involving civilians. There are indeed some cases that cast a doubt on the status of civilians. For example, how should one classify a farmer who turns into a *guerrillero* each night? How should one classify a man who carries a gun to protect his family? Is he a combatant or a civilian? It all depends on the degree of participation in hostilities; does the individual take direct part in hostilities or not? Since this concept is difficult to define, there are questions regarding the operability of the distinction. An International Committee of the Red Cross guideline sheds some light on the issue of direct participation in hostilities, but there remain some difficult issues, such as the use of human shields.

A. The Concept of Direct Participation in Hostilities

The status of combatants and civilians is mutually exclusive; one is either a combatant or a civilian. If a civilian participates directly in the hostilities, he loses his status and forfeits the protection afforded. Meanwhile, he does not become a combatant. A civilian enjoys immunity unless he takes direct or active part in hostilities. If he seems to fall in between categories, he will benefit from an *ad minima* protection.

The concept of "direct participation in the hostilities" is not clarified under international humanitarian law. There is a general understanding that "the commission of acts which, by their nature and purpose, are intended to cause actual harm to enemy personnel and *matériel* amounts to a direct participation in hostilities."[1] A farmer who takes up arms to participate in military actions would lose his immunity. A less clear case is the farmer who provides food and shelter to combatants.

There have been several attempts to clarify the notion of direct participation in hostilities. The ICRC commentary on API states that the behavior of civilians must constitute a direct and immediate military threat to the adversary to amount to direct and active participation. This criterion has been challenged by certain scholars and States advocating for the enlargement of the notion of direct participation to include, for example, the electrician who works for the municipality since he delivers electricity to both civilians and the army; he therefore, according to a broad

---

[1] Inter-American Commission on Human Rights, Third report on human rights in Colombia, Doc. OEA/Ser.L/V/II.102 Doc. 9 rev. 1, Feb. 26, 1999, Chapter IV, §§ 53 and 56.

understanding of the concept, participates directly in hostilities since without his intervention, the armed forces would not function.

There are often doubts because the situations might not be clear-cut; there can be grey areas. A good illustration is an individual who works in an ammunition factory. If the ammunition produced is used by a party to the conflict, then the factory is a legitimate target because it contributes to the war effort directly. The means used for transportation of the weapons, train, car, or truck will also be legitimate targets. It is the same for a pipeline transporting oil that will be used by a party. What about the people who work in these factories or transport the ammunition or the oil? The attacks against the means of transportation and the factories might remain lawful even though there are civilians working for the effort of war. Workers are not legitimate targets, but the factory is. Consequently, civilians lose their immunity when they enter the workplace but regain it on their way home or at home. A business that sells ammunition would not be a legitimate target except if the ammunition is used by a party to the conflict for its military actions. The reason is that the business sells and does not produce.

The existence of direct participation means that there are also indirect forms of participation. The question is then to know when a civilian indirectly participates in hostilities and when he crosses the line and becomes active. For example, a postman delivering maps to the U.S. army indirectly participates in the hostilities. He therefore remains a civilian. The same applies to the individual working for an electric company; he provides electricity to both civilians and the military, but takes no direct part in hostilities. Some have suggested extending the notion of direct participation in war by evaluating the value added to war: therefore, the delivery of maps by the postman would be evaluated with regard to his contribution to the war: if this individual adds a value to the war by delivering maps, he will directly take part in hostilities and is a legitimate target. In this situation, the impact of the participation would be analyzed rather than the form or degree of participation. These propositions have been rejected on the grounds that this would shatter the protection afforded to civilians.

There is little agreement regarding the level of participation. For some, a driver who delivers ammunition to combatants and an intelligence officer working in the territory of the enemy are considered participants in the hostilities.[2] For others, a civilian retrieving intelligence data from satellites provides less direct support to the war and therefore seems to keep his immunity.[3] There are actually as many examples as there are opinions. Some situations are clear; a civilian who is armed and attacks an army directly takes part in hostilities and loses his immunity. It is also agreed that civilians preparing or returning from combat operations are considered participants in hostilities. Another issue is knowing whether personnel and objects involved in a

---

[2] ICRC, FIGHT IT RIGHT: MODEL MANUAL ON THE LAW OF ARMED CONFLICTS 29 (Geneva: ICRC 1999).

[3] YORAM DINSTEIN, THE CONDUCT OF HOSTILITIES UNDER THE LAW OF INTERNATIONAL ARMED CONFLICTS 28 (New York/Cambridge University Press 2004).

peacekeeping mission are to be qualified as civilian. The Additional Protocols do not address such questions. Custom indicates that the protection granted to them is equivalent to that granted to civilians and civilian objects. As Professor Louise Doswald-Beck summarizes, there is an agreement that the individual who puts the bomb cartridge in the launcher is a combatant, but there is no agreement as to whether the person who delivers the cartridge is a combatant. The general agreement is that a person who manufactures the cartridge is not taking direct part in hostilities.[4]

The difficulty in defining who directly takes part in hostilities and whether civilians can be targeted while at work can be illustrated by the debate that sprang to life after the 1999 bombardment of a radio station in the Former Yugoslavia. NATO bombed the Radio Televizija Srbija (RTS) building because it was emitting propaganda and because it was also the base for military antennae. Journalists are civilians, and those working for the RTS did not work for the military but worked in a building that was actively and directly used by the army. The journalists therefore did not directly take part in hostilities, especially since emitting propaganda is not prohibited, unless it is hate propaganda that encourages killings or genocide. However, the workplace hosted military antennae, and the workplace qualified as a military target. The only way, therefore, to know whether these civilians become legitimate targets because they are in a military building is to include in the parameters the principle of proportionality; the destruction and attacks against civilians in the building or the factory should bring a military advantage. If it does not, these attacks are disproportionate and the killing of civilians is unlawful. The principle of proportionality is thus very important in the decision to destroy the factory that produces bullets and the means of transportation of the army. The best approach, which would show restraint and a respect for civilians and humanitarian law, would have been to attack the factory with ground soldiers rather than bombing from the air. Another solution would have been to attack the place by night when the workers were away. NATO justified the legitimacy of its attack against the radio station by saying it attacked by night. The problem with Radio or TV stations as well as hospitals is that they do not close at nights. The argument, which is valid for factories that are closed at night, is not acceptable in a business that works day and night; journalists work day and night, especially in times of war, and NATO could have expected civilians to be inside the building. There were indeed 120 civilians inside the RTS building on the night of June 1999. Therefore, not only did civilians who took no direct part in hostilities die, but the principle of proportionality was violated since the radio once destroyed was emitting again a few hours later; the military advantage sought was nullified, and people died while they should have been protected. This case is a good example of the limits of humanitarian law: it can be said that all measures were taken to protect civilians and that military necessity overrode civilians' protection within the boundaries of the principle of proportionality. One could argue that the

---

[4] Faisal Bodi, *What Constitutes a Legitimate Target?*, AL JAZEERA, Nov. 19, 2004.

role of humanitarian law is only to limit war. It could also be said that war could be humanized and that when 120 non combatant human beings are in a building, there should be no strike. This is particularly true in this case since the destruction served no long-term military purposes for NATO.

The matter is increasingly complex because of terrorism, the use of computerized warfare, the privatization of armed forces, and the mixing of civilian and military activities. This is why defining the concept of participation in hostilities has grown important and why some call either for a redefinition of the concept of direct participation in hostilities or an end to the distinction between civilian and combatant. What remains clear is that any interpretation of the concept should be narrow enough to protect civilians and maintain the principle of distinction, and broad enough to meet the legitimate need of the armed forces to effectively respond to violence by non combatants.[5]

The ICRC and the TMC Asser Institute have worked on a project to define the concept. This project was justified by the growing involvement of civilians in hostilities.[6] The first question the organizations tackled was how to know the difference between a "direct" or an "active" participation. Indeed the two adjectives appear in the Geneva Conventions; Article 3, common to the four Conventions, speaks of an *active* part in hostilities, while Article 51.3 API speaks of a *direct* participation. The commentary to Additional Protocol I (API) and the jurisprudence of the The International Criminal Tribunal for Rwanda (ICTR) treat "direct" and "active" as synonyms.[7]

The ICRC released an interpretive guidance on the notion of direct participation in hostilities under international humanitarian law in 2009. The aim was to clarify the concept. It took six years of meetings and discussions with experts on the issue to produce the guidance.

B. The ICRC Study

The document is remarkable in the sense that it clarifies several concepts. It first defines the concept of civilians in international armed conflict in a clearer fashion than earlier definitions, although it remains a negative definition: civilians are "all persons who are neither members of the armed forces of a party to the conflict nor participants in a levée en masse." In a non international armed conflict, civilians are "all persons who are not members of State armed forces or organized armed groups of a party to the conflict are civilians." The document also addresses the crucial

---

[5] NILS MELZER, DIRECT PARTICIPATION IN HOSTILITIES (Geneva: ICRC/TMC Asser Institute 2009).

[6] Interpretive Guidance on the Notion of Direct Participation in Hostilities under International Humanitarian Law, Adopted by the ICRC Assembly, Feb. 26, 2009. http://www.icrc.org/Web/eng/siteeng0.nsf/htmlall/participation-hostilities-ihl-311205/$File/Direct_participation_in_hostilities_2004_eng.pdf.

[7] The Prosecutor v. Jean-Paul Akayesu Case ICTR No ICTR-96-4-T, Decision of September 2, 1998, para. 629.

question of private contractors and civilian employees: "they are entitled to protection against direct attack unless and for such time as they take a direct part in hostilities. Their activities or location may, however, expose them to an increased risk of incidental death or injury even if they do not take a direct part in hostilities."[8] The document then defines "direct participation in hostilities" by establishing several elements: "In order to qualify as direct participation in hostilities, a specific act must meet the following cumulative criteria:

- The act must be likely to adversely affect the military operations or military, capacity of a party to an armed conflict or, alternatively, to inflict death; injury, or destruction on persons or objects protected against direct attack (threshold of harm),
- There must be a direct causal link between the act and the harm likely to result either from that act, or from a coordinated military operation of which that act constitutes an integral part (direct causation),
- The act must be specifically designed to directly cause the required threshold of harm in support of a party to the conflict and to the detriment of another (belligerent nexus)."

This interpretative guidance provides recommendations and does not reflect the opinions of all collaborators in the ICRC study; it remains crucial, however, since the ICRC is often considered the guardian of the Geneva Conventions. The organization clarifies the guidance and its criterion-based approach by providing examples:

"examples of causing military harm include capturing, wounding or killing military personnel; damaging military objects; or restricting or disturbing military deployment, logistics and communication, for example through sabotage, erecting road blocks or interrupting the power supply of radar stations. Interfering electronically with military computer networks (computer network attacks) and transmitting tactical targeting intelligence for a specific attack are also examples. The use of time-delayed weapons such as mines or booby-traps, remote-controlled weapon systems such as unmanned aircraft, also "directly" causes harm to the enemy and, therefore, amounts to direct participation in hostilities.[9]

According to the interpretative guidance, all persons who are not members of State armed forces or of organized armed groups belonging to a party to an armed conflict are civilians. Civilians sometimes take part in hostilities in a sporadic fashion. The ICRC clarifies this situation by saying that civilians cannot be regarded as members of an organized armed group unless they assume a "continuous

---

[8] MELZER, *supra* note 5.
[9] Direct Participation in Hostilities: Questions & Answers, ICRC, June 2009, http://www.icrc.org/web/eng/siteeng0.nsf/htmlall/direct-participation-ihl-faq-020609.

combat function". The ICRC also clarifies the matter of prosecution; civilians can be domestically prosecuted just for taking up arms.[10] This is an important clarification in the debate on the membership-based approach raised earlier: it seems that although the guidance seems to accommodate military necessity, it does not encourage the targeting of those who support a cause. It therefore does not solve the problem of, say, a temporary fighter who attends a wedding.

The ICRC also seized its opportunity to clarify other problems pertaining to the concept of direct participation. It's guidance illustrates indirect participation and explains that it "contributes to the general war effort of a party, but does not directly cause harm and, therefore, does not lead to a loss of protection against direct attack."

(Examples) include the production and shipment of weapons, the construction of roads and other infrastructure, and financial, administrative and political support [...] For example, the delivery by a civilian truck driver of ammunition to a shooting position at the front line would almost certainly have to be regarded as an integral part of ongoing combat operations and would therefore constitute direct participation in hostilities. However, transporting ammunition from a factory to a port far from a conflict zone is too incidental to the use of that ammunition in specific military operations to be considered as "directly" causing harm. Although the ammunition truck remains a military objective subject to attack, driving it would not amount to direct participation in hostilities and, therefore, the civilian driver could not be targeted separately from the truck.[11]

Another important point concerns the length of time of a civilian's participation in the conflict: civilians lose their immunity for the time of their participation in hostilities. The guidance says that members of organized armed groups belonging to a party to the conflict lose their immunity for the duration of their membership, which means for the time they assume a combat function. The extension of the membership criteria is therefore not validated by the ICRC; civilians lose protection for the duration of *each specific act* that amounts to the direct participation. This includes the preparatory phase, the deployment, as well as withdrawal.[12] The guidance stresses the obligation of parties to the conflict to try their best to identify whether an individual is a civilian or if he participates directly in hostilities. This means that civilians regain their immunity after the hostile act, and they remain liable under domestic law for taking up arms. If there is a doubt, the status of civilian will apply and the person will be protected. This clarifies the position of the ICRC on the farmer by day/fighter by night who attends a wedding or works in his field, an issue mentioned in the introduction.

[10] *Id.*
[11] *Id.*
[12] MELZER, *supra* note 5.

These guidelines are groundbreaking since the ICRC attempts to solve several matters pertaining to civilians, and in particular rejects the membership-based approach. This guidance could put an end to several of the debates mentioned before. It certainly demonstrates that a civilian who directly participates in hostilities does not fall outside the scope of the law: parties to the conflict are bound by their obligations and cannot violate their obligations of humanity. The distinction is therefore strengthened by explaining who can and cannot be targeted lawfully. The document is only a suggestion and is not legally binding. However, considering the status and the role of the ICRC as well as the aim of the guideline, which is to enhance civilians' protection, it is to be hoped that all will follow the interpretation given by the document.

C. The Protection Afforded to Civilians Who Participate in Hostilities

No situation is black or white, and it happens that civilians do directly take part in hostilities. International humanitarian law is clear: civilians who directly take part in hostilities lose their immunity for the time of the participation. They do not become combatants unless they formally become members of armed forces, which means they comply with Article 4 GCIII or Articles 43 and 44 API. As Baxter observed: "armed and unarmed hostilities, wherever occurring [whether in occupied or unoccupied areas], committed by persons other than those entitled to be treated as prisoners of war or peaceful civilians merely deprive such individuals of a protection they might otherwise enjoy under international law and place them virtually at the power of the enemy."[13] It is then crucial to afford them the right protection.

First of all, human rights conventions are still applicable to them. This brings little protection, since States can suspend some rights in times of conflict, internal disturbances, or tensions. There are rules of customary law that ignore the categorization of conflict, and there is a minimum standard of protection to be found in Common Article 3 for non international armed conflict, and in Article 75 API for international armed conflict. Therefore, civilians who directly take part in hostilities will benefit from fundamental guarantees and customary law. They qualify for the status of unprivileged combatants; they lose their immunity under GCIV, do not gain protection under GCIII, and yet they are still protected by *ad minima* rights. This is important to stress; there are no grey zones and no illegal combatants in international law.

This is controversial since, for some, the immunity should be lost until the end of the war rather than for the duration of the participation. This means that the farmer by day/fighter by night will only be a legitimate target at night.

---

[13] R. R. Baxter, *So-called "Unprivileged Belligerency": Spies, Guerillas and Saboteurs*, 28 B. Yb. Int'l L. 343, 325–45.

Another problem is again the definition of the concept: who directly takes part in hostilities, and how? The problem is particularly acute in occupied territory, as demonstrated by the Palestinian example. The Israeli High Court replied to the question of who is a legitimate target of a targeted killing by broadening the concept of direct participation to the persons who decide on the acts or plan them, and even to those who enlist others, guide them, and send them to commit the attacks. The Court added that it does not include civilians who offer assistance by means of strategic analysis, logistic and financial support, or propaganda. These activities constitute an indirect participation in hostilities, and therefore the persons engaged in them are not legitimate objects of targeted killings.[14] This is an attempt to clarify concretely the concept of direct participation. The ICRC issued the guideline document three years later, a document which has adopted the criteria approach rather than concrete explanations and examples. It is therefore interesting to see the Israeli High Court trying to solve the issue by giving categories of people who directly participate, and to compare it to the ICRC's interpretation of the concept. It is interesting to stress that the Court did not take into account the membership-based argument that transforms supporters into legitimate targets.[15] The danger of the membership approach as accepted is that it knows little boundaries: members of the Palestinian Qassam Brigades, of the military wing of Hamas, would all be legitimate targets, notwithstanding the frequency and scope of their participation in hostilities. This means that teachers, doctors, or anyone with regular jobs joining the insurgency for some time would be a target. The rationale for the membership approach is that the members pose an "ongoing threat."[16] The membership argument is by consequence an attempt to discuss the time length during which civilians who take direct part in hostilities can be a target; they should be targets until the end of the conflict, and not only during the length of their actions, because they are a permanent threat. The problem with this approach is that this definition can be extended to all of those who support Hamas in one way or another. There is also the limited membership approach, which is narrower; it does not permit the targeting of all members of an armed group at all times; only fighters can be targeted, even if they are not up in arms or directly participating. They are legitimate targets because they belong to a group. Belonging to the Qassam Brigades turns one into a legitimate targets according to this approach. Some present the limited membership approach as an improvement to the complete membership approach since it does not target supporters who do not take part directly in hostilities and the temporal scope is

---

[14] On December 13, 2006, the High Court of Justice gave its decision on the petition filed in January 2002 by the Public Committee Against Torture in Israel.

[15] Valentina Azarov, *Who Is a Civilian in Gaza? The Dangers of Adopting a Membership Approach to Direct Participation in Hostilities*, Alternative Information Center, January 2009, http://internationallawobserver.eu/2009/03/03/who-is-a-civilian-in-gaza-the-dangers-of-adopting-a-membership-approach-to-direct-participation-in-hostilities/.

[16] International Humanitarian Law and Civilian Participation in Hostilities in the OPT, Harvard Programme on Humanitarian Policy and Conflict Research, Policy Brief, October 2007, at 10.

broader than the one relying on the specific act approach.[17] Some experts suggest there should be a distinction between, on the one hand, members of Hamas and the Qassam Brigades who have a continuous, "important combat function," and those, on the other hand, who sporadically participate in hostilities on an "ad hoc" basis without being members of a brigade. They clearly do not spend the same amount of time fighting, which not only raises the question of the membership approach, but bases it upon a time-length criterion. The membership approach would then clarify the blurring of the concept of combatant. This approach is in disagreement with international humanitarian law and again accommodates war rather than limiting it; the role of humanitarian law is not to facilitate the work of armed groups and forces, but to protect civilians.[18] The membership approach, under all shapes, is unacceptable: one cannot target people who are not up in arms because of their beliefs or membership in a certain group.

Civilians who take direct part in hostilities will not be granted the status of prisoners of war (POWs) once captured; their offenses, even if they violate international humanitarian law, will be tried under domestic law. It remains unclear, however, if the participation itself can be prosecuted as an offense under domestic law or international law.[19]

D. A Sensitive Case: Human Shields

There is a debate regarding the targeting of human shields. Civilians can, for example, be moved to military objectives by a party to the conflict to prevent the other belligerent from striking these legitimate targets. The ICRC defines the phenomenon in its study on customary international humanitarian law as follows: "the use of human shields requires an intentional co-location of military objectives and civilians or persons *hors de combat* with the specific intent of trying to prevent the targeting of those military objectives."[20]

The rule is that civilians do not benefit from protection once they enter military objectives; for example, civilians working in ammunition factories or on military bases lose their protection (with respect to the principle of proportionality). The question is addressed in Article 23 GCIII, Article 28 GCIV, and in Articles 37.1, 50.3, 51.7, and 51.8 API. It is prohibited to use civilians to form human shields, and it is considered a war crime by Article 8.2 of the Rome Statute. The prohibition remains even if the civilians consent.[21]

[17] *Id.*

[18] Azarov, *supra* note 15.

[19] Melzer, *supra* note 5.

[20] Jean-Marie Henckaerts & Louise Doswald-Beck, Customary International Humanitarian Law 340 (Cambridge, UK/New York, NY, USA: Cambridge University Press 2005).

[21] *Adalah—The Legal Centre for Arab Minority Rights in Israel v. GOC Central Command, IDF* (2006) HCJ 3799/02, http://elyon1.court.gov.il/eng/home/index.html.

Some sources believe the intent of civilians should be taken into account; if a civilian volunteers, he loses his immunity. If he is compelled to be part of a human shield, he keeps the immunity. There are, according to Yoram Dinstein, three scenarios possible:[22]

1. In the first scenario, civilians choose to voluntarily be used as human shields. The aim is to deter any attack on a legitimate military target. The interpretation is that in that type of situation, civilians deliberately quit the protection. For Dinstein, this could be perceived as a direct participation in hostilities, and these civilians should lose the benefit of the protection.
2. In the second scenario, civilians are compelled by the belligerent to participate as a shield; when coerced, civilians cannot be considered as guilty of direct participation in the attacks and cannot assume their criminal conduct.
3. In the third scenario, combatants mix with the population. They might for example infiltrate refugees leaving a country. Civilians remain protected in that type of situation.

Dinstein is not the only one who insists on a strict dichotomy between civilians and combatants, or who attributes the status of unlawful combatants to all those who at first seem to fall in between categories or directly participate in hostilities. For Michael Schmitt, voluntary human shields have "a status similar to that of illegal combatant."[23] Richard Parrish says that although "neither lawful nor unlawful belligerents," voluntary human shields are not "traditional civilians."[24] An Israeli Court goes the same way:

Certainly, if they are doing so because they were forced to do so by terrorists, those innocent civilians are not to be seen as taking a direct part in the hostilities. They themselves are victims of terrorism. However, if they do so of their own free will, *out of support for the terrorist organization*, they should be seen as persons taking a direct part in the hostilities.[25]

The notion of intent, the importance of knowing whether civilians are willingly playing their part or are being compelled, seems to be the criterion.[26] The problem

---

[22] DINSTEIN, *supra* note 3, at 129 seq.

[23] Michael N. Schmitt, *Ethics and Military Force: The Jus in Bello*, Speech delivered at the Carnegie Council Workshop on European and North American Perspectives on Ethics and the Use of Force, Cambridge, UK, Jan. 7, 2002, *in* Rewi Lyall, *Voluntary Human Shields, Direct Participation in Hostilities and the International Humanitarian Law Obligations of States*, 11 MELBOURNE J. INT'L L.

[24] Richard Parrish, The International Legal Status of Voluntary Human Shields, Paper presented at the annual meeting of the International Studies Association, Montreal, Canada, March 17, 2004, citing the possession of and intent to use firearms definition of "illegal belligerency" in *ex parte Quirin*, 317 US, *in* Lyall, *id.*

[25] PCATI (2006) HCJ 769/02, [36] http://elyon1.court.gov.il/eng/home/index.html.

[26] Matthew V. Ezzo & Amos N. Guiora, *Critical Decision Point on the Battlefield—Friend, Foe, or Innocent Bystander*, U. UTAH LEGAL STUDIES PAPER 08-03, 3 (2008).

with intent-based analysis is that it is almost impossible to evaluate the willingness of civilians in such situation. How can the soldier targeting the military object protected by civilians be aware of the willingness factor, and how can he evaluate it? Doubt should play a role: when there is a doubt as to the status, the individuals should be considered civilians, as stated in the Geneva Conventions. This rule of the Geneva law seems to be forgotten. The test of the intent is too weak and law should take over.

Therefore the interpretation of Article 51 API that looks at intent is too subjective and gives the army too much leeway. In addition, one should refer to Article 51.3 API: when doubt arises regarding the status of a civilian person, he should be deemed a civilian. One approach would be to consider human shields as having the same status as journalists accompanying armed forces; this would extend the civilian protection to human shields. It is sometimes difficult to know where a person stands. This is particularly true for two types of asymmetric warfare: wars of national liberation and terrorism. Under international humanitarian law, civilians who willingly form a human shield are still protected in those situations. As perfectly stated, "under international humanitarian law, breaches of the law do not strip individuals of their status but affect the nature of the rights and protections that individuals can rely on."[27]

Having different beliefs does not make them combatants or direct participants in hostilities. Therefore, they should not be targeted. These civilians might have an indirect impact upon hostilities by protecting a military target. Therefore, one could prosecute them under domestic law for disrupting the war effort; but certainly not for war crimes. This reasoning does not apply to compulsory human shields. Combatants using human shields commit a war crime. Eventually, the best argument to prevent the targeting of voluntary human shields is the principle of proportionality, which is why foreign volunteers who rushed to Iraq in 2003 to form the human shields were not bombed; it would have come at an extremely high political cost, considering most of the civilians were Western.

II. THE BLURRING OF THE CONCEPT OF COMBATANT

If there are civilians engaging in hostilities and becoming therefore unprivileged combatants, there are also major changes regarding combatants. Combatants belonging to armed forces are defined in Article 4 GCIII and Articles 43 and 44 API. There was a major change with Protocol I since the document relaxes the criteria set in Article 4 GCIII to meet new situations and circumstances caused by wars of self-determination. A major problem is that several countries have not ratified Protocol I, and others have created a third category, namely unlawful combatants.

[27] Lyall, *supra* note 23; Josiane Haas, *Voluntary Human Shields: Status and Protection under International Humanitarian Law, in* INTERNATIONAL HUMANITARIAN LAW AND THE 21ST CENTURY'S CONFLICT: CHANGES AND CHALLENGES 191, 200 (Roberta Arnold & Pierre-Antoine Hildbrand eds., Lausanne: Editions interuniversitaires suisses, Edis 2005).

Additionally, the nature of warfare has changed today, especially in an era of resurgenct terrorism.

A. Additional Protocol I and the Extension of the Status of Combatants and Prisoners of War

The aim of the Protocols was to bring an answer to the challenges emerging with struggles for self-determination and new actors in asymmetric conflicts. Article 44 API provides us with extra information regarding combatants and prisoners of war. Paragraph 2 states that if a combatant violates a rule of international law, he will not lose his status as a combatant or as a prisoner of war, except under circumstances stated in paragraphs 3 and 4. Paragraph 3 reminds us that a combatant should distinguish himself at all times from civilians. When this is not possible because of the nature of the hostilities, the combatant will keep his status as long as he carries his arms openly during each military engagement, and when "he is visible to the adversary while he is engaged in a military deployment preceding the launching of an attack in which he is to participate." Paragraph 4 says that a captured combatant who does not meet these criteria will forfeit his right to be a prisoner of war, but will benefit from protection equivalent to the protection granted by GCIII and API to prisoners of war. This includes the same rights and protection of the combatant if tried. Paragraph 5 states that if a combatant is captured when he is not engaged in an attack or a military preparation, he will not lose his status of combatant or prisoner of war. If a soldier on holiday visits his family and is captured, he will still benefit from the status of combatant and prisoner of war.

1. Extension of the Status of Combatants

Articles 43 and 44 API give a new definition of armed forces covering the categories of Article 4 GCIII: all combatants, including those who belong to a resistance movement, are a party to the conflict, which is a novelty compared to Article 4 (a) (2) GCIII. Article 44 API relaxes two of the four cumulative criteria set in Article 4 that make an individual a member of the armed forces; the duty to carry arms openly at all times is restricted to the duration of the battle, and combatants are released from the obligation of wearing a fixed distinctive sign recognizable at a distance.[28] This takes into account the reality of warfare and the fact that a combatant might not always be dressed in a uniform during an asymmetric conflict. This is particularly true for armed groups struggling for self-determination; wearing a uniform does not agree with the type of war guerrilla groups lead since discretion and secrecy is usually part of their philosophy. The Colombian FARC is a rare example of an armed group wearing a uniform, but the Taliban or Abu Sayyaf combatants in the

---

[28] Dinstein, *supra* note 3, at 46.

Philippines usually wear local attire or a mix of military and civilian attire. Article 44 is a very complex article and is part of API's effort to adapt to the new realities of the battle field, including irregular armies.[29] One cannot expect groups who fight on behalf of the poor to the follow the same rules as a State army that benefits from advanced and expensive technology. Parties are not on an equal footing, and compromises are to be made. Besides, if wars of self-determination are to be included in the category of international armed conflict, then methods and means used in these struggles should also be taken into account.[30] This is why the conditions for combatant status set forth in Article 4 of GCIII are relaxed in Article 44 API; Article 44 (3) goes as far as allowing a guerrilla combatant to dress as a civilian if the nature of the hostilities requires it.[31] He will keep his status as a combatant while doing so, and cannot switch from the category of civilian to the category of combatant as it pleases him. Combatants using guerrilla warfare methods have to comply with the law of war; especially since they could benefit from it. The article strikes a balance between the protection of these fighters and the need for them to respect the law.

Article 44 was heatedly discussed in its drafting phase, and some States did not ratify Protocol I because they disagreed that article alone. Many states were displeased with the inclusion of self-determination fighters. For many, the alteration of Article 4 GCIII made by Article 44 API comes at the expense of civilians; combatants can pose as civilians without being endangered, which blurs the distinction.[32] The difficulty was actually to respond to the needs of combatants of armed groups while upholding civilians' protection, and for some, Article 44 API is not a viable compromise.[33] Dinstein speaks of *ad absurdum* reduction of the conditions of lawful combatancy.[34] He sees this major change as the end of the distinction between lawful and unlawful combatants, which was actually the aim of the Protocol. Indeed, the protocol cuts the ground from under the feet of those who would like to justify the existence of the category of unlawful combatant through the imperative of a secure homeland. The immunity of civilians is not threatened since the ICRC has clarified the concept of direct participation in hostilities. As stressed, the respect of international humanitarian law should remain the aim, and all organized armed groups should be enticed to respect this law.[35] If all parties understand their interests in respecting humanitarian law, there will be no blurring between categories. Jean de Preux concludes by saying that belligerents have to understand that

---

[29] Judith Gail Gardam, Non-Combatant Immunity as a Norm of International Humanitarian Law 103 (Dordrecht/Boston: Norwell, MA: M. Nijhoff 1993).

[30] *Id.*, at 102.

[31] ICRC, Commentary Article 44, http://www.icrc.org/ihl.nsf/COM/470-750054?OpenDocument.

[32] G. B. Roberts, *The New Rules for Waging War: The Case Against the Ratification of Additional Protocol I*, 26 Va. J. Int'l. L. 109–70, 129 (1985–86).

[33] Abraham D. Sofaer, *The Rationale for the United States Decisions*, 82 A.J.I.L. 784, 786 (1988).

[34] Dinstein, *supra* note 3, at 47.

[35] René Kosirnik, *The 1977 Protocols: A Landmark in the Development of International Humanitarian Law*, 320 I.R.R.C. 483–505 (1997).

"by protecting the civilian population, they protect themselves."[36] Besides, the rule is limited and applies mainly to occupied territories and conflicts covered by Article 1(4) API.

2. Extension of the Status of POW

The status of POW is also extended by Article 44 API; Protocol I extends the protection offered to Francs-tireurs, insurgents, and guerrillas in GCIII by giving them the status of POWs. As stressed in the commentary, the reason for doing so is that the problem is not so much how to get the status of combatant and POW, but how to avoid forfeiting the status. Members of armed groups are POWs unless they commit a war crime. This allows for the prosecution of terrorism. They can never be prosecuted under domestic law for taking up arms, since they are combatants. The conditions for granting POW status are therefore eased, again, to increase the protection afforded to combatants in asymmetric warfare.[37]

Consequently, the strict conditions set forth in the Hague law, the Geneva Law, and international customary law are relaxed to adapt to irregular forces and self-determination struggles. The outcome, as pointed out by several scholars, is that the distinction between combatants who respect the rules of international armed conflicts and combatants who either do not, or manipulate those rules, could become blurred. However, a better education regarding international humanitarian law, as well as better information of the belligerents' rights and protection under this law, will encourage them to respect the laws of war and to maintain the distinction. If they blur the distinction and use perfidy to trump enemies by acting as civilians, they will be severely punished and will lose POW status, therefore benefitting solely from the status of unprivileged combatant.

Article 44 is one of the reasons the United States has not ratified Protocol I. The United States divides combatants between lawful and unlawful combatants, a concept that does not exist in humanitarian law. It is a legal interpretation to which API puts an end. President Ronald Reagan felt that API, and in particular Article 44, gave legitimacy to terrorists and also limited possibilities to punish members of armed groups for their actions.[38] The consequences of this decision were heavy since one of the outcomes was the creation of Guantanamo Bay. This denial of reality is rather stunning; asymmetric wars are almost the rule today, rather than the exception, and denying rights to irregular armies that are already at a strong disadvantage would ensure that countries like the United States impose their will in the

---

[36] Jean de Preux, *The Protocols Additional to the Geneva Conventions*, 258 I.R.R.C. No. 258, 250–58 (1987).

[37] Michla Pomerance, Self Determination in Law And Practice: The New Doctrine of the United Nations 53 (The Hague/Boston: M. Nijhoff 1982).

[38] Georges H. Aldrich, *Prospects for United States Ratification of Additional Protocol I to the 1949 Geneva Conventions*, 85 A.J.I.L. (1991).

world. It also sets a negative precedent for the rest of the world since the United States is often perceived as a role model.

B. Lawful and Unlawful/Unprivileged Combatants

1. Who Are Unlawful Combatants?

Several States have decided not to ratify Protocol I for various reasons, one of which is the relaxed criteria under Article 44 API. These States refer solely to Article 4 GCIII and consider anyone who does not fulfill the four cumulative conditions (being commanded by a person responsible for his subordinates; having a fixed distinctive sign recognizable at a distance; carrying arms openly; and conducting their operations in accordance with the laws and customs of war) an illegal or unlawful combatant, the regular and lawful combatant being the one who meets all the criteria. This is why some scholars speak of lawful combatants versus unlawful combatants, or even enemy combatants.[39] This restricted approach of humanitarian law turns members of armed groups, who are civilians who take direct part in hostilities, into unlawful combatants.

This sub distinction within the category of combatants is said to allow for more protection to civilians.[40] The rule is that it is prohibited for people to wear two hats, the one of civilian and the one of combatant, since they are mutually exclusive: one cannot be a civilian and a lawful combatant at once. Therefore, the unlawful combatant is a civilian who directly engages in hostilities and loses protection both under GCIII and GCIV. Under this approach, unlawful combatants are combatants masquerading as civilians either to mislead the enemy or to avoid detection;[41] this masquerade can range from dressing as a civilian to hiding in civilians' midst. This situation also includes the farmer who works in his fields by day and turns into a combatant by night; he is neither a civilian nor a lawful combatant since he does not answer to either of the two definitions. He is an unlawful combatant for the entire period of the war. He stands in between the two categories, putting both at risk. The outcome is that he can be lawfully targeted, but cannot benefit from the protection granted by Geneva Convention III. This position is supported by the United States. One of the bases for the U.S. position on an unlawful combatant can be found in domestic case law. Under the 1942 Quirin, unlawful combatants can be captured and tried by military tribunals for their acts which "render their belligerencies unlawful." Indeed, they might have committed offenses under domestic or international law. The United States relies heavily on this third category of actors to explain its behavior toward individuals and groups fighting in Afghanistan and Iraq.

---

[39] DINSTEIN, *supra* note 3, at 29.

[40] Theodore Meron, *Some Legal Aspects of Arab Terrorists' Claims to Privileged Combatancy*, in OF LAW AND MAN: ESSAYS IN HONOR OF HAIM H. COHN 225–41 (Shoham ed., New York: Sabra Books 1971).

[41] DINSTEIN, SUPRA NOTE 3, at 29.

2. The Argument Against the Notion

Being an unlawful combatant means that one does not fit in any of the categories protected under GCIII and GCIV. This concept was used for the first time in the Quirin case, which is a domestic case. It appears in domestic military manuals as well. Domestic case law does not dictate the direction that international and universal humanitarian law should take. The issue lies in the fact that the United States has not ratified API and therefore relies on GCIII to build its argument, as well as on domestic law.[42] No combatant falls between categories and consequently, no combatants are unlawful. If a combatant does meet the criteria of Article 4 GCIII or Articles 43 and 44 API, he is then an unpriviledged combatant. The concept of unprivileged combatant revolves around the idea that there are combatants who do not meet all conditions of Article 4 GCIII or Articles 43 and 44 API, but still possess some rights. Indeed, speaking of unlawful combatant implies that between categories act in an illegal fashion that deprives them of all rights and protection. Dinstein goes as far as comparing them to war criminals.[43] This is why some organizations like Amnesty International, Human Rights Watch, and the International Committee of the Red Cross prefer to use the term unprivileged combatants.

A judgment of the International Criminal Tribunal for the Former Yugoslavia (ICTY) understood that the ICRC commentary on Geneva Convention IV holds that:

There is no gap between the Third and Fourth Geneva Conventions. If an individual is not entitled to the protection of the Third Convention as a prisoner of war... he or she necessarily falls within the ambit of [the Fourth Convention], provided that its Article 4 requirements [defining a protected person] are satisfied.[44]

There are therefore no illegal or unlawful combatants, only civilians who directly take part in hostilities and benefit from a minimal protection. There is no grey zone

---

[42] *See* the various memos of the Bush administration and its attempts to thwart international law until a Supreme Court Decision in 2006 holding that international law was violated. Charles Babington & Michael Abramowitz, *U.S. Shifts Policy on Geneva Conventions*, Wash. Post, July 12, 2006, at A01.

For a collection of memoranda, see Karen J. Greenberg & Joshua L. Dratel, The Torture Papers: The Road to Abu Ghraib (Cambridge/New York: Cambridge University Press 2005). *See also* the position of Jack Goldsmith: Jack Goldsmith & Curtis Bradley, *Customary International Law as Federal Common Law: A Critique of the Modern Position* 110:4 Harv. L. Rev. 815–76 (1997); *also*, Jason Ralph, Defending the Society of States: Why America Opposes the International Criminal Court and Its Vision of World Society (Oxford/New York: Oxford University Press 2007).

[43] Yoram Dinstein, *The Distinction Between Unlawful Combatants and War Criminals*, in International Law in Time of Perplexity: Essays in Honor of Shabtai Rosenne 103–16 (Yoram Dinstein ed., Dordrecht/Boston: Kluwer Academic Publishers 1989).

[44] ICTY, Celebici Judgment, para. 271 (1998).

in international humanitarian law, and people who are caught in between become unprivileged combatants.

The concept of unlawful combatant has given rise to an important debate in the United States, which has been mostly approached through the lens of national law, setting aside international law.[45] Others have chosen to provide specific readings of international law that support the existence of the category of unlawful combatants.[46] The argument supporting the creation of a third category, the one rejecting Protocol I since the United States has not ratified API, and the one that rests upon the primacy of U.S. law, is defeated in international law. First, part of API is customary international law and the United States is bound by these rules. For example, the United States cannot create a third category of war actors and deprive them of all protection. Article 75 API is a rule of customary international humanitarian law and provides *ad minima* protection to civilians taking part in hostilities. The United States, as a member of the international community, has ratified the Geneva Conventions and many other treaties and conventions; it cannot invoke domestic law to justify violations of international law.[47]

The most important part of the argument is the fact that since the United States did not ratify API, it is free from any obligations regarding this document and can consider unlawful combatants to be unprotected. This is an erroneous interpretation of international humanitarian law: this law provides protection to all under all circumstances. A civilian who takes part in hostilities is indeed not a combatant and will not benefit from POW status International humanitarian law covers this situation and grants an *ad minima* protection to the unprivileged combatant, a civilian who directly takes part in hostilities in violation of humanitarian law, and who can be prosecuted under domestic law for his violations.[48] He is unprivileged because he will not benefit from the protection of GCIV since he is not a full civilian, with exceptions that we will see below, or from GCIII since he does not respond to the criteria of a combatant.

GCIV applies to unprivileged combatants to a certain extent; indeed the Convention has a wide scope of application to encompass many different situations. Article 5 GCIV provides protection to protected persons such as spies and saboteurs, or any individual suspected of engaging in activities hostile to the State or Occupying Power; this encompasses direct participation of a civilian, and this article could apply to unprivileged combatants.[49] Knut Dormann also looks at Article 45.3 API to justify further application of GCIV's protection to unprivileged combatant.

---

[45] *See, e.g.,* JACK GOLDSMITH, THE TERROR PRESIDENCY: LAW AND JUDGMENT INSIDE THE BUSH ADMINISTRATION (New York: W. W. Norton & Company 2007).

[46] Joseph P. Bialke, *Al-Qaeda & Taliban Unlawful Combatant Detainees, Unlawful Belligerency, and the International Laws of Armed Conflict*, A.F.L. REV. (2004); Dinstein, *supra* note 44.

[47] GOLDSMITH, *supra* note 47.

[48] George Aldrich, *The Taliban, Al Qaeda, and the Determination of Illegal Combatants*, 96 A.J.I.L. 892, 891–98 (2002).

[49] Esbjorn Rosenblad, *Guerrilla Warfare and International Law*, 12 MIL. L. & L. OF WAR REV. 91–134, 110 (1973); Fritz Kalshoven, *The Position of Guerrilla Fighters under the Law of War*, 11:1

According to that article, "[a]ny person who has taken part in hostilities, who is not entitled to prisoner-of-war status and who does not benefit from more favourable treatment in accordance with the Fourth Convention shall have the right at all times to the protection of Article 75 of this Protocol. In occupied territory, any such person, unless he is held as a spy, shall also be entitled, notwithstanding Article 5 of the Fourth Convention, to his rights of communication under that Convention." Dormann understands this provision as containing the "implicit confirmation" that GCIV applies to unprivileged combatants who are protected persons as long as they fulfill the nationality criteria mentioned in Article 4 GCIV. Article 5 (3) GCIV states that all captured persons should be treated with humanity, and Article 5 GCIII says that they should have a fair trial to decide whether they are combatants and will be granted POW status. Common Article 3 and Article 75 API will provide the necessary protection to these civilians who took arms; they have basic guarantees, such as the right not to be tortured. Additionally, Common Article 3 and Article 75 API are considered to be customary rules. The International Court of Justice in the 1986 Nicaragua case stated that "minimum rules applicable to international and non international armed conflicts" are laid out in common Article 3 of the Geneva Conventions. Since protection is afforded in customary law, no State can avoid respecting fundamental guarantees on the grounds that they did not sign a convention or a protocol. These fundamental guarantees are applicable to both international and non international conflicts, and their status in customary law has been confirmed in the ICRC study.[50]

3. In Practice: the U.S. and Israel

Issues pertaining to the concept of unlawful combatant are relatively new. A U.S. journalist was detained in Liberia as an unlawful combatant.[51] A major debate sprang to life with the war in Afghanistan as to whether captured fighters were regular or irregular combatants. The United States decided to launch a war against al Qaeda since the group was accused of perpetrating the 9/11 terrorist attacks, and again, the Taliban was accused of supporting al Qaeda by hosting the group in Afghanistan. The United States put forward the notion that all members of the two groups captured during hostilities fell into the category of enemy combatant and were deprived from protection afforded under GCIII and GCIV. The outcome is infamous: the creation of prisons where severe abuses were committed and the outsourcing of torture. The United States is not the only country using that rhetoric. Israel also calls captured

MIL. L. & L. OF WAR REV. 55–91, 72 (1972); Knut Dormann, *The Legal Situation of Unlawful/Unprivileged Combatants*, 85:849 I.R.R.C. 45–73, 49 (2003).

[50] Jean-Marie Henckaerts, *Study on Customary International Humanitarian Law: A Contribution to the Understanding and Respect for the Rule of Law in Armed Conflict*, 87:857 I.R.R.C. 175–212 (March 2005).

[51] Amnesty International, Liberia: Human Rights Defenders Detained Incommunicado: Request for Action by West Africa Human Rights Defenders Coalitions, Public document AI Index: AFR 34/017/2002, Oct. 2, 2002.

Palestinian fighters unlawful combatants. The concept of unlawful combatant has even been legislated upon in Israel.[52] The Israeli Supreme Court has applid the concept in recent decisions pertaining to detainees captured during Israel's "Operation Cast Lead" in Gaza during December 2008–January 2009.[53] This way the detainees neither benefit from the status of civilians nor from the one of combatant. To put an end to a debate regarding the enforcement of Article 44 API, a protocol that neither country has ratified, the two countries have invented the concept of enemy combatant without even filling it with content. The danger for these two countries is the label's use by their opponents, as occurred in Liberia.

To minimize risks of having its soldiers judged for war crimes because of the refusal to grant the status of unprivileged combatant, the United States refuses to be part of the International Criminal Court and signs bilateral agreements with other countries to protect U.S. soldiers and citizens. The concept of unlawful combatant that the United States then twisted into the one of enemy combatant sprang from a 1942 U.S. Supreme Court ruling, the *ex parte Quirin* decision in which the court made a distinction between unlawful combatants and lawful combatants:

Unlawful combatants are likewise subject to capture and detention, but in addition they are subject to trial and punishment by military tribunals for acts which render their belligerency unlawful. The spy who secretly and without uniform passes the military lines of a belligerent in time of war, seeking to gather military information and communicate it to the enemy, or an enemy combatant who without uniform comes secretly through the lines for the purpose of waging war by destruction of life or property, are familiar examples of belligerents who are generally deemed not to be entitled to the status of prisoners of war, but to be offenders against the law of war subject to trial and punishment by military tribunals.[54]

With the War on Terror, the United States borrowed from this decision to further the concept of enemy combatant.[55] The term was formalized in different settings and documents related to al Qaida and the Taliban.

Al Qaeda had established its headquarters in Afghanistan, which was under the rule of the Taliban. The George W. Bush administration launched the War on

---

[52] Incarceration of Unlawful Combatants Law, 5762-2002.

[53] The two cases are *Dr. Hamdan Sofi v. State of Israel* (A.D.A 2595/09) and *Waal Atamaba v. State of Israel* (A.D.A 1510/09). For more information, see Ido Rosenzweig & Yuval Shany, *Two Unlawful Combatants Cases in the Israeli Supreme Court*, http://www.idi.org.il/sites/english/ResearchAndPrograms/NationalSecurityandDemocracy/Terrorism_and_Democracy/Newsletters/Pages/4th%20Newsletter/1/UnlawfulCombatants.aspx.

[54] Ex Parte Quirin, U.S. Supreme Court 317 U.S. 1 (1942).

[55] There was a shift on language from unlawful to enemy combatant: enemy combatant means members of al Qaeda or the Taliban held by the U.S. government as part of the War on Terror. The U.S. administration formalized the usage of this term. The category was central in the Bush administration legal construct. In 2009, the Justice Department announced it would drop the use of the term.

Terror after the events of 9/11 and targeted both groups. It designed its policy regarding captured Taliban and al Qaeda members through a constant shower of memoranda and deprived them from the status of POW on the grounds that they were unlawful combatants.[56] The decision to deprive these individuals of all protection caused an international outcry, since it was a blunt violation of international humanitarian law. Several matters of humanitarian law were relevant, all analyzed above, including those relative to Article 4 GCIII and Articles 43 and 44 API. Since the United States has not ratified API, it refers only to Article 4 GCIV and expected Taliban and al Qaeda fighters to meet all conditions set forth in Article 4. They did not meet all conditions; for example, they did not don a uniform. They also threw their weapons in bushes when U.S. soldiers captured them. The condition of wearing a uniform and wearing arms openly are two cumulative conditions that are not relaxed for irregular armies under Article 4 GCIII, but are relaxed under Article 44 API. Therefore, for the United States, the cumulative conditions were missing and Taliban and al Qaeda fighters could therefore not benefit from the POW status. Additionally, both groups had violated the rules of conflict under humanitarian law.[57] Since opponents to this analysis could not oppose Article 44 API which enforces relaxed conditions upon irregular armies, because the United States did not ratify the Protocol, they had to rely on customary law instead; the United States violated its obligations under the Geneva Conventions for the Taliban since, as stressed by Dormann, Article 4 GCIV should have applied. Besides, no fair and competent trial was established to decide whether the captured were combatants or benefited from POW status.

There is an additional legal issue regarding the status of al Qaeda fighters; they are not mercenaries and not soldiers belonging to a State. For the United States, al Qaeda fighters are terrorists. For humanitarian law, they are armed non state actors. Since there is no common legal definition of terrorism, the label of unlawful combatant cannot apply, and until a common definition is found with humanitarian consequences attached, "terrorists" benefit from humanitarian law.[58] Besides, they are also volunteers, which means they should be afforded full protection under Article 5.2 GCIII until a competent tribunal decides upon their status, and then they will benefit from fundamental guarantees.[59]

Had the United States ratified Protocol I and had Article 44 been applicable, there would have been an ethical issue with applying relaxed standards of participation in combat: indeed the Taliban and al Qaeda openly violate all rules of international humanitarian law, and it would seem to be rather unethical to enforce loosened standards of participation in hostilities to combatants who clearly have no respect for the law or for civilians' lives. This raises the matter of morality and the

---

[56] To read the documents, see GREENBERG, *supra* note 44.

[57] Bialke, *supra* note 48.

[58] Jan Klabbers, *Rebel with a Cause? Terrorists and Humanitarian Law*, 14:2 E.J.I.L. 299–312 (2003).

[59] Jennifer Leaning, *Was the Afghan Conflict a Just War*, 324 B.M.J. 353–55 (2002).

law. As stated earlier in this book, ethics is not a solid ground for humanitarian law since we all have different ethical codes. In 2009 President Barack Obama announced that the term enemy combatant would not be used anymore by the U.S. government.[60]

III. CIVILIANS OR COMBATANTS? THE PRIVATIZATION OF WAR

For some categories of people, the civilian/combatant distinction is particularly difficult because of the privatization of war. The wars in Afghanistan and Iraq have revived debates about the status of people working with or for the army as well as people working close by. Are employees of security agencies acting in Iraq to protect private companies or support the war effort civilians or combatants? What is the status of the army's medical personnel? Is a cook working for the army a combatant? Such questions were relevant already after World War II, but are more acute today with the increasing role of civilians working for the army and with the use of private companies in roles formerly reserved for the military.

A. Mercenaries

The use of mercenaries is not a new phenomenon, but there has been a sharp change with the use of private military companies and the rise of Islamic jihadists around the world.

1. Who Is a Mercenary?

Mercenaries participate in armed conflicts but are not a national or a party to the conflict. As Article 47 (2) API underlines, the mercenary is recruited for waging a war, takes part directly in the hostilities, and is motivated by private gain. He is rewarded for his participation in the conflict through a financial compensation. API approaches these actors of war by looking at their motives. Article 47 API states that a mercenary will not be granted the status of combatant or prisoner of war. Since mercenaries cannot benefit from such status when captured, they will not be repatriated at the end of the war. GCIII therefore does not apply to the mercenary. Does that mean the mercenary is a civilian, despite the fact that he takes part directly in hostilities? Mercenaries are not regular civilians since they are recognized actors of war in their own right.[61] He benefit, however, from *ad minima* protection, whether in international or non international armed conflict. International humanitarian customary law provides them with a basic protection. A mercenary who has been captured must be "treated with humanity and, in case of trial, shall not be

---

[60] Associated Press, *Obama Abandons Term "Enemy Combatant,"* AP, Mar. 13, 2009.
[61] DIETER FLECK & MICHAEL BOTHE, THE HANDBOOK OF HUMANITARIAN LAW IN ARMED CONFLICT 302 (Oxford/New York: Oxford University Press 1999).

deprived of the rights of fair and regular trial," according to Article 75 API and Common Article 3.[62] He can be tried for war crimes or other grave breaches of humanitarian law.

One of the key difficulties is to identify a mercenary; Article 5 GCIII guarantees a fair trial to determine whether someone is a combatant and will benefit from POW status. The same tribunal can determine whether the person is a mercenary or not by looking at Article 47.2 API. Article 47 sets six conditions that have been understood as cumulative:[63]

A mercenary is any person who:

(a) is specially recruited locally or abroad in order to fight in an armed conflict;

(b) does, in fact, take a direct part in the hostilities;

(c) is motivated to take part in the hostilities essentially by the desire for private gain and, in fact, is promised, by or on behalf of a Party to the conflict, material compensation substantially in excess of that promised or paid to combatants of similar ranks and functions in the armed forces of that Party;

(d) is neither a national of a Party to the conflict nor a resident of territory controlled by a Party to the conflict;

(e) is not a member of the armed forces of a Party to the conflict; and

(f) has not been sent by a State which is not a Party to the conflict on official duty as a member of its armed forces.

The definition itself is problematic. First, a mercenary must be recruited to take part in hostilities as a fighter. Furthermore, an individual is not a mercenary until he goes into combat.[64] The definition also excludes mercenaries who are integrated within an army, like the members of the Foreign Legion in France. The recruitment must be for a particular armed conflict. Instructors and advisers seem to be forgotten in the definition.[65] Yet there might be little difference between the one who advises and the one who carries out the deed.[66]

For some, this accumulation of conditions is unworkable since no mercenary can fulfill all of them.[67] The main issue is that the article takes greed and financial gain as the main component for being a mercenary and sets aside a mercenary who acts for ideological purposes. According to the definition, the jihadists who went to Bosnia in the 1990s would not be mercenaries; they would be volunteers motivated by ideological aims. However, their devotion was largely compensated as they were given houses, for instance.

---

[62] L. C. GREEN, THE CONTEMPORARY LAW OF ARMED CONFLICTS 116 (Manchester/New York/New York: St. Martin's Press 2000).

[63] DINSTEIN, SUPRA NOTE 3, at 51.

[64] Georges Aldrich, *New Life for the Laws of War*, 75 A.J.I.L. 764, 776 (1981).

[65] EDWARD K. KWAKWA, THE INTERNATIONAL LAW OF ARMED CONFLICTS : PERSONAL AND MATERIAL FIELDS OF APPLICATION 109 (Dordrecht/Boston: Kluwer Academic Publishers 1992).

[66] Fran Abrams, *British Officer Advised Gunship Killers*, THE INDEPENDENT, Sept. 7, 2000.

[67] Francois J. Hampson, *Mercenaries: Diagnosis Before Prescription*, 22:3 N.Y.I.L. 3–38 (1991).

The 1989 International Convention against the Recruitment, Use, Financing, and Training of Mercenaries keeps the same definition in its Article 1 and adds more details. A mercenary is an individual who:

1. (a) Is specially recruited locally or abroad in order to fight in an armed conflict;
   (b) Is motivated to take part in the hostilities essentially by the desire for private gain and, in fact, is promised, by or on behalf of a party to the conflict, material compensation substantially in excess of that promised or paid to combatants of similar rank and functions in the armed forces of that party;
   (c) Is neither a national of a party to the conflict nor a resident of territory controlled by a party to the conflict;
   (d) Is not a member of the armed forces of a party to the conflict; and
   (e) Has not been sent by a State which is not a party to the conflict on official duty as a member of its armed forces.

2. A mercenary is also any person who, in any other situation:
   (a) Is specially recruited locally or abroad for the purpose of participating in a concerted act of violence aimed at:
       (i) Overthrowing a Government or otherwise undermining the constitutional order of a State; or
       (ii) Undermining the territorial integrity of a State;
   (b) Is motivated to take part therein essentially by the desire for significant private gain and is prompted by the promise or payment of material compensation;
   (c) Is neither a national nor a resident of the State against which such an act is directed;
   (d) Has not been sent by a State on official duty; and
   (e) Is not a member of the armed forces of the State on whose territory the act is undertaken.

The Protocol clarifies the status to be given to mercenaries in times of armed conflict, and the protections they are to be afforded when captured. The United Nations, as well as the conventions, serve a different purpose; they seek to criminalize mercenarism and the use of mercenaries. Article 2 makes it an offense to employ a mercenary and Article 3.1 states that a mercenary who participates directly in hostilities commits an offense. That said, the Convention is not widely ratified, so Article 47 of Protocol I remains the reference for the most widely accepted definition of the notion of mercenary. The definition in the Convention is broader, and for some, this helps in including foreign Muslim volunteers who went to fight in Gaza, for example, or in Afghanistan. This is forgetting the financial gain, which is crucial to the definition of a mercenary; al Qaeda fighters did not earn anything by going to Bosnia. They were however rewarded after the war with houses and support for a family life: does that amount to financial gain? It is important to define what private gain is. Edward Kwakwa speaks as of the notion of gain a psychological element that is difficult to evaluate.[68]

2. Evolution

The status of mercenaries has evolved, with volunteers going across the globe to fight for jihad, but also with the emergence of private military companies used by States; for many analysts, these two categories of actors qualify as modern mercenaries.[69] The use of mercenaries for jihad and private contractors has raised questions: are the individuals sent across the world to fight for jihad mercenaries or volunteers? Are the British contractors sent to Iraq combatants or mercenaries? The definition of mercenary, is often political: "[i]t is difficult to define what a mercenary is. This is because the word has different meanings at different times. The different meanings it has acquired throughout history depend on the spirit of the age."[70] Some would not mind describing volunteers of al Qaeda as mercenaries to withdraw all legitimacy to them as combatants; indeed, volunteers are considered to be civilians, while the concept of mercenary is a highly negative one. Others have discussed the financial gain as being central to the definition of a mercenary. Anthony Mockler believes the true mark of a mercenary is "a devotion to war for its own sake."[71] To this, one might say that "... any definition of mercenaries which require positive proof of motivation would either be unworkable, or so haphazard in its application as between comparable individuals as to be unacceptable. Mercenaries, we think, can only be defined by reference to what they do, and not by reference to why they do it."[72] Others would like to see private military groups described as mercenary.[73] Broadening the concept of mercenary could blur the principle of distinction and affect the categories. Volunteers of al Qaeda cannot be requalified to fit a political agenda, and the use of private military companies is treated strictly under international humanitarian law, as seen above.[74]

---

[68] KWAKWA, *supra* note 67, at 110.

[69] For jihadist, see, e.g., Aliheydar Rzayev, *Foreign Mercenaries in Chechnya*, THE POLITICIAN, Mar. 30, 2005, http://www.globalpolitician.com/2504-chechnya.
For private military company employees, see, e.g., Bruce Falconer, *Showdown in Blackwater Backyard*, MOTHER JONES, Jan. 28, 2008.

[70] Holds Bashir (it is his name), quoted in Juan Carlos Zarate, *The Emergence of a New Dog of War: Private International Security Companies, International Law and the New World Disorder*, 34 STAN. J. INT'L. L. 75–162 (1998).

[71] ANTHONY MOCKLER, THE NEW MERCENARIES 35–36 (London: Sidgwick & Jackson 1985).

[72] Diplock Report, Report of the Committee of Privy Counsellors appointed to inquire into the recruitment of mercenaries, December 1972, at 2.

[73] MERCENARIES: AN AFRICAN SECURITY DILEMMA (Abdel Fatau Musah & J. Kayode Fayemi eds., London: Pluto Press 2000).

[74] DAVID SHEARER, PRIVATE ARMIES AND MILITARY INTERVENTION (Oxford: Oxford University Press, Londres 1998); Christopher Kinsey, *International Law and the Control of Mercenaries and Private Military Companies*, 52 CULTURE & CONFLICTS 91–117 (2003).

While the United States governed Iraq, U.S. armed guards did not qualify as mercenaries under Article 47 because they were nationals of a party to the conflict. When the power was transferred to the Iraqi government, these armed guards were "sent by a State which is not a party to the conflict on an official duty as a member of its armed forces" (see Article 47(1-f)) and therefore qualified as mercenaries, if one does not consider the coalition forces parties to the conflict. However, the situation remains confusing. There are also foreigners who are hired by these private military or security companies, people coming from Chile, Peru, or El Salvador.[75] Since their countries do not participate in hostilities in Iraq, they are considered mercenaries. In 2007, the United Nations released a study stating that private contractors were performing military duties. The report found that the use of contractors such as Blackwater was a "new form of mercenary activity" and identified it as illegal under international law.[76]

Another major issue is the one of prosecution; when on duty, mercenary soldiers kill civilians. In 2000, mercenaries in Sierra Leone fired on them from helicopters.[77] Kashmiris are often killed by mercenaries employed by Pakistan.[78] Mercenary forces killed twenty civilians in Pakistan, including fifteen children, in the name of the War on Terror in 2009.[79] A mercenary can be tried for his offenses under domestic law and can face execution. For example, in 1976, an Angolan Court sentenced three British citizens and an American to death; nine other mercenaries were condemned to prison terms ranging from sixteen to thirty years.[80] The French mercenary Bob Denard was tried several times.[81] In 2008, mercenaries were tried in Equatorial Guinea.[82]

[75] **Jorge Beltran** *Salvador: Soldats de Fortune et Salaires de Misère*, 932 COURRIER INTERNATIONAL, Sept. 11, 2008, translated from EL DIARIO DE HOY.

There is a scandal regarding the use of foreigners by private military and security companies in Iraq: many of those sent died of mysterious diseases upon their return. Others say they have been exposed to constant dangers See, e.g., Cesar Uco Latin American Mercenaries Guarding Baghdad's Green Zone WSWS, Dec. 28, 2005, http://www.wsws.org/articles/2005/dec2005/merc-d28.shtml; Marc de Banville Peru/Iraq : Mercenaires au rabais pour Bagdad Effet Papillon CANAL +, 2007.

[76] See The Working Group on the use of mercenaries as a means of violating human rights and impeding the exercise of self-determination, http://www2.ohchr.org/english/issues/mercenaries/index.htm.

[77] Abrams, *supra* note 68.

[78] United Nation Secretary-General, *Self Determination: Principle & the Law: Use of Mercenaries as a Means of Violating Human Rights and Impeding the Exercise of the Right of Peoples to Self-Determination*, A/49/362, Sept. 6, 1994, http://www2.ohchr.org/english/issues/mercenaries/annual.htm.

[79] *Mercenary Forces Killed 25 Civilians in Pakistan, Including 15 Children*, DAILY EXPRESS, Feb. 10, 2009.

[80] *1976: Death Sentence for Mercenaries*, BBC, http://news.bbc.co.uk/onthisday/hi/dates/stories/june/28/newsid_2520000/2520575.stm.

[81] BOB DENARD & GEORGES FLEURY, CORSAIRE DE LA REPUBLIQUE (Paris: Robert Laffont 1998).

[82] Jonathan Miller, *Equatorial Guinea: The Mercenary Confesses*, ABC, Apr. 8, 2008.

B. Private Military and Security Companies

Private military and security companies play an increasing role in armed conflicts, with deadly consequences for civilians. In 2005, a trophy video surfaced on the Internet that showed private security contractors working for Aegis Defense Service firing at Iraqi civilian vehicles in Baghdad.[83] Another scandal was later discovered involving Blackwater, another security company: in 2006, security contractors working for the company fired at fleeing Iraqi civilians.[84] The company still works in Iraq and is also employed in Afghanistan under the name of Xe. One of the outcomes of hiring private soldiers is that they often either ignore the distinction between combatants and civilians, or do not take it into consideration.

1. What are Private Military/Security Companies?

Private military/security companies have increased since the 1990s and have taken over many duties and functions that were traditionally performed by a State army: security, logistics, technical support, training, protection, intelligence gathering, analysis, custody, participation in combat, and even interrogation of prisoners are contracted. This is a real issue for humanitarian law.

Private military companies (PMC) provide special expertise or service of a military nature. The people working for these companies are often hired to protect civilians (for example, government members) or civilian infrastructure. They can also protect military infrastructure or personnel, such as the entrance to the Green Zone in Baghdad. They also protect private companies. PMCs have been used in Iraq, Afghanistan, and Colombia, where they destroy coca crops.[85] They can also train soldiers or police, provide intelligence information, or even support combat operations. In these situations, they are in direct contact and fight side by side with combatants belonging to an army and benefit from the protection of international humanitarian law. They are often denounced as employing "soldiers to hire" or mercenaries.[86] What is their status within international humanitarian law?

15 percent of the U.S presence in Iraq is represented by private contractors, and so the outsourcing of the military effort is an important phenomenon. States have also employed private military companies to help them during conflicts like those in

[83] Michel Chossudovsky, *British Mercenaries Shooting at Baghdad Motorists Is Part of "the Rules of Engagement,"* Global Research, Dec. 4, 2005, http://www.globalresearch.ca/index.php?context=va&aid=1402.

[84] Arthur Bright, *US Soldiers: Blackwater Attacked Fleeing Iraqi Civilians*, CHRISTIAN SCIENCE MONITOR, Oct. 13, 2007.

[85] Colectivo do Abogados José Alvear Restrepo, *Empresas Transnacionales de Seguridad Privada en Colombia*, Feb. 4, 2008, http://www.colectivodeabogados.org/IMG/pdf/0802_merc_wisc_esp-2.pdf.

[86] Peter W. Singer, *Outsourcing War*, Brookings Institution, March/April 2005, http://www.brookings.edu/articles/2005/0301usdepartmentofdefense_singer.aspx.

Sierra Leone and Angola. International organizations are also tempted: humanitarian aid workers are constantly being attacked by pirates in Somali waters.[87] Some speak of the possibility of having the vessels of international organizations be protected by private companies. The Dutch and Canadian armed forces protect the humanitarian ships of the Word Food Programme (WFP).[88] Some propose the involvement of NATO. This is highly problematic since humanitarian workers and the delivery of humanitarian assistance should always be neutral, which means they should not be assimilated within the armed forces of a country. By accepting military protection, the WFP went against the principle of neutral assistance, according to which no weapons should be carried or used by or around humanitarian workers. Blackwater is eyeing the high seas market: the company started offering antipiracy services in October 2008.[89] The danger of sending private military companies to fight pirates is in turning an economic phenomenon into a bloody one; most of the time, pirates shoot in the air and avoid deaths or harm. If private military companies enter the game, there will be many more casualties. The situation took a new legal turn when France arrested and deported pirates to its own soil to be judged. These Somalis were sent to France and are kept in custody in full violation of their rights. France amended its law in November 2010 to deal with these various issues.

2. Obligations under International Humanitarian Law

The employees of these companies are expected to respect international humanitarian law, and the States who employ them must ensure that they do. The Montreux document is the result of an ICRC initiative to make sure these employees know the rules of international humanitarian law;[90] it reaffirms the obligations of States to make sure that PMCs comply with humanitarian law and human rights law. There are seventy recommendations that include verifying the track record of companies and the procedures they use to recruit their staff. States should also take concrete measures to make sure the personnel of these PMCs can be prosecuted in case of serious breaches of international humanitarian law. States recruiting these companies cannot transfer their humanitarian law obligations to these companies. They have to ensure that these companies know about humanitarian law, respect it, and enforce it in the field.[91] If the PMC staff violates humanitarian law, the State that hired them might be responsible. The State of Afghanistan enacted a law to bring these companies under domestic legislation and prosecute them in Afghan courts.

---

[87] *Pirates Hijack UN Foodship Off to Somalia*, UN NEWS, Mar. 2, 2007.

[88] *Canada Saves Lives by Extending Naval Escorts to Somalia*, WFP, Sept. 25, 2008.

[89] Shanita Sinharoy, *Blackwater to Battle Pirates*, IN THESE TIMES, Jan. 26, 2009.

[90] ICRC, Montreux Document, http://www.icrc.org/web/eng/siteeng0.nsf/htmlall/montreux-document-170908/$FILE/Montreux-Document-eng.pdf.

[91] Interview with Melker Mabeck, Private Military/Security Companies "Acknowledge Humanitarian Law Obligations," Nov. 27, 2006, www.icrc.org/eng/resources/documents/interview/private-military-companies-interview-271106.htm

The Blackwater case is very informative. The security firm was at the center of a heated controversy regarding the outsourcing and privatization of war. On September 16th, 2006, several contractors killed seventeen Iraqi civilians after a car exploded near their convoy. Human rights organizations claim that U.S. regulations and Iraqi legislation allowed them to act with impunity since they could not be prosecuted under Iraqi law. Before leaving office as head of the Coalition Provisional Authority, Paul Bremer signed Coalition Provisional Authority Order 17, which says:

Contractors shall not be subject to Iraqi laws or regulations in matters relating to the terms and conditions of their Contracts, including licensing and registering employees, businesses and corporations; provided, however, that Contractors shall comply with such applicable licensing and registration laws and regulations if engaging in business or transactions in Iraq other than Contracts. Notwithstanding any provisions in this Order, Private Security Companies and their employees operating in Iraq must comply with all CPA Orders, Regulations, Memoranda, and any implementing instructions or regulations governing the existence and activities of Private Security Companies in Iraq, including registration and licensing of weapons and firearms.[92]

This created a dangerous legal vacuum.[93] Since then, the government of Iraq took legal measures, and all PMC has lost its immunity in Iraq.[94]

The outrage in Iraq and the international outcry were such that the U.S. authorities decided to prosecute the Blackwater guards under domestic laws. Five were prosecuted at the federal level in the United States; they were facing charges of voluntary manslaughter, attempt to commit manslaughter, and weapons violations.[95] This case was supposed to be shaping a precedent, since the accused were U.S. citizens working under a U.S. contract. It was the first time defense contractors working for a PMC were to be charged under the Military Extraterritorial Judiciary Act, which allows for the prosecution of civilian contractors who commit a crime while working for the U.S. Department of Defense (DOD) abroad. Indeed, the law was extended in 2004 to include non-DOD contractors who support military missions abroad. The Blackwater guards were therefore not judged for breaches of humanitarian law but under domestic law. The trial was set for early 2010, but the charges were dismissed.

Washington, DC – based Human Rights First praised the introduction of legislation authored to clarify and expand the jurisdiction of U.S. courts over serious crimes committed by private contractors deployed abroad by the United States. The Civilian Extraterritorial Jurisdiction Act (CEJA) of 2010, introduced simultaneously

---

[92] Coalition Provisional Authority Order Number 17 (Revised), Status of the Coalition Provisional Authority, www.iilj.org/courses/documents/Order17.Section4.pdf
[93] Michael Hirsch, *The Age of Irresponsibility*, Newsweek, Sept. 20, 2007.
[94] Patrick Cockburn, *Security Firms Lose Immunity in Iraq Deal*, The Independent, July 10, 2008.
[95] Nathan Hodge, *Accused Blackwater Shooters Face Trial in DC*, The Wire, Dec. 9, 2008.

by Senator Patrick Leahy and Representative David Price, clarifies and expands the jurisdiction of U.S. courts in these cases. "Failing to hold contractors accountable for serious crimes in war zones abroad has created a culture of impunity which has fostered hostility among civilian populations towards the United States. This increases the threat to U.S military personnel and contractors and undermines the U.S. mission," wrote Human Rights First President and CEO Elisa Massimino in a letter to Senator Leahy and Representative Price.

The Blackwater group still exists and now acts in Afghanistan under the name Xe Services; their men have already killed civilians. This time they have signed contracts making them liable for prosecution under Afghan laws.[96]

3. Combatants or Civilians?

Many have compared workers of PMCs to modern mercenaries. However, unless they are hired to fight in the armed conflict, and unless they take a direct part in hostilities, they do not fit within the definition of mercenaries.[97] Most contractors are civilians: guards, waterworks engineers, escorts of food convoys, logistics and communications officers. There is a problem with civilians who are armed and those who take part in hostilities during armed conflicts. There is an overlap of roles; civilians assume military roles, which is a threat to the principle of distinction. The Third Geneva Convention does not distinguish between defense contractors and private military companies. They are qualified as supply contractors. They cannot directly take part in the hostilities. The supply contractor has issues with a valid identity card from the armed forces they accompany. Private contractors and people working for private military companies seem to be neither civilians nor combatants. In fact, the categorization depends upon several factors: the nature of the contract; the level of integration within the structure; whether the contractor is armed or not; the nature of the work; and the actual operations. A case-by-case analysis is risky since it opens the path to abuses. There is again no grey zone or legal vacuum; humanitarian law is applicable, although PMCs are not directly addressed in the Geneva Conventions or the Protocols. The solution given by humanitarian law is that contractors are unprivileged combatants, as clearly said in the Military Commissions Act. They are therefore not entitled to POW status and can be prosecuted under the relevant domestic legislation. If captured, these people will benefit from the *ad minima* protection granted by customary international law (Article 75), domestic law, and international human rights law.

[96] *After Iraq, Blackwater Haunts Afghans*, ISLAMONLINE, Aug. 13, 2009, http://www.islamonline.net/servlet/Satellite?c=Article_C&cid=1248187910938&pagename=Zone-English-News/NWELayout.
[97] Jamie A. Williamson, *Status and Obligations of Mercenaries and Private Military/Security Companies under International Humanitarian Law, in* ELIMINATION OF MERCENARISM IN AFRICA: A NEED FOR A NEW CONTINENTAL APPROACH (Sabelo Gumedze ed., Pretoria: Institute for Security Studies 2008).

In the field, complex situations arise. In September 2004, a private contractor was sentenced for torturing Afghans and running a private prison in Kabul. He argued that he had been conducting a mission on behalf of NATO and the International Security Assistance Forces (ISAF). When asked, the military staff of ISAF said they thought the contractor was part of the U.S. army since he wore a U.S.-style uniform.[98] Other contractors can be compared to humanitarian workers because they work in civilian clothing and use number plates normally associated with humanitarian organizations. This is extremely dangerous as it jeopardizes the security of real humanitarians. Furthermore, private contractors try to benefit from this blurring of roles with humanitarians and from this space between the categories of civilians and combatants to appear as extensions of humanitarian action and consequently jeopardize the neutrality of humanitarian actions and organizations.

C. Civilians Working for an Army

States have enhanced civilians' roles in the army as an outcome of the privatization of armed forces in several countries and the need for expertise. Civilian experts play a crucial role, and a further increase is to be expected in years to come. These civilians working for the army operate in war zones, which exposes them to higher risks. The problem is that the army sometimes offers training to these civilians.[99]

The ICRC commentary clarifies the situation of soldiers who do not fire but have a role in the army and are therefore legitimate targets; a lawyer and an administrative assistant are both legitimate targets. This does not apply to military doctors and religious personnel; they cannot be targeted, even if they work for the army. Civilians working for the army as cooks or drivers are also clearly not lawful targets for the ICRC since they do not directly take part in hostilities.[100] The commentary concludes with the rejection of the concept of "quasi-combatants." There is no semi-civilian or semi-combatant. A civilian who is incorporated in an armed organization and takes part directly in hostilities is a combatant during the duration of hostilities.

There are complex situations arising every day. For example, in 2003, the Taliban press spokesman, Mullah Abd al-Salam Zaeef, was arrested in Pakistan. He is now at Guantanamo Bay and is considered an enemy combatant. Zaeef never seems to have directly taken part in hostilities; he performed a job as a civilian. There are therefore debates regarding the legality and legitimacy of his imprisonment at Guantanamo and his label as an enemy combatant. The question is also accurate for all Iraqi translators operating for the U.S army, but also for drivers and cooks. All these civilians have paid a heavy price working for the Allies.[101]

---

[98] Claude Voillat, *Private Military Companies: A Word of Caution*, Humanitarian Exchange Magazine 28 (November 2004).

[99] Steve Vogel, *Army Is Offering Civilian Workers More Training*, Washington Post, Feb. 4, 2009.

[100] Melzer, *supra* note 5.

[101] Pratap Chatterjee, *Civilian Translators in Iraq Thrust into Combat Roles?*, Interpress Service, Aug. 12, 2006.

The distinction between civilians and combatants has proved a challenge, in particular in the twenty-first century. There seems to be a shift from the status of civilians to that of combatant—except for the fact that such a shift is impossible. Therefore, international humanitarian law provides for all those who fall in between categories. In general, organizations such as the ICRC prefer to give a tight meaning to the concept of direct participation in hostilities so that the principle of distinction remains intact and so that those who will fall in between the two categories constitute a small group. It remains in practice difficult to distinguish between combatants and civilians for several reasons. Combatants can hide in the midst of a civilian population. For example, in Iraq it is sometimes very difficult to know who is a civilian and who is a combatant since even a young girl could be a suicide bomber.[102] Former combatants hide among refugees to leave Rwanda, and hide in camps in Congo. During the siege of Gaza in the winter of 2008–09, it was reported that Hamas fighters would mingle with the population in order to go unnoticed. Therefore, the decision whether to attack places where civilians and combatants intermix is up to the other belligerent, who often disregards the rule according to which a civilian building in which soldiers are present does not constitute a legitimate target unless it has a military purpose. This type of decision can lead to humanitarian violations, such as the killing of one thousand Somalis by American forces in the First Battle of Mogadishu, which is often depicted as a failed enterprise by the U.S army and as a disaster by onlookers and experts. According to Mark Bowden, 80 percent of the Somalis killed were civilians, caught between the U.S. military and combatants who hid among them. Mark Bowden said in an interview about the onslaught:

> If you feel the need to go to war against an enemy that is not as powerful as you are, one of the tactics of the weaker party is to hide among civilians, and use the global media to advertise the horror of the onslaught [...] The parallel with Mogadishu is that gunmen in that battle hid behind walls of civilians and were aware of the restraint of the (Army) Rangers. These gunmen literally shot over the heads of civilians, or between their legs. They used women and children for this.[103]

The blurring of categories is a reality, but when the situation becomes so complicated and burdened with doubts, one can refer to the principle of proportionality, according to which it is illegal to attack if the damage caused to civilians would be excessive in relation to the military advantaged gained.

---

[102] Martin Chulov, *Raid Uncovers al-Qaida Network of Child Suicide Bombers in Iraq*, THE GUARDIAN, Dec. 4, 2008.

[103] Interview with Jeffrey Goldberg, *Does "Black Hawk Down" Portray an American War Crime?*, THE ATLANTIC, Jan. 13, 2009.

5 Concrete Challenges: the Evolution of War— Asymmetric Conflicts, Terrorism, and Weapon Technology

The principle of distinction seems to blur when civilians take part in hostilities. However, humanitarian law addresses all situations and, additionally, the ICRC, which is depicted as the custodian of international humanitarian law,[1] issues studies such as the ones on customary law and direct participation, to clarify concepts. The Additional Protocols to the Geneva Conventions were, for example, a formalized legal attempt to respond to humanitarian issues. With this legal guidance, the principle of distinction is not only affirmed, but also clarified and protected from any attempt to create subcategories. The principle of distinction and the protection of civilians and captured, sick, or wounded combatants remain the core of this body of law, while the law of armed conflicts tries to adapt to humanitarian law for war needs. The law of armed conflicts addresses the conduct of hostilities and the protection of combatants; it hardly takes civilians into account. This is the major difference between the Hague law and the Geneva law: they complete each other in that sense. This ability to cover all situations to ensure the respect of the principle of distinction is the outcome of the work carried out mainly by the ICRC.

The difficulty of maintaining this distinction is the result of the evolution of warfare; combatants nowadays fight differently than our ancestors fought. Hand-to-hand combat is extremely rare, and bombing has become the main warring tool.

---

[1] John F. Hutchinson, *"Custodians of the Sacred Fire": The ICRC and the Postwar Reorganization of the International Red Cross*, in INTERNATIONAL HEALTH ORGANISATIONS AND MOVEMENTS 1918–1939 17 (Paul Weindling ed., Cambridge/New York, NY, USA: Cambridge University Press 1995).

The 1991 Gulf War was an illustration of a computerized war, with the use of civilian experts and little fighting on the ground. The wars in Iraq and Afghanistan have required a return to field combat in addition to air strikes. All these changes have put international humanitarian law, in particular, the principle of distinction, to the test. We will analyze in this chapter how the law has been adapted and expanded to respond to three major changes: asymmetric conflicts (self-determination struggles), terrorism, and the evolution of weapons.

I. THE DEFINITION OF ASYMMETRIC CONFLICT

Many experts declared after 9/11 that we were entering an era of asymmetric conflict.[2] This is a slightly erroneous statement, however. Asymmetric warfare has existed as long as war has existed. Examples of asymmetric conflicts include terrorism, counterterrorism, self-determination struggles, and counterinsurgencies. An illustration of an early asymmetric war would be the struggle of Kahina, Queen of the Berber, who led a coalition of tribes against the Romans in the first century CE. The reason why the term has suddenly became so popular, in particular in the news, is because in 2004, the U.S. military began using the concept and understood that it had to work on the challenges pertaining to this type of warfare. Since terrorism is a wide phenomenon in itself, it will be analyzed in the next section of this chapter.

A. What Is an Asymmetric Conflict?

A symmetric war is the classic opposition between two belligerents facing each other. The two belligerents have the same military power and use conventional warfare strategies and weapons.[3] In asymmetrical warfare, there are two or more belligerents who have different military power. A regular army often fights a ghost enemy leading the "war of the poor."[4] There is a disparity in force as well as different aims, different strategies, and different weapons.[5] Therefore, groups using asymmetry as a strategy differ in essence from a regular army. The outcome is unconventional warfare, during which the weaker party uses any means possible and searches to exploit the other belligerent's weaknesses.[6] One of the outcomes is that the

---

[2] See, e.g., John W. Jandora, *Center of Gravity and Asymmetric Conflict: Factoring in Culture*, 39 J.F.Q. 78–83 (2005).

[3] Andrew Mack, *Why Big Nations Lose Small Wars: The Politics of Asymmetric Conflict*, 27:2 WORLD POLITICS 175–200 (1975).

[4] Georges Abi-Saab, *Wars of National Liberation in the Geneva Conventions and Protocols*, 416, 416–30, 417, *in* 165 RECUEIL DES COURS (Académie de Droit International de la Haye/Hague Academy of International Law 1979).

[5] Carsten Bockstette, *Jihadist Terrorist Use of Strategic Communication Management Techniques*, George C. Marshall Center for European Security Studies paper, December 2008, http://www.marshallcenter.org/mcpublicweb/MCDocs/files/College/F_ResearchProgram/occPapers/occ-paper_20-en.pdf.

[6] Robert Tomes, *Relearning Counterinsurgency Warfare*, 2 Parameters 16–28 (Spring 2004).

strategies used might not be "militarized,"[7] which makes it difficult for regular armies and powers to respond. During asymmetric conflicts, the fighting does not take place within a definite space, there are no clear frontlines, and the weakest party uses all means available, in particular guerrilla methods. A group resorting to asymmetric methods of war is mobile, discreet, and acts by surprise. The combatants work in small units and use ambushes and raids to combat the formal army. They usually use a field that they know well, or a field that facilitates the methods they use, such as the jungle. This is why it is called the "war of the flea."[8] It is interesting to stress that the weak party in these conflicts usually wins the war or has a definitive advantage, mainly because they do not follow the rules for war: it gives them an important advantage.[9] Steven Metz and Douglas Johnston have offered the following definition regarding asymmetric warfare:[10]

In the realm of military affairs and national security, asymmetry is acting, organizing, and thinking differently than opponents in order to maximize one's own advantages, exploit an opponent's weaknesses, attain the initiative, or gain greater freedom of action. It can be political-strategic, military strategic, or a combination of these. It can entail different methods, technologies values, organizations, time perspectives, or some combination of these. It can be short-term or long-term. It can be deliberate or by default. It can be discrete or pursued in combination with symmetric approaches. It can have both psychological and physical dimensions.

As Che Guevara said when he described guerrilla warfare:

The guerrilla band is an armed nucleus, the fighting vanguard of the people. It draws its great force from the mass of the people themselves. The guerrilla band is not to be considered inferior to the army against which it fights simply because it is inferior in fire power. Guerrilla warfare is used by the side which is supported by a majority but which possesses a much smaller number of arms for use in defense against oppression.[11]

Sun Tzu's *Art of War*, written in the fifth century BC and describing how best to conduct mobile guerrilla warfare, influenced the more recent work of Mao Tse Tung. The Roman strategist Vegetius spoke about asymmetry in *Epitoma*

---

[7] EKATERINA STEPANOVA, TERRORISM IN ASYMMETRIC CONFLICT: IDEOLOGICAL AND STRUCTURAL ASPECTS (Oxford/New York: Oxford University Press 2008).

[8] ROBERT TABER, THE WAR OF THE FLEA: A STUDY OF GUERRILLA WARFARE THEORY AND PRACTISE (New York: L. Stuart 1965).

[9] ROBERT B. ASPREY, WAR IN THE SHADOWS: THE CLASSIC HISTORY OF GUERRILLA WARFARE FROM ANCIENT PERSIA TO PRESENT (London: Little, Brown 1994).

[10] STEVEN METZ & DOUGLAS V. JOHNSON MET, ASYMMETRY AND U.S. MILITARY STRATEGY: DEFINITION, BACKGROUND, AND STRATEGIC CONCEPTS (Carlisle Barracks, Pa: Strategic Studies Institute, U.S. Army War College 2001).

[11] ERNESTO GUEVARA, GUERRILLA WARFARE 3 (New York: Vintage Books 1961).

rei militaris.[12] As historian of the Peloponnesian War, Herodotus provides detailed accounts of the plans, stratagems, and tactics the Greeks utilized against a superior adversary. In the Battles of Marathon and Salamis, the Greeks were outnumbered but defeated the Persians by using unconventional methods. A more recent illustration is the opposition the Soviet troops met when they entered Afghanistan in 1979 to respond to the call of the Afghan government that wished to put the diverse mujahedeen groups under control. The Red Army was severely defeated by the mujahedeen, who used unconventional techniques of warfare.[13] The Taliban today is using the same tactics.[14] Another illustration of asymmetric warfare is the Iraqi insurgency, which sets off small explosive devices on the streets when American tanks pass by.[15] The suicide bombing technique used in the context of the Palestinian-Israeli conflict is another example of asymmetric warfare.[16] As Osama bin Laden sums it up, these groups do not find their strength in conventionally military weapons and strategies:

> The difference between us and our adversaries in terms of military strength, manpower, and equipment is very huge. But, for the grace of God, the difference is also very huge in terms of psychological resources, faith, certainty, and reliance on the Almighty God. This difference between us and them is very, very huge and great.[17]

Unconventional warfare in an asymmetrical conflict is often associated either with wars of national liberation or with terrorism.

B. Asymmetric Conflict in the Twenty-First Century: A Challenge

The phenomenon of asymmetrical warfare is not new. It goes back in history as far as the Parthians, who used asymmetric strategies to free Persia from the

---

[12] Vegetius, Vegetius: Epitome of Military Science (N. P. Milner trans., Liverpool: Liverpool University Press 1996).

[13] Ali Ahmad Jalili et al., Afghan Guerilla Warfare: In the Words of the Mujahideen Fighters (Osceola, WI: Zenith Press 2002).

[14] Thomas H. Johnson & M. Chris Mason, *Understanding the Taliban and Insurgency in Afghanistan*, Orbis 71–89 (Winter 2007).

[15] Evan Thomas & John Barry, *A New Way of War*, Newsweek, Aug. 20–27, 2007.

[16] Robert J. Bunker & John P. Sullivan, *Suicide Bombings in Operation Iraqi Freedom*, 46 Land Warfare Papers, Institute for Land Warfare, 2004, http://www.ausa.org/PDFdocs//LWP%5F46 Bunker.pdf.

[17] Foreign Broadcast Information System, Al-Jazirah Airs "Selected Portions" of Latest Al-Qa'ida Tape on 11 Sept. Attacks, Doha Al-Jazirah Satellite Channel Television in Arabic 1835 GMT Apr. 18, 2002, Compilation of Usama Bin Laden Statements 1994–January 2004 (January 2004), at 191, 194, cited in Michael N. Schmitt, *Asymmetrical Warfare and International Humanitarian Law, in* International Humanitarian Law Facing New Challenges: Symposium in Honor of Knut Ipsen 11–48 (Wolff Heintschel von Heinegg & Volker Epping eds., Berlin/New York: Springer 2007).

Seleucid rule.[18] The Parthians used the war of the poor against all invaders.[19] Other
examples include the defeat of General Edward Braddock in the French and Indian
wars,[20] and more recently, the opposition the Russian army met when it entered
Chechnya.[21] The novelty is that asymmetric warfare has transformed because of
technological developments that coincided with the postwar era of decolonization.
The spread of technology and in particular the Internet makes it possible for groups
to exchange tips and acquire new weapons, or learn techniques and strategies.
Everyday instruments like a mobile phone or an iPod become deadly weapons in the
hands of such groups. People who cannot afford to buy the latest traditional weaponry use small exploding devices to harass regular troops and cause deaths and injuries that will strike the public's imagination.[22] Other than ambushes and raids, the
fighters can also use, for example, a medical vehicle to cover an attack or to ambush
the other belligerent. For example, the belligerents in Sudan are known for ambush-
ing humanitarian aid convoys to steal the cars and medical vehicles.[23] They later
carry out attacks with them, using the emblems as a decoy.

All these changes have in a way popularized the concept, which is now well known
to the public because of its extensive use by terrorist groups like al Qaeda or Abu
Sayyaf, or groups whose identity has been blurred with time like the Colombian
FARC. Asymmetric warfare has also become popular since it is used by groups
fighting the U.S. presence in Iraq and in Afghanistan. Asymmetrical wars are also
used in internal settings—for example, Somalia, which is characterized as a
noninternational armed conflict, has a weak government struggling with various
Islamic groups. These groups harass the government by striking regularly in an
unconventional fashion, and often turn to tactics prohibited by the *jus in bello*. On
February 22, 2009, the group called al-Shabaab conducted a suicide car bomb attack
against an African Union military base in Mogadishu and killed six Burundian
peacekeepers.[24] During the ongoing Siege of Badoia that started in July 2008, conducted by the Islamic Courts Union's Al Shabaab, Islamist fighters attacked an
Ethiopian army convoy, killing two soldiers and one civilian.

The most important issue with asymmetric warfare today is its use by terrorist
groups and groups that are fighting for self-determination. One should not,
however, associate asymmetric warfare with terrorism since asymmetric warfare is
only part of terrorism. In addition, there is an issue with the concept of terrorism
and who uses it, for example, a self-determination group such as the ANC in

---

[18] ADAM LOWTHER, HISTORY OF WARFARE AND MILITARY THOUGHT 10 (Glenn Segell/LPCS:
London 2006).

[19] Vincent Goulding, *Back to the Future with Asymmetric Warfare*, PARAMETERS 21–30 (2000).

[20] RENE CHARTRAND, MONONGAHELA, 1754–1755: WASHINGTON'S DEFEAT, BRADDOCK'S DISASTER
(United Kingdom: Osprey Publishing 2004).

[21] *Ivan Safranchuk*, Chechnya: Russia's Experience of Asymmetrical Warfare, Center for Defense
Information, 2002, http://www.cdi.org/terrorism/chechnya-pr.cfm.

[22] Johnson, *supra* note 14.

[23] *Humanitarian Convoy Attacked in Darfur*, REUTERS, FRANCE, 24, Sept. 22, 2007.

[24] *Bombs Kill Somalia Peacekeepers*, BBC, Feb. 22, 2009.

South Africa in the 1960s might use asymmetric warfare as a strategy. It was labeled a terrorist group by the apartheid regime of the time, but was considered a self-determination group by the international community.[25] Another example is the Kashmiris, who fight for self-determination according to some, but are labeled terrorists by others.

The Additional Protocols have set up rules regarding civilians and combatants in the setting of a struggle for self-determination. The most important step was Article 44 Additional Protocol I (API), which relaxes the standards to be considered a combatant so that self-determination fighters would be better protected. However, despite this major legal step, there are still issues: civilians participate in hostilities in various ways but are also often caught between parties to a conflict. It is then difficult to distinguish between combatants and civilians for several reasons: they tend to intermix. Combatants can hide in the midst of a civilian population. For example, during the siege of Gaza in the winter of 2008–09, it was reported that Hamas fighters would mingle with the population to go unnoticed. The brief following study will shed light on how humanitarian law protects actors in asymmetric conflicts, and what recent challenges have arisen.

II. WARS OF SELF-DETERMINATION AND ARMED STRUGGLES: THE DISTINCTION DURING WARS OF NATIONAL LIBERATION

The two most recurrent types of asymmetrical wars are self-determination wars/national liberation struggles and terrorism.

A. War of Self-Determination

Wars of national liberation often feature groups that are weaker than the State or the other party; these groups struggle for self-determination and call themselves freedom fighters, while their opponents often think of them as terrorists. They mostly use guerrilla warfare. These wars are not a new phenomenon. One can go back as far as 66–73 BCE during the First Jewish-Roman War, which was a war of national liberation, during which the Jews of Judea tried to put an end to the Roman occupation, in vain.[26] The zealots led a guerrilla war and one of its factions, the Sicarii (knife wielders) were urban freedom fighters (terrorists to the Roman Empire) who killed the people who collaborated with the Romans.[27] The Scots' opposition to the British invasion in the thirteenth and fourteenth centuries was also a struggle for

---

[25] Anisseh Van Engeland & Rachael Rudolph, From Terrorism to Politics (Aldershot, UK: Ashgate 2008).

[26] John Haralson Haynes & Sarah R. Mandell, The Jewish People in Classical Antiquity: From Alexander to Bar Kochba (Louisville, Ky.: Westminster John Knox Press 1998).

[27] Gerard Chaliand & Arnaud Blin, Histoire Du Terrorisme: De L'antiquite A Al Qaeda 59 (Paris: Bayard 2004).

self-determination. One of its heroes, William Wallace, believed in guerrilla warfare to overcome the enemy.[28] More recently was the First Indochina War (1946–1954), during which guerrilla warfare was used against the French in remote areas. The Việt Minh progressed through raids, skirmishes, and guerrilla attacks. This war also demonstrates the use of tactics aimed at harassing the colonial power so that the costs of occupation would become too high to carry on.[29] Another illustration is the sabotage campaign of the ANC that aimed at harassing the apartheid regime and at making the discrimination regime quite expensive.[30] The period following World War II was very active, with countries fighting to gain their independence. It is to answer that challenge that the Additional Protocols were drafted. Since decolonization was not a peaceful process most of the time, the AP provided more protection to freedom fighters than to unprivileged combatants.

B. International Humanitarian Law and Wars of Self-Determination

1. Applicable Law

The Geneva Conventions hardly address wars of national liberation. Fighters who took part in such struggles were not considered combatants and could not be POWs. The first matter was to know whether the Geneva Conventions could be applicable to wars of national liberation. Indeed, many wondered whether national liberation movements could be bound by the Conventions, referring to Article 59 GCII regarding accession to the Conventions: "From the date of its coming in force, it shall be open to any Power in whose name the present Convention has not yet been signed, to accede to this Convention." Common Article 2 (3) was also referred to: "Although one of the Powers in conflict may not be a party to the present Convention, the Powers who are parties thereto shall remain bound by it in their mutual relations. They shall furthermore be bound by the Convention in relation to the said Power, if the latter accepts and applies the provisions thereof." Therefore, it was understood that national liberation movements could accede to the Geneva Conventions. There were many criticisms about this interpretation, with objectors saying that the powers included only States and that non state armed groups should not be included. The drafters probably never intended to have national liberation movements becoming a party to the Conventions, or to be bound by them.[31] Others said this extrapolation

---

[28] D. J. GRAY, WILLIAM WALLACE: THE KING'S ENEMY (London: R. Hale 1991).

[29] MICHEL BODIN, LES COMBATTANTS FRANÇAIS FACE A LA GUERRE D'INDOCHINE (Paris, L'Harmattan 1998).

[30] VAN ENGELAND, *supra* note 25.

[31] Antonio Cassese, *Wars of National Liberation and Humanitarian Law*, 316 in STUDIES AND ESSAYS ON INTERNATIONAL HUMANITARIAN LAW AND RED CROSS PRINCIPLES 313–24 (Christophe Swinarski ed., Geneva: CICR/Martinus Nijhoff Publishers 1984).

was necessary in order to answer the new challenges that arose in the 1960s, when wars of national liberation raged.[32]

There was another problem: since at the time, wars of national liberation were regarded as non international conflict, they fell outside the scope of the largest part of the Geneva Conventions, except for Common Article 3. Self-determination fighters were consequently unprivileged combatants benefiting at the time from Common Article 3's protection. This qualification had an impact on the protection of civilians, since until the drafting of Protocol II (APII), Article 3 only afforded the basic protection in non international armed conflicts. Civilians benefited therefore from the ad minima protection granted by Common Article 3. The nature of these wars evolved, and soon it was clear that the approach of the Geneva Conventions was not satisfying and did not bring enough protection to civilians and combatants. The debate intensified with the decolonization process, and that is why the Additional Protocols were drafted. Wars of national liberation were approached as international armed conflicts, mostly thanks to UN resolutions.[33] During the Travaux Préparatoires for the Protocols, the first ICRC's draft of the Protocols did not reflect this evolution, and there was no reference to wars of national liberation. The pressure of Third World Countries had an effect, and eventually, the ICRC had to review its position. The most important step was to include wars of national liberation in the category of international armed conflicts, which meant that more laws were applicable to the issue. This step also afforded citizens better protection, in particular, the protection set forth in Protocol I. Article 1 of Protocol I sets forth general principles and the scope of application. Its paragraph 2 speaks of the distinction between combatants and civilians, and the protection from which they benefit is strengthened "in cases not covered by this Protocol or by the other international agreements, civilians and combatants remain under the protection and authority of the principles of international law derived from established custom, from the principles of humanity and from the dictates of public conscience."

The other important innovation was the extension of the status of combatants and POWs to self-determination fighters (Article 44 API) taking part in hostilities, as long as they are part of an armed force. The standards to be considered a combatant are lowered in regard to Article 4 GCIII. The four cumulative criteria—subordination to a responsible command, a fixed distinctive emblem, arms carried openly, and respect of international humanitarian law—are therefore to be found in GCIII, and only a combatant who meets all the criteria will be granted POW status. Article 44 API loosened the conditions to take into consideration the evolving notion of a combatant.

---

[32] Dietrich Schlindler, *The Different Types of Armed Conflicts According to the Geneva Conventions and Protocols*, RECUEIL DES COURS 135 (1979).

[33] Georges Abi-Saab, *Wars of National Liberation and the Laws of War*, 3 ANNALS OF INTERNATIONAL STUDIES 93–118 (1972).

2. Limits of These International Documents

There are, however, limits. Article 1 API does not cover all cases of national liberation; it targets in paragraph 4 "armed conflicts in which peoples are fighting against colonial domination and alien occupation and against racist regimes in the exercise of their right of self determination." In reality, very few wars of national liberation fall within the scope of Article 1. This could mean that many civilians involved in wars of national liberation not cited in Article 1.4 are not provided with adequate protection. Classic cases of war of national liberation, such as the ones witnessed in the post–World War II period, are covered. However, the Protocol might not apply to situations of struggle for self-determination by a small entity included in a State, such as the Mindanao case in the Philippines, because there is no alien occupation *stricto sensu* and no racist regime. Another issue lies with Article 44; it does not specify how a combatant is supposed to distinguish himself from a civilian. There is no rule, norm, or sign that would help make the distinction, except if the combatant were to fulfill the rules set up in Articles 43 and 44 API regarding uniforms or arms carried openly. What would happen if a combatant belonging to an armed group wore no insignia or uniform and threw away his weapons when the other party reached him? What would distinguish him from a civilian? Another problem with Protocol I is that it has not been ratified by all countries that have ratified the Geneva Conventions. The reason is that most of the time, States consider freedom fighters to be terrorists. This is also why the United States chose not to ratify API.

These issues are problematic since in this type of conflict, it is very difficult to uphold the distinction between civilians and combatants. Besides, fighters hide within the population or have the support of civilians. Therefore, the distinction relies on the capacity to give a clear-cut definition of each actor: who is a combatant and who is a civilian in wars of national liberation? A combatant in such wars benefits from protection, thanks to Article 44 API, which says that the fighters will enjoy the status of privileged combatants and are not compelled to carry arms at all times, or to wear a uniform. The aim of Article 44 was to adapt Article 4 GCIII to reality; it was indeed difficult to find members of national liberation movements who would fulfill the four criteria to be a combatant, and therefore, they benefited from little protection as unprivileged belligerents. The first criterion of Article 4 GCIII is rather easy to respect; the combatants have to be part of a group that is a party to the conflict. This is clearly a way of putting aside banditism. The problem is that with time, some groups who claim to fight wars of national liberation have become bandits, like the FARC. In addition, it might be difficult to assess the linkage of a group with a party to the conflict. In Darfur, parties to the conflict change on a weekly basis, with groups seceding from other groups. Is each one still a party to the conflict? The matter of the internal hierarchy is not really an issue since every movement has an internal structure. Then it is said that the movement must act in accordance with the laws and customs of war. This raises some practical issues, since most combatants ignore the Geneva Conventions until they understand that they have an interest in respecting humanitarian law: humanitarian law will apply to them, and it will protect them.

It remains that the FARC is very well versed in the Geneva Conventions, but doesn't follow them, or rather, adapts them to its own needs. The problem is more about the fixed distinctive sign recognizable at a distance, and carrying arms openly. Very rarely do combatants belonging to national liberation movements wear insignia, for fear of being recognized and targeted, and rarely do they carry arms openly for the same reason. This is why Article 44 API presents relaxed criteria. There are practical problems regarding the application of these rules to these groups. Therefore, Additional Protocol I had to reconcile the spirit of humanitarian law—which is to protect civilians—with the nature of these movements—which is to be discreet and to move swiftly around in order to puzzle the enemy. Acting like a State army is rarely an option for these groups.

There is an issue with the Geneva Convention regarding the protection of civilians during asymmetric wars: the Fourth Convention focuses on two legal concepts, nationality and occupied territory, as legal criteria for protection. These two concepts are rather difficult to apply in wars of national liberation. A possible interpretation would be to qualify the colonial or alien power as an occupation power in the territory fought for. Therefore, civilians would benefit fully from the Fourth Geneva Convention. It is, however, difficult to speak of an occupation without taking sides. Saying that Mindanao is an occupied territory comes down to agreeing with the request of the Muslims of Mindanao for independence; humanitarian law would then become a political tool. For the Filipino government, Mindanao is part of the country, and there is no occupation. Therefore, although this interpretation provides protection to the civilians, it also somehow grants legitimacy to the claims of self-determination groups.

All these questions are still open to debate, and do concretely affect wars of national liberation. An important step would probably be to define clearly what terrorism is, in order to differentiate it from freedom fighters' actions. There have been numerous attempts to define terrorism, but it is a highly controversial topic. In the meantime, humanitarian law provides protection to combatants and civilians engaged in a war for national liberation.

3. Protection of Civilians

Since national liberation movements resort to guerrilla methods, the civilian population finds itself exposed to grave dangers; the invisibility and the mobility of the groups, as well as the non conventional warfare methods, often require the participation of the population. They might be forced to host *guerrilleros*, or to have them living in their midst. Other civilians might openly support the movements for political reasons, and provide shelter. This cannot be punishable; as Abi-Saab underlines, this support is often natural since the community as a whole seeks to fulfill self-determination and considers the *guerrilleros* freedom fighters.[34] At other times,

---

[34] Georges Abi-Saab, *Wars of National Liberation and the Laws of War*, 3 ANNALES D'ETUDES INT'L. 101–03 (1972).

however, civilians are the victims of national liberation groups. In these types of conflicts, it is again difficult to distinguish the civilians from the combatants. The issue is that the support brought by civilians is an argument used by the other party to the conflict to commit atrocities. For example, the French in Algeria systematically targeted civilians supporting the National Liberation Front (NLF) during the Algerian War of Independence. The NLF use tactics that resembled the tactics used by groups in Asia (the hit-and-run tactics formalized by Mao Tse Tung) that the French army already had to struggle with in Indochina. The FLN also massacred Pieds-Noirs civilians near the town of Philippeville (Skikda today) in August 1955, including old women and babies.

Additional Protocol I completes the Fourth Geneva Convention and addresses more clearly the issue of wars of national liberation and guerrilla warfare methods. Protocol I was drafted in part to answer the issues raised by the application of the Fourth Geneva Convention to wars of national liberation and guerrilla warfare. Article 1-4 and Article 96-3 include special provisions about wars of national liberation. This actually creates a linkage between a war of self-determination and an occupying power. Articles 1, 4, and 96 (3) bring the solution to the issue of the two concepts of "nationality" and "occupied territory"; the interpretation set above is definitive. The colonial or alien power fought against is seen as an occupation power. The Protocol also deals quite extensively with guerrilla warfare strategies and methods to protect civilians in all possible situations. Article 48 places a positive obligation on the parties to the conflict to clearly distinguish civilians from combatants, as well as civilian objects from military objectives. Article 50 (3) states an extremely important rule in the case of wars of national liberation: the presence of non civilians amid civilians does not deprive the latter of their civilian character. As stated earlier, the population cannot be attacked because combatants are living with civilians, hiding among them, or because the population supports the fighters (Article 51-2). The civilian population cannot be the target of indiscriminate attacks (Article 51 (3) and (4)), and there can be no attacks against civilians as a way of reprisal (Article 51 (6)). These rules are an ameliorated version of the Hague body of laws, and complete the Geneva Convention. They provide for a better protection of civilians and for ways to differentiate combatants from non combatants.

The problem is that even if the belligerents are committed to distinguishing between combatants and non combatants, the reality of guerrilla warfare makes it difficult to enforce this rule. The methods used in guerrilla, counterguerrilla, insurgency, and counterinsurgency warfare expose the civilians to risks. In addition, it is not always easy to distinguish a civilian from a member of a guerrilla band. An illustration of this is the systematic targeting of Karen civilians, who live in the jungle with their combatants. Unfortunately, this argument is also being used by Burma to commit ethnic cleansing of the Karen people.[35] The My Lai massacre in Vietnam is also the outcome of the belief that the enemy was hiding among the

---

[35] BERG, FORGOTTEN VICTIMS OF A HIDDEN WAR: INTERNALLY DISPLACED KAREN IN BURMA (Bangkok, Thailand: Burma Ethnic Research Group and Friedrich Naumann Foundation 1998).

civilian population. Another example is the daily victims in the streets of Iraq, such as passers-by who fall victim to an explosive device aimed at U.S. forces.[36] Other violations of humanitarian law involve suicide bombers activating their charges near children. In July 2005, an Iraqi suicide bomber killed twenty-four children who were taking candies from U.S. soldiers.[37] Some of these attacks on civilians could be avoided if the armies and combatants were more careful in their field evaluations. In other cases, regular armies are ill-equipped and cannot deal with situations where the distinction between civilians and combatants is not clear; accidents are the outcome of this lack of clarity.[38] For example, bombs are thrown on an area full of insurgents where locals live as well; Afghan civilians have paid a high cost from both sides bombing each other.[39]

Because it is difficult to distinguish concretely between combatants and civilians in the field, and in particular during asymmetrical conflicts, some have called for the end of the distinction. Others have suggested that humanitarian standards should be lowered for guerrillas engaged in wars of self-determination and civilians helping or supporting these groups. This is how the membership-based argument sprang to life. This proposal is not acceptable; lowering standards for combatants or civilians in such conflicts would only worsen the situation.

The membership-based argument was elaborated on the basis of the support civilians can bring to national liberation groups. The idea is to extend the status of combatants to civilians at different degrees, according to the level of participation in the conflict. This argument flirts dangerously with a form of collective punishment and a violation of several human rights. If an individual is not armed, he cannot be considered a combatant under Article 44 API, or even under Article 4 GCIII. The targeting of civilians is often used as a form of a collective punishment, but also as a way to eradicate support of the movement (collective punishment is prohibited by Article 33 GCIV). One strategy is to prevent the movements from reaching their popular bases; for example, the army can enter a village known for its support and settle there. But at no point can they mistreat the civilians to get information about the whereabouts of the group (Articles 31 and 32 GCIV). The membership-based argument is in the end not so different from a collective form of punishment; it aims at punishing civilians for the support they brought to those whom they see as freedom fighters. The humanitarian rules regarding the prohibition of collective forms of punishment include other rules. A party cannot take hostages (Article 34 GCIV). In occupied territories, parties to a conflict cannot massively arrest civilian populations, nor can they intern them, deport them, expel them, execute them, or apply collective punishment (Articles 79–135). An example of humanitarian law

---

[36] Naseer al Nahr, *Children Killed in Iraq Attack*, Arab News, Apr. 26, 2004.

[37] Borzou Daraghi & Raheem Salman, *Iraq Suicide Blast Targeting U.S. Troops Kills 24 Children*, L.A. Times, July 14, 2005 at A1.

[38] *See* Abi-Saab, *supra* note 33.

[39] Human Rights Watch, *The Human Cost: The Consequences of Insurgent Attacks in Afghanistan*, Washington DC: HRW, Apr. 15, 2007, http://www.hrw.org/en/reports/2007/04/15/human-cost-0.

violations includes the village of Lucanamarca, in Peru; in April 1983, the Shining Path entered the village and killed sixty-nine people with machetes. The attack was a punishment because the village had resisted guerrilla activities in the area.[40] Some belligerents take radical actions from the start and consider everyone to be a potential combatant, so they take no chance. This is clearly a violation of the principle of distinction. The reasons for such violations vary. For example, groups fight for a goal and think all means are acceptable. They also want to make their struggle public. The Ogaden National Liberation Front is a separatist group which fights for the independence of the territory of Ogaden in Ethiopia. The Ethiopian government considers the group a terrorist movement. In April 2007, the group attacked a Chinese-run oil field in Abole, killing only civilians.[41]

III. TERRORISM AND THE PRINCIPLE OF DISTINCTION

Since 9/11, the debate about whether international humanitarian law is applicable to terrorism has been intense. The problem with terrorism is that it willingly violates humanitarian law, and intentionally violates the distinction between civilians and combatants.

A. What Is Terrorism under International Humanitarian Law?

International humanitarian law does not provide a definition of terrorism. It only prohibits acts of terror committed during times of armed conflicts in Article 33 GCIV and Article 4 API. During armed conflicts, it is prohibited to spread terror (Article 51.2 API and Article 13 APII). Attacks on civilians, indiscriminate attacks (Article 51.4 API), or the taking of hostages (Article 75 API, Common Article 3, and Article 4.2 APII) are all prohibited actions under the Geneva Conventions and the Additional Protocols. Terrorist acts committed in peacetime are not covered by humanitarian law, but rather by domestic law and human rights law. Measures taken in response to terrorism do not amount to an armed conflict if carried out in times of peace. Intelligence activities, police cooperation, sanctions, extraditions, and financial investigations, and others are not acts of war; therefore, humanitarian law does not apply either. Terrorism is multifaceted, and one should remember that international humanitarian law applies only to terrorism during an armed conflict.

Transnational armed groups have always been part of conflicts, and this is why their terrorist actions when they carry arms are covered by humanitarian law. The relationship between terrorism and humanitarian law is therefore clear. The question at the core of most debates is whether a terrorist group can be a party to the Geneva Conventions and Additional Protocols. Are non state actors party bound by the Geneva Conventions? The ICRC has requested the application of the Geneva

---

[40] Jeremy M. Weinstein, Inside Rebellion: The Politics of Insurgent Violence 250–51 (Cambridge; New York: Cambridge University Press 2007).

[41] Jeffrey Gettleman, *Ethiopian Rebels Kill 70 at Chinese-Run Oil Field*, N.Y. Times, Apr. 24, 2007.

Conventions "wherever a situation of violence reaches the level of an armed conflict."[42] However, it is problematic to apply the Geneva Conventions and the Protocols to groups that, first, have not signed the Conventions, and second, do not respect humanitarian law. Terrorist groups have not signed the relevant treaties. They often show the utmost disrespect for these texts. Many argue that under these circumstances, terrorist groups acting in times of war do not benefit from any protection. These groups have duties under domestic law and under international law. States are reluctant to admit that non state actors, including terrorist groups, could have a standing under international law as this could grant legitimacy to these groups. Instead, States claim that terrorist groups are liable under domestic criminal law. This would mean that terrorist groups, or other non state actor groups that use violence, are not bound by the Geneva Conventions. It is however quite clear that the Conventions are binding on any party to the conflict (see, for example, the wording of Common Article 3); it is, besides, in the interests of all to have terrorists abide by humanitarian law and to create duties for these groups. It is generally accepted that these groups are bound by humanitarian law and are parties to the conflict. Terrorist groups are therefore parties to the Geneva Conventions although they have not signed them. Furthermore, the fact that a terrorist group could be a party to the conflict is crucial since it means that it would have the same obligations as the States when it comes to the principle of distinction.[43] There is, of course, a debate as to who is a terrorist and what is a national liberation group benefiting from the Geneva Conventions and the Protocols without having to ratify them as long as criteria set in Articles 43 and 44 API are met.

Sporadic terrorist actions that occur around the world and that are organized by various networks and groups, or even individuals, cannot be considered armed conflict. For example, the attacks carried out by the Red Brigades in Italy in the 1970s were carried out in times of peace, or rather during internal disturbances, but not during a conflict, so humanitarian law could not apply. The question remains important for terrorist acts carried out around the world by subgroups that are loosely attached to al Qaeda. Questions arise as to actions, such as the various sporadic attacks carried out in Indonesia, London, Madrid, Egypt, Pakistan, and other countries, and that are thought to be linked to al Qaeda cells. Are these attacks considered to be carried out in times of peace, or are they sporadic manifestations of a long-term war resulting from the War on Terror? From the qualification of the type of conflict we choose, a different set of laws will apply. If we consider that the War on Terror is taking place in times of peace, international human rights and domestic law will apply to terrorist actions. If instead we are of the belief that the War on Terror is an armed conflict, then humanitarian law applies. The question is to know

---

[42] ICRC, *International Law and the Challenge of Armed Conflicts*, 28th International Conference of the Red Cross and Red Crescent, Dec. 2–6, 2003, at 8.

[43] More can be found in Cedric Ryngaert, *Non-State Actors and International Humanitarian Law*, Institute for Inernational Law, Katholieke Universiteit Leuven, Working paper, 2008, https://www.law.kuleuven.be/iir/nl/onderzoek/wp/WP146e.pdf.

whether the War on Terror rises to the level of an armed conflict. The view of Gabor Rona is that it may amount to an armed conflict when the War on Terror "amounts to the use of armed force within a State, between that State and a rebel group, or between rebel groups within the State, a) if hostilities rise to a certain level and/or are protracted beyond what is known as mere internal disturbances or sporadic riots, b) if parties can be defined and identified, c) if the territorial bounds of the conflict can be identified and defined, and d) if the beginning and end of the conflict can be defined and identified."[44] This means that a balance must be found between the application of different sets of law according to the qualification of the conflict in a certain situation. The George W. Bush administration believed that the War on Terror is an armed conflict. With this argument, it reduced the scope of rights applicable to terrorists. The core argument is to declare the September 11, 2001 events acts of war and to look at the continuation of events like the war in Afghanistan and sporadic terrorist attacks carried out by groups affiliated with al Qaeda all parts of one single armed conflict. This shortcut is risky since all acts carried out in the name of the War on Terror would qualify as an armed conflict, including, for example, targeted killings. Meanwhile, British authorities always referred to the London bombings in 2005 as crimes and not as acts of war, which demonstrates a will to act according to domestic law rather than international law. This is in agreement with the former policy that regarded the Irish Republican Army (IRA) as a criminal organization governed by domestic criminal law, not as a party in an armed conflict. Spain chose the same path in 2004.[45] Therefore, the debate is still open as to whether these acts were committed in times of peace or times of war. In the end, either domestic law coupled with human rights law or humanitarian law will apply, so that all actors are covered, but the protection is not the same. The protection afforded by humanitarian law is more the threshold of humanity's protection.

The interaction between international human rights law and international humanitarian law has been analyzed with regard to the War on Terror. There is a debate as to whether or not international human rights apply during armed conflicts; for some it does, while others believe that international humanitarian law as a lex specialis should be the only applicable law. An argument is that the concept of armed conflict could be widened to include situations like the War on Terror so that actors to that conflict would benefit from both branches of law. Indeed, the current definition of armed conflict might not, as stressed by Gabor Rona, include the conflict with al Qaeda, while the conflicts in Afghanistan and Iraq would be armed conflicts. The reason is that a war against a transnational terrorist group is unclear: there is no clear time line or no clear territory, and classic approaches to

---

[44] Gabor Rona, *When Is a War Not a War?—The Proper Role of the Law of Armed Conflict in the "Global War on Terror,"* International Action to Prevent and Combat Terrorism—Workshop on the Protection of Human Rights While Countering Terrorism, Copenhagen, March 15–16, 2004, http://www.icrc.org/web/eng/siteeng0.nsf/html/5XCMNJ.

[45] Anthony Dworkin, *The London Terror Bombs: Were They a Crime or Act of War?,* July 11, 2005, http://www.crimesofwar.org/onnews/news-london.html.

war do not apply. It makes it again very difficult to distinguish between civilians and combatants since everyone is a target, everywhere. By contrast, the wars in Afghanistan and Iraq fall under the definition of armed conflicts since they take place in the framework provided by the law. The concept of armed conflict is therefore under pressure because of transnational terrorism, which is why it is so difficult to decide which sets of law apply and therefore which sets of protection apply to both civilians and combatants.[46]

B. The War on Terror

Some scholars have argued that international humanitarian law is outdated for many reasons and cannot protect civilians as well as it should. The case often referred to is terrorism; there is a so-called legal vacuum since everyone is targeted everywhere and the very aim of terrorism is to terrorize civilians as well as government officials and combatants. Terrorists act in times of peace as well as in times of war, therefore, the usual distinction between international humanitarian law applied in times of war and international human rights applied in times of peace seems to be blurred. The outcome is that terrorist acts committed during peacetime are not regulated by international humanitarian law: "[w]hen armed violence is used outside the context of an armed conflict in the legal sense or when a person suspected of terrorist activities is not detained in connection with any armed conflict, humanitarian law does not apply. Instead, domestic laws, as well as international criminal law and human rights govern."[47] It sounds clear on paper, but situations can be blurred; the July 2005 London bombings were carried out by a loose terrorist group probably affiliated with al Qaeda. The United Kingdom is engaged in Iraq and Afghanistan, where these groups play a role. Is the 2005 bombing a terrorist act committed in times of peace, or a terrorist act committed during an armed conflict?

In the post-9/11 world, there has been vivid opposition to the enforcement of the Geneva Conventions and the Protocols for combatants captured in Afghanistan, while the human rights community has fought for the enforcement of those treaties as well as international human rights law to provide the widest protection possible. The debates demonstrate how a law that was designed primarily to protect civilians and individuals *hors de combat* can be manipulated to justify the unjustifiable, such as routine torture. The first question that has to be answered is whether the War on Terror is an armed conflict. If it is not, domestic law and human rights law will apply, but not humanitarian law.

---

[46] Natasha T. Balendra, *Defining Armed Conflict*, New York University School of Law, Public Law and Legla Theory Research Paper Series, Working paper 07-22, Dec. 2007, http://papers.ssrn.com/sol3/papers.cfm?abstract_id=1022481.

[47] ICRC Official Statement, *The Relevance of IHL in the Context of Terrorism*, http://www.icrc.org/Web/Eng/siteeng0.nsf/html/terrorism-ihl-210705.

1. Is the War on Terror an Armed Conflict?

If we are to declare the War on Terror to be an armed conflict, we must identify parties to the conflict. In this particular case, the first question is whether a terrorist group can be a party to a conflict. As seen above, an armed transnational group using terrorism can be considered a party to the conflict, but the problem is that there is no definition of terrorism. Therefore, until there is an international agreement about who is a terrorist and what terrorism is, it will be difficult to agree on the inclusion of terrorist groups as parties to the conflict. Besides, in the specific framework of the War on Terror, al Qaeda has no tie to a government or a State. Even though there is no clear definition of terrorism, there is little doubt that al Qaeda is an organization of a terrorist nature. It does not claim to be any other type of movement, including a national liberation group; al Qaeda asserts its nihilism.[48] Another issue is that the Geneva Conventions and the Protocols apply to a territory. Al Qaeda does not have a territory as such, although it has ties and bases in various countries. Meanwhile, the 9/11 attacks were carried out in the United States, and this suffices to qualify as a territory. However, al Qaeda as an armed non state actor is bound by humanitarian law and must respect it. The Allies are at war with the movement, and there is no doubt that al Qaeda satisfies the criteria of a party to the conflict.[49] What is clear is that al Qaeda is involved in an armed conflict.

The war taking place in Afghanistan today is without doubt an armed conflict. This is a major factor in the decision to qualify the War on Terror as an armed conflict; since the United States attacked the Taliban in Afghanistan because of its support for al Qaeda, the War on Terror qualifies as an international armed conflict, and humanitarian law applies. There is another layer to the conflict: the government of Afghanistan backed up by the foreign coalition struggles with local and international armed non state actors, which makes the qualification of the conflict even more difficult. The part of the War on Terror that takes place in Afghanistan actually qualifies as an armed conflict because there are belligerent parties to the conflict, and these parties have a certain structure. As stressed by Gabor Rona, it might not be the best fit, but it applies.[50] The fact that there is an international armed conflict has never been denied by the United States, which insisted on the fact that the War on Terror is an international armed conflict but considers the Geneva Conventions to be useless because of the so-called novelty of the conflict, forgetting that asymmetric conflict and terrorism are certainly not new in history. The U.S.'s main argument in refusing the application of ad minima standards to captured members of the Taliban was that they did not respect the standards set in Article 4 GCIII and that the United States had not ratified API, so Article 44 could not apply. The United States also argued for the enforcement of international humanitarian law as a

---

[48] VAN ENGELAND, *supra* note 25.

[49] HELEN DUFFY, THE "WAR ON TERROR" AND THE FRAMEWORK OF INTERNATIONAL LAW 251 (Cambridge, UK/New York: Cambridge University Press 2005).

[50] Rona Gabor, *Interesting Times for International Humanitarian Law: Challenges from the "War on Terror,"* 27:2 FLET. FORUM WORLF AFF. 55–74 (Summer/Fall 2003).

lex specialis. It declared: "The United States is engaged in an armed conflict with al Qaida, the Taliban and their supporters. As part of this conflict, the United States captures and detains enemy combatants, and is entitled under the law of war to hold them until the end of hostilities. The law of war, and not the Covenant, is the applicable legal framework governing these detentions."[51]

2. International Humanitarian Law Does Not Apply to Terrorists?

One argument against the application of humanitarian law to terrorism is that it is anachronistic and does not apply to post-9/11 events. Another argument is that the law needs to be revised in order to take into account recent developments, in particular, regarding terrorism and armed conflicts.[52] These arguments have been used by the Bush administration and its Allies to reject the applicability of humanitarian law to the War on Terror. The United States did not deny that there is an armed conflict in Afghanistan or Iraq, or even with al Qaeda. Instead, the government chose to discuss the validity of the Geneva Conventions. Therefore, rather than saying that there is no war, the U.S. government declared the Conventions to be obsolete. This is an attack upon the Geneva Conventions, and in particular Protocol I. This has prompted a debate on whether humanitarian law covers current situations of terrorism, in particular transnational terrorism. One has to understand that this strategy is aimed at denying any credibility of international law in order to justify the Guantanamo anomaly; the lawyers of the Bush administration turned all humanitarian rules and the concept of torture on their heads to justify a philosophy of war.

The Bush administration built a very complex argument, twisting humanitarian law so that it would justify the concept of an unlawful combatant. Bush rejected the enforcement of the Protocol since it was not ratified by the U.S.; rejected the applicability of customary law; rejected the enforcement of international human rights; rejected the application of Common Article 3; and decided to use, misuse, and abuse Article 4 GCIII. This demonstrates a will to empty humanitarian law of its content to fulfill an agenda. Consequently, the U.S. government applied only part of the Geneva Convention; Article 4(A)3 GCIII was applicable. According to that article, the Taliban was not a regular armed force since it did not meet all the required conditions set forth. Secretary of Defense Donald Rumsfeld addressed this issue at a February 8, 2002, press conference:

[51] USA, Follow-Up Response to the Human Rights Committee by State Party, UN Doc. CCPR/C/USA/CO/3/Rev.1/Add.1 (2008), at 2, 3.
[52] Gabor Rona, *When Is a War Not a War?—The Proper Role of the Law of Armed Conflict in the "Global War on Terror,"* International Action to Prevent and Combat Terrorism—Workshop on the Protection of Human Rights While Countering Terrorism, Copenhagen, March 15–16, 2004—Presentation given by Gabor Rona, legal adviser at the ICRC's Legal Division, http://www.icrc.org/web/eng/siteeng0.nsf/html/5XCMNJ.

The Taliban did not wear distinctive signs, insignias, symbols or uniforms... To the contrary, far from seeking to distinguish themselves from the civilian population of Afghanistan, they sought to blend in with civilian non-combatants, hiding in mosques and populated areas. They [were] not organized in military units, as such, with identifiable chains of command.[53]

The problem with this argument is that it means the Taliban were not eligible for treaties' coverage. The outcomes of this interpretation were the blunt violations of humanitarian law and the practice of torture by the United States. One has to understand the consequences if these humanitarian obligations are rejected; if we decide that part of humanitarian law, including customary law, does not apply to terrorism, terrorists will be deprived of protection, which is contrary to the spirit of humanitarian law. If an act of terrorism is committed during an armed conflict, humanitarian law applies fully and not according to political circumstances or domestic interpretations.

3. Humanitarian Law Does Apply to Terrorists

As demonstrated above, humanitarian law applies to terrorism; acts of terror during armed conflicts are prohibited, which means that attacks carried out by the Taliban in Kabul and elsewhere in Afghanistan are acts of war. Therefore, humanitarian law—far from being useless—and Geneva Conventions—far from being quaint and obsolete—offer an answer to modern challenges of terrorism, even though as admitted earlier, it might not be the best fit, since transnational armed terrorist groups like al Qaeda are not expressly mentioned in humanitarian law. The qualification of a conflict involving a transnational group in an armed conflict and the application of humanitarian law to transnational terrorism will indeed depend on the facts, the nature of the conflict, and the intensity of the hostilities.

The debate regarding the qualification of the conflict is crucial for the protection of those who are terrorists and have been captured. Terrorists benefit from protection; they can either be approached as unprivileged combatants, or if one wishes to go further, they can be compared to self-determination groups, which would put an end to the debate as to whether a group is a terrorist group or struggles for national liberation. This approach would cause an ethics debate since it is fundamentally wrong to grant full humanitarian protection to individuals and groups who deliberately violate humanitarian law. Since non state armed groups do not hold a privileged position under humanitarian law, a protection afforded by Common Article 3 and Article 75 API, as well as the protection granted by customary law, in addition to human rights law, seems sufficient; it provides fundamental guarantees to the captured respectively in international armed conflicts and in non international ones. Some have denounced this as complicating the War on Terror, considering

---

[53] Donald H. Rumsfeld, U.S. Department of Defense news conference, Feb. 8, 2002, at http://usinfo. org/usia/usinfo.state.gov/topical/pol/terror/02020818.htm.

that humanitarian law might lower protection afforded against armed transnational groups.[54] The role of humanitarian law is to protect civilians and persons *hors de combat*, and certainly not to facilitate any policy. Humanitarian law does not grant any privileges to terrorists either, since terrorist attacks are prohibited.[55] It does not grant any legitimacy to these transnational armed groups. Rather, it fulfills a mission, which is to protect civilians and protect combatants *hors de combat* and the captured.

The issue of the enforcement of humanitarian law and the distinction between civilians and combatants in the case of transnational terrorism should be approached on a case-by-case basis. Civilians are clearly protected from terrorism during armed conflicts. As for individuals who participated in acts of terror during armed conflicts and were captured, both human rights and humanitarian law apply.

IV. WEAPONS AND THE PRINCIPLE OF DISTINCTION

Scientists constantly deliver new weapons. There are, for example, bombs that explode into multiple little bombs before hitting the ground. This is an area of concern, since most weapons used today—booby traps, cluster bombs, and landmines—do affect civilians. The use of weapons whose effects are difficult to control is prohibited under international humanitarian law because it targets civilians in an indiscriminate fashion. The effect of some bombs and weapons is so broad and destructive that it goes well beyond the principle of proportionality. Weapons of mass destruction are an obvious example of a method of warfare that destroys far too many lives to be allowed. The outcome is that a weapon must distinguish between civilians and combatants.

A. A New Behavior

Warfare methods have evolved, and the battlefield is often extended ad infinitum; new technologies allow for less one-to-one combat in the field. Strategies have changed as well, and hostilities take place from the sky through bombardments or through a guerrilla type of fighting. During the Israeli incursion into Gaza in the winter of 2008–09, the death toll rose to more than 1300 civilians (410 of them children), and more than 5300 civilians (1830 children) were hurt during the twenty-two days of the attack,[56] while only ten Israeli soldiers were killed (officially)[57] and

---

[54] Ted Lapkin, *Does Human Rights Law Apply to Terrorism*, XI:4 M.E. Quart. (Fall 2004).

[55] Toon Vandenhove, *The Relevance of International Humanitarian Law to Contemporary Armed Conflicts*, Feb. 14, 2008, http://www.icrc.org/web/eng/siteeng0.nsf/html/ihl-sri-lanka-feature080214.

[56] OCHA, *OPT: Situation in Gaza Strip as of Jan. 18, 2009*, http://www.reliefweb.int/rw/fullMaps_Sa.nsf/luFullMap/5CEC2BEFAFDEAA2585257543007A8B74/$File/CE-2008-OPT_VMU_011809_lowres.pdf?OpenElement.

[57] *Death Toll from Israel Offensive Soars Amid Diplomatic Moves*, AFP, Jan. 16, 2009.

more or less forty-eight Hamas combatants (officially).[58] This is explained by the types of weapons used by both sides of the conflict. Thus we see that the type of weapons and war strategies used today allow for less differentiation between combatants and civilians. This not an entirely new phenomenon; the Thirty Years War is an example. It was fought between 1618 and 1648 in Germany, and almost all European powers were involved. The civilians' toll amounted to 30 percent of the conflict because of armed conflict, famine, and disease. The difference is that technology plays a heavy role today, and combats turn into scenes of butchery. The Israeli army was accused of using phosphorus bombs, which melt human skin, during the attack on Gaza.[59] These bombs are not prohibited, but the military usually avoids using them in crowded areas with civilians. The use of cluster bombs, which are illegal, was also reported in that attack.[60]

These are not the only weapons whereby civilians can be hurt or killed; the advent of nuclear weapons carries the possibility of total annihilation. Ground warfare is still an option, as we have seen in Iraq and Afghanistan. The U.S. army is over-equipped and facing light and invisible improvised exploding devices such as roadside bombs. This type of weapon is a favorite of guerrilla groups, such as the Tamil Tigers in Sri Lanka. Guerrilla warfare is also a problem; it is fought by groups of irregular troops, who benefit from international humanitarian law but usually do not respect it. There are the possibilities of biological warfare, chemical warfare, and nuclear warfare, the very nature of which is to ignore the difference between combatants and non combatants. Illustrations of modern warfare techniques and weapons are countless, and all of them affect civilians. The best illustrations for this are probably the 1991 Gulf War and NATO's behavior in the Former Yugoslavia, during which aerial bombings were used to extremes and civilians paid a high price.

B. The Regulation of Weapons under International Humanitarian Law: Protection of Civilians

The principle of distinction cannot be affected by the development of new weapons and technologies. It is up to the parties to uphold it. The fast-paced evolution of technology, in particular new weapons, remains a matter of concern for the distinction. Bombing is accepted, but there are limits enumerated in the Geneva Conventions and the Protocols. It is prohibited to target the civilian population (Article 51 API and Article 13 AP II); medical units (Article 19 GCI, Article 23 GCII, Article 18 GCIV, Article 12 API, and Article 11 APII); cultural objects and places of worship (Article 53 API); objects indispensable to the survival of the civilian population (Article of 54 of API), works and installations containing dangerous

---

[58] Aschraf Khalil, *Hamas Reclaims Gaza as Fragile Cease-Fire Holds; Israelis Seek Full Pullout by Inauguration*, L.A. TIMES, Jan. 20, 2009.

[59] Richard Norton-Taylor, *Video Shows Evidence of Phosphorus Bombs in Gaza*, THE GUARDIAN, Jan. 16, 2009.

[60] Amira Hass, *Is Israel Using Illegal Weapons in Its Offensive on Gaza?*, HA'ARETZ, Jan. 16, 2009.

forces (Article 56 API); and non defended localities and demilitarized zones (Article 15 GCIV and Articles 59 and 60 of API). Additionally, camps for prisoners of war and places of internment must be sheltered against aerial bombardments and any other attacks (Article 23 GCIII and Article 88 GCIV). Extensive destruction, when not justified by military necessity, is prohibited (Article 50 GCI, Article 51 GCII, Article 130 GCIII, and Article 147 GCIV). Protocol I prohibits the bombing of specific targets. Indiscriminate bombardment is also prohibited; it is considered such a bombardment if it "treats as a single military objective a number of clearly separated and distinct military objectives located in a city, town, village or any other area containing a similar concentration of civilians or civilian objects" (Article 51.5.a API). Bombardment to spread terror among the civilian population (Article 51 API) is prohibited. In the first phases of the war against the United Kingdom, when Adolf Hitler still hoped the British would surrender, the Fuhrer prohibited terror raids by the Luftwaffe. Hermann Goring declared at the time:

The war against England is to be restricted to destructive attacks against industry and air force targets which have weak defensive forces.... The most thorough study of the target concerned, that is vital points of the target, is a pre-requisite for success. It is also stressed that every effort should be made to avoid unnecessary loss of life amongst the civilian population.[61]

German bombers however accidentally hit non military targets in the residential areas of London. When the Royal Air Force (RAF) retaliated to bombings by attacking Germany's civilian areas, Hitler allowed the Luftwaffe to carry out terror bombings. Any violation of these prohibitions amounts to a war crime according to the Rome Statute, even though the statute uses the word bombardment only in relation to international conflict (Article 8.2.b.v of the International Criminal Court [ICC] Statute).

The International Court of Justice reiterated the principle of distinction, but also the protection from hostilities in its advisory opinion of 1996: "Legality of the Threat or Use of Nuclear Weapons." The distinction between civilians and combatants is as follows: "[s]tates must never make civilians the object of attack and must consequently never use weapons that are incapable of distinguishing between civilian and military targets."[62] Indeed civilians must be protected from the effects of war. Some weapons breach this principle because they cause either direct or indiscriminate attacks against civilians. Therefore any weapon violating the principle of distinction is illegal. The second principle the Court states is that "it is prohibited to cause unnecessary suffering to combatants." Therefore, combatants do not have "unlimited freedom of choice of means in the weapons they use."

---

[61] *In* DEREK WOOD & DEREK DEMPSTER, THE NARROW MARGIN: THE BATTLE OF BRITAIN AND THE RISE OF AIR POWER 1930–1940 at 117 (Pen & Sword Military Classic 2003).

[62] Advisory Opinion on Legality of the Threat or Use of Nuclear Weapons, 1996, ICJ Rep 226, at 257.

C. Prohibition to Use Weapons Causing Unnecessary Suffering

The principle prohibiting unnecessary suffering can be found in the 1868 St. Petersburg Declaration and in the Hague Law. Article 35 (2) of Protocol I of 1977 states that "it is prohibited to employ weapons, projectiles and material and methods of warfare of a nature to cause superfluous injury or unnecessary suffering." There is also the 1980 Convention on Prohibitions or Restrictions on the Use of Certain Conventional Weapons. Using such weapons is considered a war crime under the Rome Statute of the International Criminal Court. The issue is to know what type of injury or suffering is considered unnecessary. A test is proposed by the International Court of Justice: "a harm greater than that unavoidable to achieve legitimate military objectives." There must be, therefore, some proportionality in the injury done and the military advantage gained. Therefore, a weapon is not banned because of the unnecessary injuries it might cause. It is the use of this weapon in certain situations that might be banned. This is why some weapons are in use even though they cause pain, injury, and death. This is again an illustration of the pragmatism of international humanitarian law yielding to military necessity. Weapons designed to hurt are, however, prohibited as stressed by Article 3 (a) of the Statute of the International Criminal Tribunal for the Former Yugoslavia. The difficulty is to evaluate the degree of calculation, since by nature all weapons are designed to hurt and kill. There are also treaties that have been acknowledged as being part of customary law that directly prohibit the use of certain weapons.[63] For example, the use of poison is prohibited by the Hague Regulations of 1899 and 1907. Using poison is a war crime under Article 8(2)(b) (xvii) of the Rome Statue for the International Criminal Court. Booby traps are also prohibited by Article 6 of Protocol II of the 1980 Convention. The issue is that they are often used in a guerrilla war. During the Vietnam War, many U.S. soldiers lost their lives to Punji sticks, hidden in high-grass areas. When fired upon, the soldiers would hide in the grass and fall on the spikes. The IRA made extensive use of booby traps, attaching such bombs to vehicles that would blow up when started. During the Battle of Jenin, the Israeli Defense Force (IDF) encountered massive booby traps in the streets.

D. Violations of the Principle of Distinction in Practice— The Principle of Distinction versus Military Necessity

A basic rule of international humanitarian law is that attacks must at all times distinguish between civilians and combatants, as well as between civilian objects and military objectives. It is therefore prohibited to carry out indiscriminate attacks. Military commanders must take precautionary measures while preparing and carrying out attacks to make sure they are not indiscriminate (Articles 57 and 58 API).

---

[63] Yoram Dinstein, The Conduct of Hostilities under the Law of International Armed Conflict 61 (New York: Cambridge University Press 2004).

How do these rules reconcile with the principle of military necessity and the realities of increasingly technological warfare and weapons?

There are many types of weapons that violate the principle of distinction between civilians and combatants, or that cause unnecessary suffering to combatants. Cluster bombs are an example. They are air-dropped or ground-launched; they eject smaller submunitions called a cluster of bomblets. The aim of these bombs is to kill or hurt as many combatants and combatant vehicles with one bomb as possible. The first problem is that it is hard to control the release of the little bombs, and therefore civilians in the vicinity might be hurt or killed. In addition, if they do not explode, they can kill or maim people sometimes a long time after the attack or the conflict. These munitions are prohibited by the 2008 Convention on Cluster Munitions. However, they were used during the two Chechen wars. In the 1995 war, a cluster bomb attack led by Russian aircraft caused fifty-five deaths in the Chechen town of Shali. The bombs hit the market, a gas station, a hospital, a school, and other locations. There were no military targets in Shali. The United States and Britain used cluster bombs in Nis, Yugoslavia, in 1999; the bomblets fell all over the city. The U.S. airforce explained that the cluster bomb container failed to open somewhere else, but opened after an attack. The cluster was also used in Afghanistan in 2001 despite the lessons learned by the Pentagon after the Nis accident. The village of Shaker Qala, near Herat, was attacked with cluster bombs. The major issue is that the bomblets were yellow, the color of the humanitarian package distributed by the United States. Children picked them, believing they were food packages, and were either killed or maimed.[64] Israel used cluster bombs during its war against Hezbollah in the summer of 2006. Many of these bomblets still lie in the South of Lebanon, where they may kill or maim children, who often ignore the dangerousness of these objects. Human Rights Watch reported that the Russian air force used cluster bombs in populated areas during the war in Georgia in 2008. It is important to understand that bomblets can spread across a broad zone—up to three football fields in size—from the place where they were shot. Cluster bombs still kill people in Vietnam today. White phosphorus shells are another problem; they are used as smoke screens. The problem is that this product burns the skin and can set fire to cloth or any combustible. This agent is used in bombs and mortars. Short-range missiles, for example, burst into burning flakes that hurt anyone they impact. They were used in Vietnam and are being used in Iraq. Israel used these in its Gaza siege in 2008–09.

Therefore most of the problems with weapons come from increasing technological sophistication that meets military requirements of efficiency but that misses the humanitarian test, but also from the fact that these weapons come from the air. Aerial bombings have been at the core of the issue of indiscriminate attacks against civilians. Scholars already wondered after World War II what could be done to limit civilian casualties resulting from aerial bombings, while stressing the fact that armies

---

[64] *Red Cross Warns Afghan Children Off Cluster Bombs*, REUTERS, June 29, 2002.

would never renounce them because of the military gain.[65] Indeed aerial bombings bring a definitive advantage, as demonstrated in NATO's war in the Former Yugoslavia. The problem is that this military advantage comes at the expense of civilians and causes many violations of the principle of proportionality in the name of military necessity. The problem with aerial bombing is that very few weapons actually fall where they are supposed to, and collateral damage is almost impossible to avoid. Human victims are considered collateral damage.

Military necessity is argued to justify an attack intended for a legitimate military target but carries adversarial effects on civilians. Military necessity is always counterbalanced by the principles of distinction and proportionality; and the military gain cannot cause the deaths of civilians, or unnecessary suffering for combatants. Total war at all costs is not acceptable. While taking military realities into account, international humanitarian law has interlinked the principles of military necessity with proportionality and distinction. However, when States use weapons like phosphorus shells, they know perfectly well that they have very little control on the effects of these bombs. They also act in blunt violation of humanitarian law, and they are aware that there is a risk they will violate the principle of distinction. Yet, the extended interpretation of military necessity and the process of dehumanization of the victims lead to these senseless attacks.

V. CONCLUSION

This brief study allows us to see and analyze the concrete challenges to the principle of distinction between civilians and combatants. In humanitarian law, there are no good sides or bad sides, no political agenda, and no higher good; the sole purpose is to protect civilians and even combatants from the foolishness of war.

---

[65] Lester Nurick, *The Distinction Between Combatant and Noncombatant in the Law of War*, 39:4 A.J.I.L. 680–97, 690 (October 1945); *Death from Skies in War Would Strike Down Civilians*, 35:2 SCIENCE NEWS LETTER, 183 (Mar. 25, 1939).

Conclusion:
Is the Principle of
Distinction Still Useful?

It is increasingly difficult to protect civilians and persons *hors de combat* because of the evolution of technology and asymmetrical conflicts. Civilians are sometimes deliberately targeted; for example, Suleiman Abu Ghaith, spokesman for al Qaeda, has evaluated the number of Muslims killed in the world during armed conflicts by the United States, and says that four million Americans should be killed in return.[1] There are *fatawa* justifying the killing of civilians, such as the one of Ali bin Khudeir al-Khudeiri, who justifies the killing of civilians in the September 11, 2001 attacks:

It is legitimate to kill all infidel Americans [...] it is astonishing to mourn the [American] victims as being innocent. Those victims may be classified as infidel Americans which do not deserve being mourned, because each American is either a warrior or, a supporter in money or opinion, of the American government. It is legitimate to kill all of them, be they combatants or non-combatant like the old, the blind, or non-Muslims.[2]

The same reasoning applies to Israeli citizens: most Palestinian Islamic movements consider that since the military service is obligatory in the country, all Israeli citizens are soldiers and therefore legitimate targets.[3] Armed groups are not the only ones

---

[1] Cited in Peter L. Bergen, The Osama Bin Laden I Know: An Oral History of Al Qaeda's Leader 346 (New York: Free Press 2006).
[2] Ali bin Khudeir al-Khudeiri, *fatwa* published in al-Hayat, Feb. 13, 2002.
[3] Michael L. Gross, *Killing Civilians Intentionally: Double Effect, Reprisal, and Necessity in the Middle East*, 120:4 Poli. Sci. Quart. 555–79 (Winter 2005–06).

defying humanitarian law. The military also tries to dodge international humanitarian rules by invoking the concept of military necessity, or rather an extended and all-encompassing version of military necessity. Military necessity in armed conflict is used to justify the recourse to violence. An attack or action must be intended to help in the military defeat of the enemy. It must be an attack on a military objective, and the harm caused to civilians or civilian property must be proportional and not excessive in relation to the concrete and direct military advantage anticipated. If an attack or an action is not justified by military necessity, it will be prohibited under international humanitarian law. The concept must respect principles of distinction and of proportionality. This demonstrates that international humanitarian law instead of being a pacifist law accommodates war as a reality in the human realm. The tendency is now to stretch the concept of military necessity: there is an ongoing debate about the definition of the concept and its relation to the principle of distinction and the principle of proportionality. Indeed, humanitarian law seeks to strike a compromise between military necessity and humanitarian considerations to fit the realities of war, a compromise which is now threatened.

The shelling of the city of Dubrovnik is a vivid example of this tendency to expand the concept of military necessity: the city was besieged by the Yugoslavian People's Army and suffered continuous heavy shelling toward the end of 1991 and during 1992. The heaviest shelling took place on December 6, 1991, and came to be known as the St. Nicholas Day bombardment, during which thirteen civilians were killed and sixty were wounded.[4] An analysis conducted by the Institute for the Protection of Cultural Monuments, in conjunction with UN Educational, Scientific, and Cultural Organization (UNESCO), found that, of the 824 buildings in the Old Town, 563 (or 68.33 percent) had been hit by projectiles in 1991 and 1992. Was the shelling a necessity? Were there no other means to ensure the fall of the city? The commanders of the Yugoslavian People's Army said there was no other option when confronted by the International Criminal Tribunal for Former Yugoslavia (ICTY). The ICTY answered by charging four commanders for war crimes. Miodrag Jokic, one of the four commanders, was convicted among other charges for devastation not justified by military necessity and for unlawful attack on civilian objects: "The Trial Chamber also considers the crime of devastation not justified by military necessity and the unlawful attack on civilian objects to be very serious in the present case, in view of the destruction caused by one day of heavy shelling upon the Old Town."[5] Another example illustrates how far-reaching the uses of military necessity can be. In 2006, the lawyers of the U.S. soldiers responsible for the Haditha massacre in Iraq intended to use military necessity as a defense. The argument was that insurgents had used small-arms fire, triggering a response from the Marines of Kilo Company, which led to the deaths of civilians as collateral damage. It seems

[4] William J. Fenrick, *The Battle of Dubrovnik*, Final report of the United Nations Commission of Experts established pursuant to Security Council Resolution 780 (1992) Annex XI.A, S/1994/674/Add.2 (Vol. V), Dec. 28, 1994.
[5] ICTY, Judgment in the case *The Prosecutor v. Miodrag Jokic*, 2004.

rather that the Marines executed the civilians, including seven women and three children, after the killing of a Marine by a homemade bomb that blew up the Humvee he was driving.[6] Lawyers chose to focus on the fact that armed insurgents might have been armed and that the concept of military necessity could be invoked without denying the killing of civilians, but presenting them instead as an unexpected outcome of the battle during which the soldiers defended themselves and gained a military advantage.[7] As for the protection of persons *hors de combat*, the interpretations made of the Geneva Conventions and the Protocols by the United States have been a complete denial of the existence and spirit of both international law and humanitarian law.

Therefore the distinction between civilians and combatants, its efficiency, and its relevance at the beginning of the twenty-first century is constantly being challenged. It is harder to protect civilians since they are either deliberate targets or the use of new weapons such as the white bomb hurts them in the war process. It is also more and more difficult to actually establish a clear-cut distinction between who is a civilian and who is a combatant. The question was central to the war in Afghanistan. The Taliban is not an army in the way Carl Von Clausewitz would have described it, and the Taliban did not use common strategies at war. A major problem was that the members did not wear uniforms or any specific signs that clearly indicated they belonged to an armed group. It was therefore difficult to know whether a man who had just thrown his weapon in a bush was a combatant or a civilian. This is an illustration of the blurring between the two categories that is also at the core of a heated debate regarding the status of the civilian who becomes a combatant. This *de facto* situation has increased the vulnerability of civilians in the field as well as the vulnerability of those who fall in between categories. The answer of the ICRC to this challenge has been to reinforce the status of civilians by constantly reminding the U.S. administration of the existence of the concept of unprivileged combatant and by issuing an important guideline regarding direct participation in hostilities. There are yet many challenges ahead regarding the principle of distinction.

Some have even gone as far as arguing that the distinction is meaningless in modern wars. These scholars and military experts rely on concrete examples. They look at civilians whose work is so intertwined with military strategies, and the success of the army relies so much on their work, that it is difficult to say whether that person is a civilian, a combatant, or falls in the in-between categories. A technician or a computer expert working for the army is a civilian but the army would not be able to be successful without him. Therefore, he is both a civilian and a combatant, and the distinction becomes irrelevant. This argument can go to extremes. Some scholars have argued that the man working for an electric company is a legitimate military target since his company delivers electricity to both civilians and the military.

[6] Tom McGirk, *Collateral Damage or Civilian Massacre in Haditha?*, TIME, Mar. 19, 2006.
[7] Mark Benjamin, *Defending the Haditha Killings: Lawyers for Marines Say that Kilo Company Was Responding to Small-Arms Fire when 24 Civilians Were Killed*, http://www.salon.com/news/feature/2006/06/16/haditha/.

As James Turner Johnson observes, the best way to evaluate whether someone is a civilian or a combatant would be to use the degree of cooperation with the military activities as the yardstick rather than setting the whole distinction aside as being irrelevant.[8] The problem with this case-by-case evaluation is that there is no objective norm, or yardstick, to decide who is a combatant, who remains a civilian, and who becomes an unprivileged combatant. This is why the 2009 ICRC guideline on direct participation is an important document: it gives criteria to follow to determine who directly participates in hostilities.

Another argument has been made against upholding the distinction between civilians and combatants: as war weaponry has developed, distinguishing between categories of people is almost impossible. The rationale is that reality is catching up with humanitarian law to the point it sometimes could seem to be obsolete, reminding one strongly of Counsel Alberto Gonzales's declaration regarding the Geneva Conventions.[9] This argument is not valid since it comes down to accepting a "technological determinism."[10] War is a reality and there will be casualties; the role of international humanitarian law and the distinction is to limit these casualties to the minimum, not to abandon the field to military philosophy, such as the one of total war. The reality of war cannot serve as an excuse for harming civilians. There are indeed ambiguities regarding the distinction that should be solved for the well-being of both categories at stake and the credibility of international humanitarian law, but in no way should the distinction between combatants and civilians be abolished: it is still very relevant today.

There have been renewed calls to either change the principle of distinction or to drop it altogether. For example, Colm McKeogh says that two principles should be modified: civilian death in war should not be outlawed, and the distinction between combatant and civilian should be abandoned in regard to civilian property in war as long as the civilian property is not vital to survival.[11] Not only are these mitigations morally wrong, they only blur the already difficult distinction between the two categories of human beings. The reality is that civilians are increasingly victims of warfare. However, it is not because armies are developing new technologies or because of armed groups' new strategies that the principle of distinction should be preserved. The role of international humanitarian law is to regulate the conduct of conflict and to protect civilians and individuals *hors de combat*, not to facilitate the war. This is why we should insist on the concept of humanitarian law and should not pretend that the law of armed conflict is a synonym of humanitarian law. Consequently, not only is the principle of distinction still useful, it is crucial to prevent further harm. People at war already try to twist or dodge international humanitarian law, giving us an idea of what would happen if such a limit to war did not exist.

[8] James Turner Johnson, *Protection of Noncombatants*, 37: 4 J. Peace Res. 423 (July 2000).

[9] Roland Watson, *Geneva Accords Quaint and Obsolete, Legal Aide Told Bush*, Timesonline, May 19, 2004.

[10] Johnson, *supra* note 8, at 424.

[11] Whitley Kaufman, *What Is the Scope of Civilian Immunity in Wartime?*, 2:3 J. Mil. Ethics 186–194 (2003)

Index

Abu Ghaith, Suleiman, 159
Abu Ghraib prison, 77
Abu Sayyaf, 113–14
Afghanistan
  civilian deaths in, 16, 144
  combatants vs. non-combatants in, 37
  definition of armed conflict and War
    in, 147–48
  fall of Kabul, x
  journalists targeted in, 84
  private military companies and, 128, 130
  rules of engagement in, 20, 33
  Soviet invasion, 136
  Taliban conquest of, 23
Afghanistan Islamic Emirate Rules and
  Regulations (2009), 22–23
Aguilar Moreno, Guillermo, 85
Ahmed, Sultan Hashem, 35
Albright, Madeleine, 93
al Firdos bunker, Baghdad, 18
Algeria, 83, 84
Algerian War of Independence, 143
al Ghanouchi, Rashid, 5–6, 5n24
Ali bin Khudeir al-Khudeiri, 5
al Jazeera, 92
Allies
  war crimes and, xv, 19, 24, 34, 53
  War on Terror and humanitarian
    law, 150
al-Majid al-Tikriti, Ali Hassan Abd, 35
Al Mawardi, 2
al Qaeda
  code of ethics, 22
  goals of, xv
  justification for targeting civilians, 2, 5
  as mercenaries, 125
  message to Americans regarding their
    government, 17
  press and, 92

Taliban and, 41
  terrorists acts by groups linked
    to, 146, 147
  unlawful combatant status and, 121
  war with the United States, 149–50, 159
Al Shabaab, 137
Al Shaybani, 2
Ambrose of Milan, 7
Amnesty International, 19, 51, 58
Angola, 126, 128
antipersonnel mines, 27
Aquinas, Thomas Saint, 11, 11n56
Arbre des Batailles (Bonet), 11
Aristizabal, Carlos Enrique, 85
Aristotle, 7
armed conflicts See war/armed conflicts
armed forces, defined, 30
Art of War (Sun Tzu), 8, 135
asymmetric conflicts
  combatant status and attire, 113–14
  guerrilla methods, 12, 40, 41, 54, 114,
    135, 139, 142, 153, 155
  historical conflicts, 134, 135–36,
    136–37, 138–39
  human shields, 112
  modern conflicts, 115, 137–38
  overview, 134–36
  reality of modern war, 115
  self-determination conflicts, 16, 40, 41,
    64, 112, 113–14, 115–16, 134, 137,
    138–45
Attila (King), x
Augustine of Hippo, Saint, 8–9, 11n56

Balkans, 17, 19–20, 19n87, 49
Baxter, R. R., 40
BBC crews, 89–90
Belgium, 34
Bible, 2–3, 4, 6

Bin Laden, Osama, 2, 136
Blackwater (Xe), 126, 127, 128, 129–30
Blair Doctrine, xiv–xv
Bonet, Honoré, 11
booby traps, 155
Bosnian-Herzegovian War, 35, 72, 74, 80–81, 82
Boutros Ghali, Boutros, 75
Bowden, Mark, 132
Braddock, Edward, 137
Bremer, Paul, 129
Britain, 156
Brussels Declaration (Draft) (1874), 14
Bush, George W.
    Blain Doctrine and, xiv–xv
    definition of torture, 35
    international humanitarian law and, 94
    justification for 9/11 and, 5
    unlawful combatants and, 35–36, 37, 41
    War on Terror, 120–21, 147

Caesar, 4
Cambodia, 33, 73
Cassese, Antonio, xv
Catholic Church See Christian and Catholic Church/Philosophy
Central Tracing Agency of the ICRC, 81
Chad, 75
Chang Kai Chek, 8
Charles V (king), 11
Chechen wars, 156
Chechnya, 84
children
    acts of belligerency and, 31
    in ancient wars, 2–3
    child combatants, 48, 78, 132
    Enlightenment thinking regarding, 12
    fundamental guarantees for, 48
    guns pulled by, 36
    Iraqi, 144
    killed by cluster bombs, 156
    killing as collective punishment, 16
    in the Middle Ages, 10
    in occupied territories, 96
    protections granted to, 32, 75–76, 78–81
    safe zones for, 72–73
    war crimes prosecution of, 78–79
    War on Terror and, 126
The Children of Herakles (Euripides), 4

Christian and Catholic Church/Philosophy, x, xi–xii, 7, 9, 10, 11n56, 21
Cicero, 7, 11n56
Civilian Extraterritorial Jurisdiction Act (CEJA) of 2010, 129–30
civilian objects/property
    cultural objects, 32, 35, 68, 70–71
    dual-use, 53–54, 70, 91
    media equipment, 91–94
    protection of, 31–33, 68, 70–71
    reasons to spare, 59
    vs. military targets, 49
civilians
    classification of, 29–31, 35–36, 105–8
    collective punishment of, 16, 64, 95
    deaths due to modern technology, xii, 18–20, 27, 152–53
    early attempts at protecting, 6–10, 7
    emergence of an ethic of protection regarding, 11–13
    fundamental guarantees for, 48
    Geneva Convention and Additional Protocols protections for, 31–33
    modern technology and death of, 18–20, 27
    reasons to spare, 59
    refugees and internally displaced persons, 32–35, 81–83
    right to receive assistance, 32
    as shields, xiii, 31, 64, 110–12
    status of
    targeting of, 17–18
    torture of, 63
    as victims of war prior to Nation States, 2–6
    working for an army, 131
    See also children; direct participation in hostilities; distinction between civilians and combatants; Geneva Conventions and the Additional Protocols; journalists; sick/wounded people; women
Clark, Wesley, 19
Clausewitz, Carl Von, 5, 14
cluster bombs, 76, 156
CNN team, 89
Coalition Provisional Authority Order, 17, 129
Code of Manu, 8

collateral damages
　　Bible on, 6
　　in the Former Yugoslavia, 28, 49, 52, 65
　　humans as, 18, 51, 53, 155–57
　　increased harm to civilians and broader
　　　　use of the term, xiii, xiii*n*21, xv–xvi
　　intent and, 49–51
　　in Lebanon, 51
　　legitimate military targets and, 49–54
　　military necessity and, 160–61
　　principle of proportionality and, 49–50
Colombian FARC, 113, 141, 142
Columbia, 36, 46, 85
combatants
　　children as, 80
　　in civilian buildings, 71
　　defined, 30–31, 37–40
　　mercenaries, 43–44, 48, 122–26
　　prisoners of war, 45–48
　　rebels, terrorists, and insurgents
　　　　(irregular armies), 40–42, 46
　　spies, 44–45, 48
　　status of
　　unlawful, 36, 37, 45, 47, 54, 56, 116–22
　　unprivileged, 37, 41–42, 42–43, 44, 96,
　　　　117–18, 130–31
　　See also direct participation in
　　　　hostilities; sick/wounded people
Convention on Cluster Munitions, 156
Convention on Prohibitions or Restrictions
　　on the Use of Certain Conventional
　　Weapons, 155
Crane, David, 78
Croatia, 73
Crusades, x
cultural objects and places of worship, 32,
　　35, 68, 70–71

DeCamp, Philip, 86
Declaration of St. Petersburg (1868), 14
demilitarized or neutral zones, 32, 73–74
Democratic Republic of Congo, ix
Denard, Bob, 126
Dinstein, Yoram, xviii, 38, 39, 111, 114
direct participation in hostilities
　　concept of, 102–5
　　Geneva Conventions on, 36
　　ICRC on, 105–8
　　protections for citizens that have,
　　　　108–10

as qualifier for combatant status, 36, 38
unprivileged combatants status for
　　civilians, 42–43
distinction between civilians and combatants
　　antipersonnel mines and, 27
　　attire worn and the, 38, 40–41, 44,
　　　　46–47, 54, 85, 87, 88, 113, 120–21,
　　　　131, 141, 151, 161
　　in the Bible, 2–3, 4
　　civilians changing role in armed
　　　　conflicts, 101–2
　　combatant status extension, 112–15
　　difficulty in determining the, 28–29
　　ethics and, 20–24
　　holding fire principle, 20
　　identification of combatants, 38
　　Islamic philosophy/rules regarding,
　　　　2, 3–4, 6–7
　　laws of war and the, 13–16
　　legitimate military targets, 49–54
　　military targets and, 18–20
　　modern weapon technology and the,
　　　　105, 134, 155–57
　　overview, 24–25
　　proportionality principle and the, 16–17
　　twenty-first century challenges
　　　　regarding, xii–xix, 16–20, 159–62
　　violations of the principle of, 33–35
　　See also civilians
Dormann, Knut, 118, 121
Doswald-Beck, Louise, 104
double effect, 51, 51*n*53
Dresden bombardment, 24, 68
Duke of Burgundy, 10

East Timor, 88
Eduans, 4
Egypt, 146
Ejército Nacional de Liberacion (National
　　Liberation Army, ELN), 85
elderly
　　Enlightenment thinking regarding, 12
　　facilities for elderly classified as
　　　　hospitals, 76
　　just war theory and the, 12
　　in the Middle Ages, 9
　　protections for, 75
　　safe zones for, 72–73
ELN (Ejército Nacional de Liberacion), 85
Elon Moreh settlement, 98

enemy combatants, 116, 119–22, 120n55, 122, 131, 150
  See also unlawful combatants
environment, protecting the, 6, 8, 32, 66, 70
Epitoma rei militaris (Vegetius), 135–36
Equatorial Guinea, 126
ethics, 20–24
Ethiopia, 145
ethnic cleansing, 77, 82
Euripides, 4

First Indochina War (1946–1954), 139
Fisk, Robert, 53
foreigners, protection granted to, 32
Former Yugoslavia
  aerial bombings in, 157
  civilians/civilian objects and military targets in the, 19–20, 19n87, 52–53, 53nn62, 64, 69
  cluster bombs used in, 156
  ethnic cleansing in the, 77
  journalists killed in, 84
  media in the, 91, 93, 104–5
  military necessity and bombardment of, 17, 160
France, 40, 64, 68, 74
Francs Tireurs et Partisans, 40
Free French Air Forces, 50

General Order number 100 (Lieber Code), 13
Geneva Conventions and the Additional Protocols
  Bush administration use of, 150
  civilians that take part in hostilities under, 42–43
  classification of civilian in, 29–31
  combatant status under the, 37–40, 42, 112–14, 112–15, 116, 116–17, 120–21, 123, 141
  customary laws and, 54, 55–56
  direct participation in hostilities under the, 101–2, 105, 108, 133
  extra protections for civilians under the, 75–81
  human shields under the, 110, 112
  journalists under the, 84–85, 87–88, 89, 90, 90–94
  laws of war humanized by the, 15–16
  medical installations and personnel under the, 48–49

mercenaries under, 43–44, 122–23
military vs. civilian targets under the, 19, 19n87, 49–50, 52, 53
occupied territories and, 94–99
opposition to the enforcement of the, 148, 150–51
overview, 61–62
principle of distinction in the, xii, 1, 28
prisoners of war under the, 45–46, 46–48, 115
private contractors under, 130
protection from the effects of war and attacks under the, 63–64
protection of civilian property under the, 70–71
protection of civilians under the, 17, 24, 31–33, 62–63
protections in international armed conflicts under the, 64–66, 69
protections in non international armed conflicts under the, 66–69
refugees and internally displaced persons under the, 32, 81–83
rights and fundamental guarantees under the, 48, 68–69
Safe Zones under the, 72, 72–75
self-determination conflicts and civilians and combatants under the, 40–41, 138, 139–42
spies under, 44–45
terrorism/terrorists under the, 145–46, 151
unlawful combatants and the, 116–19, 120–21
weapons technology under the, 153–54, 155, 162
  See also international humanitarian law
genocide, 33–34, 34nn16–17, 35, 52, 83, 92–93, 92n117
Germany, 50, 64, 153
Gibson, Shawn, 86
Gonzales, Alberto, 162
Grdelica train bombing, Balkins, 19–20, 19n87
Grotius, Hugo, 11n56
Guantanamo Bay detention center, xvii, 57, 102, 131
guerrilla methods, 12, 40, 41, 54, 114, 135, 139, 142, 153, 155
  See also asymmetric conflicts

Guevara, Che, 135
Gulf War (1991), 18, 134

Hagenbach, Peter Von, 10
Hague Conventions of 1899, 14, 46, 97, 155
Hague Regulations of 1907, 14, 15, 46, 94,
    97–98, 133, 155
Halabja, Iraq, 34–35, 34n, 35n18
Hamas, 36, 42–43, 95, 109–10, 132
Herodotus, 7, 136
Hindu law, 8
Hiroshima bomb, 24
History of the Peloponnesian War
    (Thucydides), 4–5
Hizb al-Nahda, 5
Hobbes, Thomas, 11n56
Hohenstafen, Conradin von, 10
homosexuals as targets in war, 77
hospitals *See* medical personnel, installations,
    and means of transportation
Hotel Palestine, Iraq, 86, 91
Hugo Grotius, Hugo, 4
humanitarian aid and human rights
    purposes, 23–24, 35, 128
humanitarian corridors, 75
humanity, principle of, 13–14
Human Rights First, 129, 130
human shields, xiii, 31, 64, 110–12
Hussein, Saddam, xiii, xiv, 24, 34, 64, 65

ICC (International Criminal Court), 79, 82,
    94, 120
ICJ (International Court of Justice), 62,
    119, 154
ICTY *See* International Criminal Tribunal
    for the Former Yugoslavia (ICTY)
Indonesia, 39, 146
Inter-American Commission on Human
    Rights, 90
internally displaced persons and refugees,
    32–35, 81–83
International Committee of the Red Cross
    (ICRC)
    child combatants and the, 80
    customary rules of international
        humanitarian law study, 17, 21, 57–58
    on direct participation in hostilities,
        xviii, 36, 102, 105–8, 109, 114
    on the distinction between civilians and
        combatants, 102

family reunification and the, 81
on human shields, 110
Montreux document and the, 128
Palestinian Occupied Territories and
    the, 95, 97
refugees and the, 82
safe zones and the, 72, 73
services during internal disturbances
    and tensions, 67
spies and the, 45
on terrorism/terrorists, 145–46
International Convention against the
    Recruitment, Use, Financing, and
    Training of Mercenaries, 124
International Convention for the
    Protection of Journalists engaged in
    Dangerous Missions in Areas of Armed
    Conflict, 85
International Court of Justice (ICJ), 62,
    119, 154
International Covenant on Civil and
    Political Rights (ICCPR), 69
International Criminal Court (ICC), 79, 82,
    94, 120
International Criminal Tribunal for
    Rwanda, 52
International Criminal Tribunal for the
    Former Yugoslavia (ICTY), xv, 19n87,
    33, 35, 53, 87, 91, 117, 155, 160
international humanitarian law
    change in ethics at war and, 94
    customary rules of, 54–58
    disregard for, 54
    distinction principle in twenty-first
        century, 13–14, 16–20
    evolution of warfare and, 133–34
    irregular forces and self-determination
        struggles and, 115–16
    manipulation of during war, xii–xix,
        xiiin21, 160–62
    private military companies obligations
        under, 128–30
    terrorism/terrorist and, 148–52
    unprivileged combatants protection
        under, 41–42, 48
    unprivileged vs. unlawful combatant
        in, 37
    war and, 61
    See also Geneva Conventions and the
        Additional Protocols

International News Safety Institute, 90
internees, civilian, 32
Iran-Iraq War, 65
Iraq
    Abu Ghraib prison, 77
    anti-Americanism in, 21
    armed guards in, 126
    attack on Iraqi Kurds in Halabja, 34–35,
        34n, 35n18
    children in, 36
    civilian deaths in, 16, 18, 144
    civilians used as shields in, xiii, 64
    cluster bomb used in, 156
    definition of armed conflict and War
        in, 147–48
    international humanitarian law and,
        xiii–xiv
    Iran-Iraq War, 65
    journalists killed or targeted in, 84, 86
    journalists working in, 87, 89
    Osirak Iraqi nuclear reactor
        bombardment, 65–66
    private contractors used in, 127, 129
    safe zones in, 74–75
Irish Republican Army (IRA), 147
irregular forces See asymmetric conflicts
Islamic philosophy/rules, distinction
    between civilians and combatants, 2,
    3–4, 6–7, 9
Islamic republic of Iran, 18
Israel
    citizens as combatants in, 5–6
    cluster bomb use by, 156
    Lebanon attack in 2006, 18, 51–52
    Osirak Iraqi nuclear reactor bombarded
        by, 65–66
    Palestinian conflict, xiv, 31, 64, 72, 76,
        85–86, 94–98, 109–10, 119–20, 136,
        152–53, 156, 159–60
    Sabra and Shatila refugee camps, 33–34
    unlawful combatants and, 119–20
Israeli Defense Force (IDF), 155
Israeli Defense Forces, 94
Israeli High Court, 109
Israeli Supreme Court, 97, 120
Italy, 146

jihad, rules for, 22–23
Johnston, Douglas, 135
Jokic, Miodrag, 160

Jordan, 38–39
journalists
    armed or with bodyguards, 89, 89–91
    civilian status of, 84–87
    deaths in war, 84
    embedded, 87–88
    freelance, 88–89
    media equipment, 91–94
    military, 89
just war
    Augustine of Hippo, 8–9, 11
    development of theory of, 11–12, 11n56
    ethics and, 20–24
    sources in Christianity, 8–9, 11, 11n56, 21
    Thomas Aquinas, 11, 11n56
Juvenal, 5

Kahan commission, 33–34
Kahina (Queen), 134
Karadzic, Radovan, 74
Kassem and Others, 38–39
Khadr, Omar, 79
Khmer Rouge, 33
Kinne, Adrienne, 86
Koi jurisprudence, 39
Kosovo War, 23, 28
Kouchner, Bernard, 75
Kurds, Iraqi, 34–35, 34n, 35n18
Kwakwa, Edward, 125

Laws (Plato), 7
laws of armed conflict/war, 13–16, 38, 133
    See also Hague Conventions of 1899;
        Hague Regulations of 1907; war/
        armed conflicts
The Laws of Nations (Vattel), 12
Leahy, Patrick, 130
Lebanon, xvii, 18, 33–34, 51–52, 83, 156
*Legality of the Threat or Use of Nuclear
    Weapons* (ICJ), 62
Les Voeux du Héron (anonymous), 11
Liberia, 120
Lieber Code, 13
Lieber, Francis, 13
Lincoln, Abraham, 13
London bombings, 146, 147, 148

Madrid bombings, 146
Malaysia, 39
Manu, Code of, 8

Manu Smriti (anonymous), 8
Mao Tse Tung, 8, 135
Martens, Fyodor, 55
Massimino, Elisa, 130
Maurice, Emperor, 7
McChrystal, Stanley, 20, 33
McKeogh, Colm, 162
media workers *See* journalists
medical personnel, installations, and
    means of transportation
    protections granted to, 28, 32, 48,
        48–49, 72, 76
    See also sick/wounded people
Ménard, Robert, 90
Mengele, Josef, 64
mercenaries, 43–44, 48, 122–26
    See also privatization of war/private
        military companies (PMC)
Metz, Steven, 135
Middle Ages, civilian treatment during war
    in the, 9–12
Military Commissions Act, 130
Military Extraterritorial Judiciary Act, 129
military necessity
    change in ethics at war and, 94, 159–62
    distinction balanced with the, 18, 160
    just war theory and, 21–22
    military targets and the, 18–20
    modern weapons technology and, 155–57
military targets
    hospitals, 28
    legitimate, 49–54
    military necessity and, 18–20
Milosevic, Slobodan, 93
Mine Ban Treaty (1997), 27
Mladic, Ratko, 74
Mockler, Anthony, 125
modern weapon technology
    Additional Protocol I protections
        regarding, 64–65
    civilian deaths due to, xii, 18–20, 27,
        152–53
    cluster bombs, 76, 156
    distinction between civilians and
        combatants and, 105, 134, 155–57
    prohibition against unnecessary
        suffering and, 155
    regulation of, 153–54
    smart bombs, 76
    warfare methods, 152–53

Mohamed Ali et al. v. Public Prosecutor, 47
Mohammed, Hussein Rashid, 35
Montreux document, 128
Morocco, 83
Muhammad Omar, Mullah, 23
Muhammed, Prophet, 3, 6
mujahedeen, 22–23
Mullah Omar, 23
My Lai massacre, xvi–xvii, 143–44

National Liberation Front (NLF), 143
national liberation wars *See* self-
    determination conflicts
Nation States, emergence of, 4–6
NATO
    Belgrade hospital bombing by, 28
    Belgrade radio station attacked by, 52
    Former Yugoslavia and, xv, 17, 19–20,
        19n87, 28, 49, 52–53, 53nn62, 64,
        76, 91, 104–5
    humanitarian aid and, 128
    propaganda regarding, 93
no-fly zones, 75
nuclear weapons and power stations, 65
Nuremberg Trials, 10, 17, 52

Obama, Barack, 122
occupied territories
    children in, 78
    prisoners of war, 46
    protection granted to civilians in, 32,
        75, 94–99
    See also Palestinian-Israeli conflict/Oc-
        cupied Territories
Ogaden National Liberation Front, 145
Omar, Mullah, 23
open cities, 74
Oxford Institute for Ethics, Law and Armed
    Conflict, 22

Pakistan, 126, 146
Palestinian-Israeli conflict/Occupied
    Territories, xiv, 31, 64, 72, 76, 85–86,
    94–98, 109–10, 119–20, 136, 152–53,
    156, 159–60
    See also occupied territories
Paris Principles and Guidelines on Chil-
    dren, 78–79, 79n52
Parrish, Richard, 111
Pax Dei, 9

peacekeeping missions, 104
Peace of God (*Pax Dei*), 9
Peloponnesian War, x, 4–5
Peru, 145
Petraeus, David, 33
Phalangists, 33–34
Plato, 7
Popular Front for the Liberation of Palestine, 38–39
Praljak, Slobodan, 35
precaution, principle of *See* principle of precaution
Price, David, 130
principle of distinction *See* distinction between civilians and combatants
principle of humanity, laws of war based on, 13–14
principle of precaution, Additional Protocol I regarding, 20, 33, 49, 66, 70, 155
principle of proportionality
  Additional Protocol I regarding, 66
  change in ethics at war and, 94
  collateral damages and, 49–50
  instruments used to measure proportionality, 93–94
  just war theory and, 21
  military necessity and, 160
  military targets and the, 18–20
  principle of distinction and the, 16–17
prisoners of war
  in ancient wars, 5, 8
  civilians who take direct part in hostilities, 110
  civilian vs. combatant status, 31
  combatants, 37, 45–48
  defined, 30
  irregular forces, 113, 115–16
  killing of, 8
  mercenaries, 44
  refugee camp as detention center for, 83
  spies, 48
  status of, 39–40
  Taliban rules regarding, 23
  tribunal decision regarding, 96
  women, 6
privatization of war/private military companies (PMC), 43, 89–90, 105–8, 127–31
  See also mercenaries

proportionality, principle of *See* principle of proportionality
protection afforded to civilians

Qassam Brigades, 109–10
Quirin, ex parte, 37, 47, 116–17, 120
Quran, on the distinction between civilians and combatants, 3–4, 6–7

Radio des Mille Collines, 52
Radio-Télévision Libre des Mille Collines, 92–93, 92n117
Radio Televizija Srbija (RTS), 52, 53–54, 91–92, 93, 104–5
Randal case, 87
ransoms, during the Middle Ages, 10
rape/sexual exploitation, x, xi, xvii, 10, 69, 77, 79
Reagan, Ronald, 54, 115
Red Brigades, 146
refugees and internally displaced persons, 32–35, 81–83
relief and humanitarian personnel, protection granted to, 32
Reporters Sans Frontières/Reporters Without Borders (RSF), 86, 88, 90
Republic (Plato), 7
Responsibility to Protect project, 24
Rome Statute of the International Criminal Court, 82, 94, 155
Rona, Gabor, 147, 149
Rousseau, Jean-Jacques, 12
Royal Air Force (RAF), 154
RSF (Reporters Without Borders), 86, 88, 90
RTS *See* Radio Televizija Srbija (RTS)
Rumsfeld, Donald, 150
Russia, 148
Rwanda, 52, 74, 75, 77, 83, 84, 92–93, 92n117

Sabra and Shatila refugee camps, xvii, 33–34
Safe Zones, 15, 72–75
Saladin, 10
Satires (Juvenal), 5
Schwarzenberger, Georg, 39
self-determination conflicts, 16, 40, 41, 64, 112, 113–14, 115–16, 134, 137, 138–45
September 11, 2001 attacks, as acts of war, 5, 17, 119, 147
sexual exploitation/rape, x, xi, xvii, 10, 69, 77, 79

Sharon, Ariel, 34
Shea, Jamie, 49
Sherman, William T., xiii–xiv, 18
shields, human, xiii, 31, 64, 110–12
Shining Path, 145
sick/wounded people
    Enlightenment thinking regarding, 12
    hors de combat, 48–49
    immunity granted to hospitals, 76
    pregnant women classified as, 77
    protections granted to, 75–76
    safe zones for, 72–73
    See also medical personnel, installations,
        and means of transportation
Sierra Leone, 126, 128
slavery, 69
Somalia, ix, 84, 132, 137
sovereignty, principle of, 24
Soviet Union, 136
Special Court for Sierra Leone (SCSL), 78
spies, 44–45, 48
Srebrenica, Bosnia and Herzegovina, 72
Srebrenica, Bosnia-Herzegovina, 74
Sri Lanka, xv, 58, 63, 73, 76
SS officers, 39
stateless persons, protection granted to, 32
Statute of the International Criminal
    Tribunal for the Former Yugoslavia, 155
Stone, Julius, 62
St. Petersburg Declaration (1868), 155
Strategica (Articles of War) (Emperor
    Maurice), 7
suicide attacks, 22–23, 94, 132, 136, 144

Taliban
    acts of war, 151
    attire and status as combatant,
        113–14, 121
    code of ethics, 22–23
    combatant vs. civilian, 36, 40, 41, 47
    execution of civilians, 33
    fall of Kabul and the, x
    press and the, 92
    press spokesman for the, 131
    rules of engagement and the, 20
    U.S. doctors treatment of wounded, 48
Talibani, Jalal, 90
Tamerlane, x–xi, xi, 17
Tamil Tigers, ix–x, xv, 63, 73
technology *See* modern weapon technology

terrorism/terrorists
    Additional Protocol I protections
        regarding, 66
    asymmetric conflicts and, 137–38
    distinction between civilians and
        combatants and, 105
    international humanitarian law and,
        121, 145–48
    prosecution for, 115
    spreading terror among civilian
        populations, 31
    targeting of civilians, 17–18
Thirty Years War, xi, 153
Thoenes, Sander, 88
Thomas Aquinas, Saint, 11, 11n56
Thucydides, x, 4–5
TMC Asser Institute, 36, 105
torture, xvii, 35, 37, 41, 45, 56, 63, 67, 69,
    77, 105, 119, 150–51
transnational wars, emergence of, 5–6
treason and rebellion within an army,
    39–40
The Tree of Battles (Bonet), 11
Tunisia, 5

UK Judicial Committee of the Privy
    Council, 39
UN Charter, prohibition regarding use
    of force, 23–24
UN Children's Emergency Fund
    (UNICEF), 80
UN General Assembly, resolution regarding
    Palestinian Occupied Territories, 98
UNHCR (UN High Commissioner for
    Refugees), 82
UN High Commissioner for Refugees
    (UNHCR), 82
UNICEF (UN Children's Emergency
    Fund), 80
United Kingdom, 74, 98, 148
United Nations, on contractors as
    mercenaries, 126
United States
    armed guards in Iraq, 126, 126n77
    child combatants and, 79
    cluster bombs use by, 156
    journalists in Iraq and the, 86
    military necessity as defense for human
        collateral damages, 160–61
    occupation of Iraq, 98–99

United States (cont.)
  Osirak Iraqi nuclear reactor
    bombardment and, 65
  Protocol I and, 54, 115–16
  safe zones in Iraq and the, 74–75
  unlawful combatants and, 35–36, 37,
    41, 56, 116, 118, 119, 120–22
  war with al Qaeda, 149–50, 159
  See also War on Terror
unlawful combatants, 36, 37, 45, 47, 54, 56,
  116–22
unprivileged combatants, 37, 41–42, 42–43,
  44, 96, 117–18, 130–31
UNPROFOR (UN Protection Force), 72, 74
UN Protection Force (UNPROFOR), 72, 74
UN Relief and Works Agency (UNRWA), 76
UN Resolution 688, 75
UNRWA (UN Relief and Works Agency), 76
UN Security Council, 86, 97, 98–99
U.S. Air Force Intelligence Targeting
  Guide, 50
U.S. Defense Department, 91
U.S. Department of Defense (DOD), 51, 129

Vattel, Emerich de, 12
Vegetius, 135–36
Vietnam War, xvi–xvii, 87, 143–44, 148, 156
Vitoria, Francisco de, 11–12, 11n56
Vows of the Heron, (anonymous), 11

Wallace, William, 10, 139
Walzer, Michael, xiv, 24, 50, 51
war/armed conflicts
  ancient history of, x, 2–5, 8
  civilians changing role in, 101–2
  early attempts at limiting, xi–xii, 6–10
  humanitarian and human rights
    purposes for, 23–24
  international humanitarian law and, 61
  international vs. non-international, 29,
    29n6, 32–33, 55, 62
  in the middle ages, x–xi, 9–12
  non international armed conflicts,
    66–69, 105
  protections during international armed
    conflicts, 64–66, 69
  terrorism and concept of, 147–50
  types of attacks prohibited, 32
  See also asymmetric conflicts; just war;
    laws of armed conflict/war; modern

weapon technology; war crimes;
  War on Terror
war crimes
  Allies, xv, 19, 24, 34, 52n62, 53
  Belgian law regarding, 34
  distinction principle and prosecution
    for, 17
  first prosecution for, 10
  Former Yugoslavia, xv, 53n62
  media and, 52
  violation of the principle of distinction
    as, 33
  World War, II, 24
War on Terror
  as armed conflict, 146–48, 147–50
  children killed as a result of the, 126
  international law and, 148–52
  unlawful combatants and the, 120–21
weapon technology See modern weapon
  technology
Wolford, Philip, 86
women
  in ancient wars, 2–3
  Enlightenment thinking regarding, 12
  killing as collective punishment, 16
  in the Middle Ages, 9, 10
  Old Testament rules regarding, 6
  protections granted to, 32, 75–77
  rape/sexual exploitation, x, xi, xvii, 10,
    69, 77, 79
  safe zones for, 72–73
World Food Programme (WFP), 128
World War, II, 24
World War II
  French resistance, 40
  German war crimes, 64
  journalists in, 87
  rules adopted as a result of, 68
  safe zone during, 72
worship, places of See cultural objects and
  places of worship

Xe See Blackwater (Xe)
Xerxes, (King), 7–8

Yassin, Sheikh, 24
Yugoslavia, Former See Former Yugoslavia
Yugoslavian People's Army, 160

Zaeef, Abd al-Salam Zaeef, 131